Top 500 Fagor Pressure Cooker Recipes

The Complete Fagor Pressure Cooker Cookbook

Damon Mann

Copyright © 2018 by Damon Mann

All rights reserved worldwide.

ISBN: 978-1986282420

No part of this book may be reproduced or transmitted in any form or by any means, electronic or mechanical, including photocopying, recording or by any information storage and retrieval system, without written permission from the publisher, except for the inclusion of brief quotations in a review.

Warning-Disclaimer

The purpose of this book is to educate and entertain. The author or publisher does not guarantee that anyone following the techniques, suggestions, tips, ideas, or strategies will become successful. The author and publisher shall have neither liability or responsibility to anyone with respect to any loss or damage caused, or alleged to be caused, directly or indirectly by the information contained in this book.

Contents

Introduction 4

Breakfast 9

Lunch 27

Snacks and Appetizers 45

Dinner...60

Vegetables and Eggs 68

Soups and Stews 76

Poultry..99

Red Meat 123

Seafood and Fish 143

Desserts 153

Introduction

The Fagor Pressure Cooker is a kitchen gadget that will make you wonder how on Earth you lived without it. This multifunctional programmable pressure cooker will help you prepare all your favorite delicious meals in no time, and the fact that it is super easy to use will make you love it even more.

This pressure cooker is specially designed to help people who love spending time outside the kitchen but who also love good, healthy food. Fagor Pressure Cooker is here to shorten the time you spend in the kitchen and replace the use of too many pots and pans. Fagor Pressure Cooker will replace up to seven traditional kitchen appliances, including slow cookers, pressure cookers, rice cookers, Sauté pans, steamers, and warmer and stock pots. This pressure cooker will save up to eighty percent of your precious time and energy, and the best part is, you will never again have to invest in expensive, useless kitchen appliances.

This cookbook will help you learn new and healthy recipes easy to prepare in your Fagor Pressure Cooker. When was the last time you decided to prepare a nice roasted meat and potatoes? A pot roast or fish? Pasta or a stew? That's right, spending too much time in the kitchen requires time and energy, and in these modern times, it is a real luxury to spend a few hours in the kitchen preparing a meal.

Fagor Pressure Cooker combined with this cookbook equals a perfectly delicious meal that requires nothing more than putting all the ingredients in the cooker, closing the lid, and letting it do its business while you do something else.

By reading this cookbook, you will learn there is no such thing as a bad cook; the only thing you don't have is a great kitchen pal, and that pal is called Fagor Pressure Cooker.

Before we dive into recipes, let's learn a little bit more about the magic that is Fagor Pressure Cooker.

Multifunctional Programmable Pressure Cooker

As mentioned in the introduction, Fagor Pressure Cooker is a real kitchen pal that will help you prepare even the most complicated meals you crave but never had the time or energy to cook. This cooker comes with one-touch settings and patented designed steam technology ideal for shortening the time for cooking yet still delivering a healthy meal.

Fagor Pressure Cooker comes with five cooking accessories, including the extra glass lid for slow cooking, extra silicone sealing ring, soup spoon, rice ladle, and measuring cup.

We talk about a kitchen gadget that not only will do the cooking for you, but it can also be cleaned in the dishwasher.

By combining fifteen smart cooking programs, you can easily cook meat, poultry, vegetables, rice, beans, soups, and so on.

Fast cooking, healthy meals

Why is it so important to cook your meals in the Fagor Pressure Cooker? The simplest reason is that it cuts down the time for cooking. This way you are not only saving energy and money, but you also save precious minutes (you can do whatever you want during the cooking time) and still end up having a delicious, healthy meal.

The entire meal is cooked by the trapped steam inside, which builds up the pressure, raises the cooking temperature, and its seal locks keep the heat, moisture, and all the flavors and nutrition inside. If you had any doubts that Fagor will cook less healthy or less tasty meals because of the shortened time, we hope you changed your mind. All those tasty soups, stews, chili, and other complicated, time-consuming meals can be prepared in much shorter time. Fagor Pressure Cooker is not only ideal for preparing healthy lunches and dinners, but also desserts such as Crème Brûlée or cheesecakes.

Cook everything in just one cooker

Multifunctional and beyond powerful, Fagor Pressure Cooker is designed to prepare a wide range of meals from sauté to slow cook. This cooker comes with a manual mode so the user can customize the cooking time for any meal. Anyone can use Fagor, thanks to its push-button controls that are beyond easy to use; the big LED display shows all the important information, making everything neat and understandable. The designers thought of everything when they created Fagor with the cool-to-the-touch side handles, so no more burned hands and fingers because safety comes first with this cooker.

As mentioned before, Fagor is super easy-to-clean and comes with the measuring cup of 160 mL, a spoon, and a ladle to make the entire cooking experience even easier.

Fagor Pressure Cooker will become your ultimate go-to cooker that will prepare your favorite pot roasts, pasta, cheesecakes, or any dish you like. The only thing you have to do is simply put all the ingredients inside the cooker, add liquid, and set your cooking mode. No more stress and wasted time on poorly cooked meals, because Fagor does all the work and saves you time and energy.

Fagor Pressure Cooker Makes the Tastiest Meals

This is a pressure cooker with one main goal – cooking fast and cooking tasty. Every ingredient you put inside the firmly sealed pot will release its natural juices so the taste and the aroma will remain inside. This makes the cooking with Fagor smart and unique. While cooking in old fashioned pots and pans requires much more time, they will never provide you with nearly the same taste as Fagor Pressure Cooker will. In this cookbook, you will find a plethora of recipes that will taste ten times better just because they were cooked the right way.

Healthy Meals

What is a meal without all the vitamins and minerals? We gain our energy and valuable nutrition from food, and poorly cooked (undercooked or overcooked) meals can harm us more than we think. Cooking with the Fagor Pressure Cooker is a real gain for the entire family because it provides meals that not only are delicious but also rich in vitamins and minerals. You wonder how that works? All the ingredients placed in the firmly sealed pot are surrounded by steam, which is the healthiest way to cook a meal. No more overheated oils or butter, just the ingredients' natural steam, colors, and tastes. The steam will evenly cook all your vegetables, soups, rice, meat, and in general every ingredient you place inside. The ingredients will remain in their natural shape and will not lose their natural color.

Fagor Pressure Cooker Is Environment Friendly

We live in a time when every minute of used electric energy causes immense damage to the environment. This is why it is important to be smart and use gadgets that don't harm our planet. Fagor Pressure Cooker was specially designed to use less time for cooking otherwise complicated meals, and at the same time, it saves not only your nerves, but energy and your money. Compared to using other kitchen appliances such as steamers, oven, pots, and so on, Fagor Pressure Cooker actually saves up to seventy percent of energy, which, if we are honest is a lot. You save more than half the time and energy, and your electric bills will significantly change. Investing in this cooker will positively effect on your budget, but you will also take care of the environment.

What To Expect From Your Fagor Pressure Cooker

First of all you will get a large cooker capable of preparing dinner for more people. If you have a family of four, consider that you can cook more than enough food in this cooker. People who use it claim this is perhaps one of the best pressure cookers, because they can put enough ingredients inside for one meal and still have leftovers for the next. If you are trying to refresh your family budget, this is an excellent way to cook food for two meals at the same time.

The Fagor Pressure Cooker is easy to use.

At the top, there is a switch that allows you to set the cooker from pressure to steam mode (depending on your preference of cooking).

- This cooker has a very easy lock system. All you have to do is simply twist the lid to the left or to the right.
- Safety first! During cooking, there is no way you can open the lid. The designers made sure the lid cannot be open if there is too much pressure inside the cooker. The auto-shut off option is also there (in case of extremely high pressure).
- The timer set in the Fagor Pressure Cooker is great. This makes Fagor a real kitchen pal because you can set the timer for any time you want. Literally, your meal for tomorrow can be cooked while you sleep, shower, do housework, or while you watch a movie.
- The clear lid (that closes the pot firmly) can be swapped out when cooking is finished. The lid can also be used for storing leftovers; just remove the inner pot, place the clear lid on, and you can bring your food to the table, store it in the fridge or any place you want without the need to move the entire cooker.
- Fagor Pressure Cooker has multiple pre-sets, which will help you worry less about the time you spend cooking. No more thinking how many more minutes you should cook your lunch or dinner. The pre-sets examples include stew, meat, fish, and so on.

How It Works

Fagor Pressure Cooker, as the name says, needs to develop pressure inside (this is why you need to add enough water to the ingredients). Once the water boils, the pressure starts developing (thanks to the firmly closed lid). The pot develops much higher temperature than 100 degrees Celsius (the temperature necessary for the water to boil) and the pressure inside the Fagor Pressure Cooker can rise up to 115 degrees Celsius. With this temperature and the steam trapped inside the pot (which will transfer inside much better than air and will evenly cook every ingredient), Fagor will cook your meals much faster than your oven or any other regular pot.

When using your Fagor Pressure Cooker you need to make sure you have read the manual and observed the display and \ buttons on the surface. For instance, if you want to cook rice, you must select the "Rice" function. If you want to cook soup or poultry, select the suitable functions for that.

Next, you need to select the cooking time, because you cannot cook soup just as long nor in the same temperature as you usually cook your poultry or rice. In case you do not know how long your meal should be cooked, leave it all to Fagor Pressure Cooker; simply select a preprogrammed cooking time and your kitchen pal will do its business perfectly.

By pressing 'Pressure/Temp' (press + or – in order to set the desired pressure level, which ranges from 1 to 6 and set the temperature from 40 to 160 degrees Celsius).

Once you have selected the 'Start' button, your Fagor Pressure Cooker will start cooking your meal. Once the meal is completely finished, the pressure cooker will start beeping, warning you (this is a very smart solution for people who cannot stay in the kitchen during the entire cooking time). If you are not able to return to the kitchen or from some reason you cannot consume your meal right away, Fagor Pressure Cooker will automatically switch to keep the meal warm in the next six hours.

We are sure that by now you are fully convinced that Fagor Pressure Cooker is the ultimate appliance for your kitchen. No wonder it became the favorite pressure cooker of thousands of people around the world.

Safety First

Forget about burned hands and fingers or possible malfunctioning that can cause a fire or minor explosions. Fagor Pressure Cooker was specially designed to keep the user and the kitchen safe. Every part of this pressure cooker is made with a purpose.

- Fagor comes with a pressure limiter; it keeps the pressure inside and makes the cooker safe for use.
- The lid lock safety is crucial; thanks to this you cannot open the cooker while it is under high pressure. There is no chance to do it even if you try. Fagor is safe for everyone.

- The anti-clog protection keeps every piece of food away from blocking the pressure release valve. Not even the tiniest particles of food can block the valve.
- The lid position monitor is built in so the Fagor will be disabled in case the lid is misplaced. This way you will be reminded that you haven't sealed your Fagor well.
- Fagor has a micro-limit switch protection, which means this pressure cooker has a watch that ensures the lid is firmly sealed and secure. Thanks to this limit switch protection Fagor works with zero potential danger.
- Pressure auto-control guard is another safety function that will keep the inside pressure in a safe range (at all times!).
- Fagor Pressure Cooker will automatically turn off if the pressure exceeds the safe levels, thanks to its electrical current monitor.
- Pressure protection releases the pressure inside in order to avoid even the slightest chance of dangerous situations.
- Temperature controller makes cooking with Fagor Pressure Cooking a really pleasant experience; thanks to this setting, the food will be evenly cooked and not.
- The excess temperature monitor will cut the power to the temperature fuse in case the temperature inside passes the safety limits.

Preparing meals

- The moment of truth is here. Finally, let's see how to prepare an actual meal in the Fagor Pressure Cooker. In this cookbook you will find all sorts of recipes (sweet, savory, meaty, and so on), but even though cooking with Fagor is beyond easy, following the recipe is a must. Once you have all the needed ingredients, set the cooker to sauté or brown (this way extra flavor is added to your meal). If you are cooking vegetables or meat, set them on brown before adding the liquid (this step is right before you start the pressure cooking). In most recipes (as you will see in this cookbook) the liquid is water, but in some of them, the liquid can be wine, for example.
- Once the ingredients and liquid are inside the pot, lock the lid (watch so you seal it right, otherwise Fagor will not function). With the lid lock and your preferred way of cooking selected, your pressure cooker will automatically start cooking. All you have to do is select your wanted pressure level and cook time and you no longer have to do anything. Fagor Pressure Cooker will do its work on its own.

What Happens After The Cooking Is Finished

Once the pressure cooking is finished (you will hear the beeping sound that will inform you the process is done), turn off the cooker (click the "Cancel" button). There are two ways to release the pressure before you open the lid: quick or natural, depending on the food you are preparing. The quick pressure release requires you to open the valve and let the air out. The natural way require you to do nothing. You simply let the pressure decrease by itself. It can take up to half an hour, and you will know the entire pressure is released when the valve drops and the lid opens by itself.

What Each Function Means

Fagor Pressure Cooker comes with a very comprehensive front that has display and functions you need to select before the cooker starts cooking your meal. Before you continue reading the recipes in this cookbook, it would be quite useful to learn what each function means.

- Sauté – If you select this function, you will be able to cook your meal without the protective lid on the cooker. By pressing this function twice you have set the browning function; by pressing sauté and function and adjusting the button twice your cooker is ready for simmering.
- Keep the food warm/Cancel – If you select this function you can cancel the previously selected function or simply turn off your Fagor.
- Manual (+ and -) – This is the function needed for recipes that require a specific temperature that otherwise cannot be reached. As the name says, you will have to manually set the preferred temperature.

- Meat – As the name says, this function is for cooking meat and stew. Adjusting the cooking time will set the cooker to cook the meat to the desired texture.
- Poultry – This is the function suitable for cooking chicken and turkey meat or any poultry dish. You can set your desired pressure level as well as cooking time depending on your preferences or based on the requirements in the recipe you follow.
- Rice – If you are cooking rice (any type of rice) set this function. The cooker will automatically cook your rice under low pressure; the time needed for the cooking will depend on the level of water you poured into the pot.
- Steam – Suitable for steaming vegetables or seafood, this function works better if you use it with the quick pressure releasing in order to avoid overcooking (which can happen if you let your Fagor release its pressure naturally).
- Soup – This is the function you need when cooking soups and broths. You can manually adjust the cooking time by clicking the 'Adjust' button (it all depends on how you want your soups, or based on your recipe).
- Beans/Chili - Fagor Pressure Cooker comes with this function that helps you prepare the best chili or beans. You can manually adjust the cooker from thirty to forty minutes, depending on how you prefer your chili or beans.

Fagor And Your Cooking

This cookbook will hopefully become your favorite now that you use the Fagor Pressure Cooker. The first time you use the Fagor Pressure Cooker you will get used to perfectly cooked, healthy, and delicious meals and will never settle for less.

You will forget about the undercooked meat or poultry, all the mushy vegetables you have ruined using other pots. It is likely you will become more interested in cooking, and the process will no longer seem like a chore because when you have this pressure cooker, you do not have to worry about anything but getting the right ingredients and setting the right function. The rest is Fagor's job.

There is no meal Fagor cannot prepare for you, and even the most stubborn foods will become tender under the pressure inside this pot. Living healthy and eating healthy does not only require exercising and eating clean, healthy food; it also takes cooking your meals in good pots without the use of oils that are bad for your health.

We know what Fagor can do, and we are absolutely in love with its endless possibilities. That is why we are so inspired to share all these yummy recipes for you.

This cookbook will surely help you learn new recipes, and it will inspire you to use your Fagor Pressure Cooker literally every day. It does not matter whether you are in a hurry or you have some time on your hands, this cookbook offers you a variety of recipes that Fagor Pressure Cooker can prepare within the time range of fifteen to forty minutes.

Below you will find our choice of recipes.

Happy cooking!

Breakfast

1. Oatmeal with Blackberries

(Time: 45 minutes \ Servings: 2)

INGREDIENTS:

1 cup oats
1 cup blackberries
1 cup cream milk

¼ cup caster sugar
4 tablespoons honey
2 tablespoons butter, melted

DIRECTIONS:

- Combine the oats, cream milk, sugar and butter in a bowl.
- Transfer the oats mixture to the Fagor Pressure Cooker and place the blackberries on top, cover with a lid. Cook on SLOW COOK mode for 35 minutes. Drizzle honey on top.

2. Oatmeal Pancakes

(Time: 25 minutes \ Servings: 4)

INGREDIENTS:

1 cup oats
1 cup all-purpose flour
½ cup caster sugar
¼ teaspoon baking soda
½ teaspoon baking powder
2 eggs

1 cup milk
2 tablespoons sour cream
4 tablespoons honey
1 pinch salt
4 tablespoons butter
strawberries for garnishing

DIRECTIONS:

- Sift flour, sugar, baking powder, baking soda, salt and set aside.
- Beat the eggs for a minute and add in milk, and sour cream, mix well.
- Add the sifted flour mixture and oats, mix thoroughly with a spatula.
- Melt butter in the Fagor Pressure Cooker on SAUTÉ mode.
- Ladle the butter in the pressure cooker and spread in a form of cake.
- Cook for 2-3 minutes on one side, then flip and cook until brown.
- Transfer to a serving platter and drizzle honey. Top with strawberries.

3. Zucchini Frittata

(Time: 15 minutes \ Servings: 3)

INGREDIENTS:

3 eggs
1 large zucchini
1 onion, chopped

½ teaspoon thyme, chopped
¼ teaspoon white pepper
2 tablespoons olive oil

DIRECTIONS:

- Cut the zucchini into thin strips and set aside.
- Crack the eggs in a medium bowl and whisk for 1 minute.
- Add the zucchini strips, onion, thyme, salt, and pepper, mix well.
- Add 3-4 cups of water into the Fagor Pressure Cooker and place a trivet or stand inside it.
- Spray a medium-sized baking dish with olive oil, transfer the eggs mixture into a pan and place on a trivet. Cover the cooker and cook on MANUAL mode for 10 minutes on high pressure.

4. Peachy Oats Crumble

(Time: 35 minutes \ Servings: 3)

INGREDIENTS:

2 cups oats
½ cup peach juice
1 peach, sliced
1 cup milk
¼ cup brown sugar

4 tablespoons maple syrup
1 pinch salt
1 cup sour cream
2 tablespoons butter, melted

DIRECTIONS:

- Combine the oats, milk, peach juice, maple syrup, sour cream, brown sugar, and salt in a bowl.
- Brush the Fagor Pressure Cooker with butter.
- Transfer the oats mixture to the Pressure cooker and cover with a lid.
- Cook on SLOW COOK mode for 35 minutes.
- Transfer to a serving dish and place the peach slices on top.
- Drizzle some maple syrup on top.

5. Cheesy Spinach Casserole

(Time: 25 minutes \ Servings: 4)

INGREDIENTS:

1 cup spinach, chopped
half lb. cheddar cheese
half lb. mozzarella cheese
1 onion, chopped
4 eggs, whisked

l yellow bell pepper, chopped
¼ teaspoon salt
¼ teaspoon black pepper
2 tablespoons olive oil

DIRECTIONS:

- In a bowl add the eggs, spinach, mozzarella cheese, cheddar cheese, bell pepper, and onion, mix well.
- Season with salt and pepper. Grease the Fagor Pressure Cooker with olive oil.
- Transfer the spinach mixture to the Fagor Pressure Cooker and cover with a lid.
- Cook for 25 minutes on SLOW COOK mode.

6. Oatmeal with Cranberry

(Time: 40 minutes \ Servings: 5)

INGREDIENTS:

2 cups oats
2 cups milk
1 egg, whisked
1 cup cranberry sauce
½ cup brown sugar

2 tablespoons honey
½ teaspoon ginger powder
1 pinch salt
4 tablespoons butter, melted
2 tablespoons olive oil

DIRECTIONS:

- Grease the Fagor Pressure Cooker with olive oil.
- Combine the oats, milk, egg, butter, cranberry sauce, honey, brown sugar, ginger powder, and salt in a bowl. Transfer to the greased cooker and cover with a lid.
- Cook on SLOW COOK mode for 40 minutes.

7. Eggs with Honey
(Time: 21 minutes \ Servings: 3)

INGREDIENTS:

3 eggs
4 slices bread
2 tbsp. mayonnaise
1 tbsp. honey

3 slices baked ham
½ cup mozzarella cheese, shredded
salt to taste

DIRECTIONS:

- Whisk eggs in a bowl. Add baked ham, honey and mayonnaise.
- Get a rond baking tray and pour the mixture in it.
- Sprinkle it with cheese and salt.
- Cook for 15 minutes in the Fagor Pressure Cooker on medium pressure on MANUAL setting.
- When done, serve with pieces of bread and enjoy the delicious breakfast.

8. Potatoes and Bacon
(Time: 10 minutes \ Servings: 4)

INGREDIENTS:

½ cup of potatoes
3 eggs
2 tbsp. bacon, chopped
½ tbsp. bacon fat

2 slices jalapeno peppers
1 cup onion, chopped
½ bunch cilantro, chopped
½ cup taco seasoning

DIRECTIONS:

- Place the potatoes in the Fagor Pressure Cooker and cook on high pressure on MANUAL for about 2 minutes.
- Put eggs, bacon, bacon fat, onion, jalapeno peppers and cilantro into a bowl. Mix well.
- When potatoes are ready, pour egg mixture over it and cook on high pressure in the pressure cooker for 5 minutes.
- When it beeps, release the pressure. Dress it with taco seasoning and serve.

9. Mushroom and Eggs
(Time: 15 minutes \ Servings: 3)

INGREDIENTS:

1 cup mushrooms, sliced
4 eggs
2 tomatoes, chopped

1 cup basil, chopped
1 tbsp. butter
salt and pepper, to taste

DIRECTIONS:

- Whisk eggs in a bowl.
- Add salt and pepper, tomatoes, basil and mushrooms.
- Mix well.
- Grease a round baking tray and pour the mixture into it.
- Place it in the Fagor Pressure Cooker and cook for 10 minutes on high pressure.
- When done, enjoy this delicious mushroom meal.

10. Easy Pumpkin
(Time: 16 minutes \ Servings: 4)

INGREDIENTS:

2 tbsp. butter
½ cup oats
2 cups water
2 cups pumpkin puree

½ cup maple syrup
1 tbsp. cinnamon powder
2 tbsp. pumpkin pie spice
salt to taste

DIRECTIONS:

- Put the butter in the Fagor Pressure Cooker and let it melt for 1 minute on SAUTÉ mode.
- Add oats, water, maple syrup, pumpkin puree, pumpkin spice, cinnamon powder and salt.
- Cook on high pressure for 10 minutes.

11. Eggs Mixed with Bacon
(Time: 19 minutes \ Servings: 4)

INGREDIENTS:

4 eggs
1 cup milk
3 slices bacon
1 lb. ground sausage

1 cup ham, diced
3 green onions, chopped
2 cups cheddar cheese
salt to taste

DIRECTIONS:

- Whisk eggs with milk in a bowl. Add salt to mixture and then pour it into the pressure cooker.
- Mix bacon, ham and sausage in the pressure cooker. Sprinkle with green onions and cover it all with cheddar cheese.
- Cook for 15 minutes in the pressure cooker on MANUAL setting.

12. Delicious Chocolaty Oats
(Time: 15 minutes \ Servings: 4)

INGREDIENTS:

1 tbsp. butter
2 cups oats
1 cup almond milk

2 cups shredded coconut
1 cup chocolate chips
½ cup sliced almonds

DIRECTIONS:

- Sauté the butter in the Fagor Pressure Cooker. Add almond milk, oats, salt and chocolate chips.
- Cook it on high pressure for 10 minutes. When ready, take it out and sprinkle with shredded coconut and sliced almonds.

13. Cheese Mix
(Time: 15 minutes \ Servings: 3)

INGREDIENTS:

4 slices bread
1 cup spinach, chopped
½ cup cheese, shredded

1 tomato, chopped
salt and pepper, to taste

DIRECTIONS:

- Place the bread as a layer into a round baking tray. Add spinach, tomato and cheese.
- Sprinkle with salt and pepper. Cook in the Fagor Pressure Cooker for 10 minutes on high pressure.

14. Artichokes with Eggs

(Time: 20 minutes \ Servings: 2)

INGREDIENTS:

2 cups artichokes, peeled
1 tbsp. fennel
2 tbsp. cream
3 egg s

4 garlic cloves, minced
1 tbsp. nutmeg powder
salt and pepper, to taste

DIRECTIONS:

- Whisk the eggs in a bowl.
- Add fennel, cream, nutmeg powder, salt and pepper.
- Blend well and then add artichokes.
- Pour the mixture into a round baking tray.
- Cook in the Fagor Pressure Cooker for 15 minutes on high pressure.
- When ready, serve with bread and enjoy!

15. French Toast with Cranberries

(Time: 15 minutes \ Servings: 4)

INGREDIENTS:

2 ½ cups cranberries
½ cup orange juice
½ cup sugar

½ tsp. cinnamon powder
salt to taste

FRENCH TOAST

3 tbsp. butter
½ cup sugar
2 ½ cups whole milk
2 eggs

2 orange zest
½ tsp. vanilla extract
½ loaf of bread, cubed

DIRECTIONS:

- Put orange juice, sugar, cinnamon powder, salt and cranberries in the Fagor Pressure Cooker.
- Cook on low pressure for 10 minutes.
- When done, put in a container and set aside.
- Whisk eggs and butter in a bowl. Add sugar. Whisk well.
- Add milk, orange zest and vanilla extract.
- Meanwhile, place the layer of bread in the pressure cooker.
- Pour the mixture over it.
- Cover the lid and cook on medium pressure for 20 minutes.
- When ready, serve with the sauce that you made in step 1.

16. Oats with Chocolate
(Time: 14 minutes \ Servings: 3)

INGREDIENTS:

2 cups water
1 ½ cups milk
½ cup oats
1 tbsp. sugar
2 tbsp. espresso powder

1 tbsp. vanilla extract
½ cup whipped cream
1 cup chocolate, grated
salt to taste

DIRECTIONS:

- Put milk, oats, water, sugar, espresso powder, salt and vanilla extract in the Fagor Pressure Cooker.
- Cover the lid and cook for 10 minutes on high pressure.
- When it beeps, take it out and serve in a bowl.
- Dress it with whipped cream and any grated chocolate of your choice.

17. Ricotta Pancakes
(Time: 15 minutes \ Servings: 4)

INGREDIENTS:

4 eggs
½ cup sugar
2 ½ cups ricotta cheese
1 cup vanilla yogurt
2 tbsp. vanilla extract

½ cup white wheat flour
1 tbsp. baking powder
2 cups sweet yogurt glaze
salt to taste

DIRECTIONS:

- Mix eggs, sugar, vanilla extract and white wheat flour in a bowl.
- Put it in the Fagor Pressure Cooker and mix with vanilla yogurt and salt. Stir well.
- Add baking powder. Cook on MANUAL on high pressure for 10 minutes.
- When ready, take it out and serve it dressed with the sweet yogurt glaze.

18. Veggie Eggs
(Time: 20 minutes \ Servings: 2)

INGREDIENTS:

½ cup milk
6 oz. chopped spinach
1 cup cheese, shredded
½ onion, chopped
½ bell pepper, chopped

4 eggs
Salt and pepper, to taste
½ cup mint, chopped
1 tbsp. oil

DIRECTIONS:

- Whisk eggs in a bowl.
- Add milk, cheese, spinach, onion, bell pepper, salt and pepper, and mint.
- Grease the round baking tray with oil.
- Pour the mixture into a tray.
- Cook in the Fagor Pressure Cooker for 15 minutes on high pressure.

19.   Oats with Raisins
(Time: 15 minutes \ Servings: 4)

INGREDIENTS:

2 tbsp. butter
½ cup oats
2 cups water

salt to taste
½ cup raisins

FOR TOPPING:

1 cup brown sugar
½ tbsp. cinnamon

½ cup cream cheese
½ tbsp. sugar

DIRECTIONS:

- Put oats, water, butter, salt and raisins into the Fagor Pressure Cooker.
- Cook on high pressure for 10 minutes.
- Meanwhile, put cinnamon, brown sugar, cream cheese and sugar into a bowl.
- Whisk it well until it turns into a thick texture.
- When the pressure cooker beeps, serve and top it with the brown sugar topping.

20.   Scrambled Eggs with Spinach
(Time: 14 minutes \ Servings: 3)

INGREDIENTS:

6 eggs
1 cup milk
2 cups baby spinach, chopped
½ cup seeded tomato

2 green onions, chopped
2 cups cheddar cheese
salt and pepper, to taste

DIRECTIONS:

- Mix eggs with milk in a bowl.
- Put it into the Fagor Pressure Cooker.
- Add salt and pepper, seeded tomato, baby spinach, green onion and cheddar cheese.
- Cover with the lid and cook on high pressure for 10 minutes. When done, serve and enjoy!

21.   Asparagus and Eggs
(Time: 20 minutes \ Servings: 2)

INGREDIENTS:

2 bread slices
3 slices avocado
3 sticks asparagus

½ tomato, sliced
1 egg
1 tbsp. oil

DIRECTIONS:

- Whisk egg in a bowl.
- Add in the avocado and asparagus.
- Mix well.
- Grease a round baking tray with oil.
- Place tomato slices on the mixture and put in the Fagor Pressure Cooker.
- Place the bread pieces on the sides of the baking tray.
- Cook on MANUAL for 15 minutes on high pressure.
- When done, serve and enjoy!

22. Cinnamon with Raisins

(Time: 15 minutes \ Servings: 4)

INGREDIENTS:

2 tbsp. butter
1 cup brown sugar
2 cups whole milk
2 eggs
2 tsp. vanilla extract

½ tbsp cinnamon powder
6 slices cinnamon bread
¼ cup raisins
salt, to taste

DIRECTIONS:

- Place layers of cinnamon bread in the Fagor Pressure Cooker.
- In a bowl, whisk the eggs with brown sugar and milk.
- Add to the pressure cooker. Mix with the butter, vanilla extract, salt, raisins and cinnamon powder.
- Spread mixture all over the bread.
- Cook on MANUAL for 10 minutes on high pressure.
- When ready, enjoy by serving it with any of your favorite sauces.

23. Oats with Chia Seeds

(Time: 15 minutes \ Servings: 2)

INGREDIENTS:

1 tbsp. butter
½ cup oats
2 cups water
½ cup cream

½ cup chia seeds
1 cup strawberries, sliced
2 tbsp. brown sugar
salt to taste

DIRECTIONS:

- Put butter into the Fagor Pressure Cooker and select the sauté option.
- When the butter melts, add oats, cream, water, chia seeds, brown sugar and salt. Mix well.
- Cook on MANUAL on high pressure for 10 minutes.
- When it beeps, take it out and serve with the strawberry slices on top.

24. Quinoa Vanilla

(Time: 15 minutes \ Servings: 3)

INGREDIENTS:

1 cup uncooked quinoa
2 cups water
2 tbsp. Maple syrup
1 tsp. vanilla

2 tbsp. cinnamon powder
a pinch of salt
toppings: fresh berries, cherries, crushed
    almonds

DIRECTIONS:

- Mix water, maple syrup, quinoa, vanilla, salt and cinnamon in the Fagor Pressure Cooker.
- Set the pressure to high and cook for 1 minute.
- When the sound beeps, turn it off and let it rest for 10 minutes.
- Release the pressure and then open the pressure cooker.
- Remove the quinoa from the bowl and dress it with any of your favorite toppings mentioned above.

25. Scallion Scrambled Eggs

(Time: 10 minutes \ Servings: 4)

INGREDIENTS:

2 eggs
1 cup water
½ lb. scallions, chopped

½ cup sesame seeds
½ tsp. garlic powder
salt and pepper, to taste

DIRECTIONS:

- Mix water and eggs in a bowl.
- Add scallions, sesame seeds, garlic powder, and salt and pepper in the Fagor Pressure Cooker.
- Add the egg mixture.
- Set to MANUAL, high pressure, and the timer to 5 minutes.
- When the timer goes off, release the pressure of the pressure cooker.

26. Cheese, Bacon and Eggs

(Time: 14 minutes \ Servings: 4)

INGREDIENTS:

5 eggs
½ tsp. lemon pepper seasoning
3 tbsp. cheddar cheese, grated

2 green onions, chopped
3 slices bacon, crumbled

DIRECTIONS:

- Whisk the eggs in a bowl and put them in the Fagor Pressure Cooker.
- Mix the cheddar cheese, green onion and bacon with the eggs.
- Cook on MANUAL for 10 minutes on high pressure.
- When done, season it with lemon pepper and enjoy!

27. Sweet Potatoes and Peanuts Smash

(Time: 45 minutes \ Servings: 4)

INGREDIENTS:

4 sweet potatoes, peeled, boiled
1 cup milk
½ cup coconut milk
¼ cup coconut flakes
1 cup peanuts
2 eggs, whisked

1 teaspoon vanilla extracts
¼ teaspoon green cardamom powder
½ cup brown sugar
¼ cup all-purpose flour
1 pinch salt
4 tablespoons butter, melted

DIRECTIONS:

- Mash the sweet potatoes and combine with peanuts and coconut flakes.
- In a separate bowl, combine the flour, brown sugar, salt, cardamom powder, eggs, milk, coconut milk, and vanilla extract, mix well.
- Add the sweet potatoes and transfer to the Fagor Pressure Cooker.
- Cook on SLOW COOK mode for 40 minutes.

28. Granola with Dates

(Time: 35 minutes \ Servings: 2)

INGREDIENTS:

2 cups granola
1 cup dates, seeded, halved
1 cup milk
¼ cup peanuts
½ cup coconut milk

¼ cup coconut flakes
1 egg, whisked
¼ cup brown sugar
1 pinch salt
2 tablespoons butter, melted

DIRECTIONS:

- In a bowl, add the dates and the milk and mash using a fork until smooth.
- Add the brown sugar, granola, salt, butter, peanuts, and egg, and mix very well.
- Transfer to a greased Fagor Pressure Cooker and cook for 35 minutes on SLOW COOK mode.

29. Mango Crunch with Strawberries

(Time: 25 minutes \ Servings: 5)

INGREDIENTS:

2 cups strawberries, sliced
2 cups mango, chunks
1 cup mango juice
1 package butter cookies, crumbled
½ cup all-purpose flour, sifted

1 cup milk
1 egg, whisked
¼ cup caster sugar
4 tablespoons butter, melted

DIRECTIONS:

- In a bowl, add all-purpose flour, cookies, egg, sugar, mango juice, and milk and mix well.
- Spread into a greased baking dish and press using a spoon.
- Drizzle butter and top.
- Add the mango chunks and the strawberries.
- Place a trivet into the Fagor Pressure Cooker and add 3-4 cups of water.
- Put a baking dish on a trivet and cover the pressure cooker with a lid.
- Cook on MANUAL mode, high pressure for 15 minutes.

30. Spinach and Tomato Cheesy Braise

(Time: 50 minutes \ Servings: 4)

INGREDIENTS:

1 cup baby spinach, sliced
2 tomatoes, chopped
1 cup mushrooms, sliced
1 teaspoon ginger powder
1 teaspoon garlic paste
¼ lb. parmesan cheese, shredded

½ lb. mozzarella cheese, shredded
1 egg, whisked
¼ pinch salt
¼ teaspoon thyme
¼ teaspoon black pepper
2 tablespoons butter, melted

DIRECTIONS:

- In the Fagor Pressure Cooker, add the butter and sauté garlic for 30 seconds on SAUTÉ mode.
- Add the spinach, tomatoes, thyme, salt, black pepper, egg, ginger powder, and mushrooms and mix well.
- Add the parmesan cheese, and mozzarella cheese and mix thoroughly.
- Cover with a lid and cook on SLOW COOK mode for 45 minutes.
- Serve hot and enjoy.

31. Lava Chocolate

(Time: 30 minutes \ Servings: 3)

INGREDIENTS:

1 cup raw chocolate, crumbled
½ cup cocoa powder
½ cup all-purpose flour
1 cup milk

1 egg, whisked
¼ cup caster sugar
4 tablespoons butter, melted
1 cup cream, whipped

DIRECTIONS:

- In a bowl, add the all-purpose flour, egg, cocoa powder, chocolate, sugar, butter, and milk, beat with a beater for 1-2 minutes.
- Transfer this mixture into the Fagor Pressure Cooker and cook on high pressure for 30 minutes.
- Transfer to a serving dish and top with whipped cream.
- Sprinkle with chocolate flakes.

32. Stir Fried Potato and Squash

(Time: 30 minutes \ Servings: 5)

INGREDIENTS:

3 potatoes, peeled, sliced
1 onion, chopped
1 cup yellow squash
½ teaspoon cayenne pepper

2-3 garlic cloves, minced
¼ teaspoon salt
¼ teaspoon cumin powder
2 tablespoons butter

DIRECTIONS:

- Melt butter on SAUTÉ mode and fry onion for 1 minute.
- Add the garlic and fry for 30 more seconds.
- Add the potatoes and squash; fry for 10 minutes.
- Season with salt, cayenne pepper, and cumin powder.
- Add 1-2 splashes of water and cook on MANUAL, low pressure for 15 minutes.

33. Spicy Potatoes

(Time: 15 minutes \ Servings: 3)

INGREDIENTS:

4 potatoes, peeled, boiled, diced
½ teaspoon chili flakes
1 teaspoon garlic paste
¼ teaspoon salt

¼ teaspoon cumin powder
¼ teaspoon black pepper
¼ teaspoon thyme
2 tablespoons olive oil

DIRECTIONS:

- Heat oil in Fagor Pressure Cooker on SAUTÉ mode and fry garlic for 30 seconds.
- Add the potatoes and fry for 10 minutes.
- Add salt, garlic paste, chili flakes, thyme, and cumin powder.
- Transfer to a serving platter and serve.

34. Creamy Spinach Simmer

(Time: 20 minutes \ Servings: 4)

INGREDIENTS:

2 cups baby spinach, chopped
1 cup heavy cream
½ cup coconut milk
¼ teaspoon white pepper

½ cup cheddar cheese
¼ teaspoon salt
2 tablespoons caster sugar
2 tablespoons olive oil

DIRECTIONS:

- Add the spinach to the Fagor Pressure Cooker and mix with the oil, milk, cream, cheese, sugar, salt and pepper.
- Cover with a lid and cook on BEANS mode for 20 minutes.

35. Bowl Egg

(Time: 15 minutes \ Servings: 1)

INGREDIENTS:

1 egg
1 bun (bread roll), cut from the top
1 pinch salt

¼ teaspoon dill, chopped
1 tablespoon red bell pepper, chopped
2 tablespoons olive oil

DIRECTIONS:

- Brush the bin with oil and crack the egg inside it. Sprinkle salt, dill and red bell pepper.
- Transfer to the Fagor Pressure Cooker and cook on high pressure for 10 minutes.
- Top with the cap of the bun.

36. Egg and Chicken Casserole

(Time: 30 minutes \ Servings: 4)

INGREDIENTS:

¼ lb. chicken breast, cut into small pieces
3 eggs, whisked
1 onion, chopped
3-4 garlic cloves, minced
½ lb. mozzarella cheese, shredded

2 oz. parmesan cheese
¼ teaspoon salt
¼ teaspoon black pepper
¼ teaspoon thyme
2 tablespoons butter

DIRECTIONS:

- Melt butter in the Fagor Pressure Cooker on SAUTÉ mode. Fry onion and garlic for 1-2 minutes.
- Add the chicken and fry until golden brown.
- Add salt, black pepper, thyme and mix well.
- Add the eggs, parmesan cheese, mozzarella cheese and mix thoroughly.
- Cover with a lid on and cook on MANUAL on high pressure for 20 minutes.

37. Potatoes and Eggs

(Time: 25 minutes \ Servings: 3)

INGREDIENTS:

2 potatoes, peeled, chopped
3 eggs, whisked
½ teaspoon chili powder
¼ teaspoon salt

¼ teaspoon cumin powder
¼ teaspoon cinnamon powder
¼ teaspoon black pepper
3 tablespoons olive oil

DIRECTIONS:

- Heat 2 tablespoons of oil on SAUTÉ mode and add the whisked eggs.
- Cook for 1 minute then flip over and cook the other side for another minute.
- Transfer the eggs to a platter and let cool. Crumble the eggs using a fork.
- Add the remaining oil and fry the potatoes for 4-5 minutes until softened.
- Season with salt, chili powder, black pepper, cumin powder and cinnamon powder.
- Transfer the crumbled eggs and stir well.

38. Creamy Egg Casserole

(Time: 15 minutes \ Servings: 3)

INGREDIENTS:

4 eggs, whisked
1 onion, sliced
1 green chili, chopped
1 red bell pepper, chopped
½ lb. mozzarella cheese, shredded

¼ teaspoon salt
¼ teaspoon black pepper
¼ teaspoon dried basil
2 tablespoons butter

DIRECTIONS:

- Melt butter on SAUTÉ mode and sauté onion for 30 seconds.
- Add the bell pepper and fry for a minute.
- Add the eggs, mozzarella cheese, green chilies, and season with basil, salt and pepper.
- Cover with a lid and cook on MANUAL on high pressure for 10 minutes.

39. Sautéd Cauliflower and Potato

(Time: 25 minutes \ Servings: 3)

INGREDIENTS:

3 potatoes, peeled, chopped
1 onion, chopped
1 cup cauliflower, chopped
¼ teaspoon garlic paste

½ teaspoon black pepper
¼ teaspoon salt
¼ teaspoon cumin powder
2 tablespoons olive oil

DIRECTIONS:

- Heat oil on SAUTÉ mode and sauté onion for 1 minute.
- Add the potatoes and cook until golden.
- Season with salt, black pepper and cumin powder. Transfer the cauliflower and mix well.
- Cook for 5 minutes and stir continuously. Serve hot.

40. Scrambled Eggs

(Time: 15 minutes \ Servings: 2)

INGREDIENTS:

4 eggs, whisked
¼ teaspoon salt
1 cup chicken broth

¼ teaspoon black pepper
¼ teaspoon dill, chopped
2 tablespoons olive oil

DIRECTIONS:

- Heat oil in the Fagor Pressure Cooker on SAUTÉ mode and pour the whisked eggs.
- Crumble the eggs using a fork and add the chicken broth. Season with salt and pepper.
- When the chicken broth is dried out, transfer the scrambled eggs to a serving dish and top with dill.

41. Creamy Sweet Potato Casserole
(Time: 25 minutes \ Servings: 2)

INGREDIENTS:

2 sweet potatoes, peeled, sliced
1 cup mayonnaise
1 cup heavy cream
1 cup chicken broth

1 red onion, sliced
½ teaspoon chili powder
¼ teaspoon salt
2 tablespoons olive oil

DIRECTIONS:

- Heat oil in the Fagor Pressure Cooker on SAUTÉ mode and sauté onion for 1 minute.
- Add the sweet potatoes and stir for 1-2 minutes.
- Add the chicken broth, and salt and cook on SOUP mode for 20-25 minutes until the potatoes soften.
- Stir in the mayonnaise and the heavy cream.
- Top with chili powder and serve.

42. Traditional Chickpea with Potatoes
(Time: 25 minutes \ Servings: 3)

INGREDIENTS:

1 cup chickpea, boiled
1 onion, chopped
1 tomato, chopped
2 potatoes, boiled, peeled, sliced

¼ teaspoon salt
½ teaspoon chili powder
2 tablespoons olive oil

DIRECTIONS:

- Heat oil in the Fagor Pressure Cooker on SAUTÉ mode and sauté onion for 1 minute.
- Add the tomatoes and fry well.
- Add the chickpea and the potatoes and stir for 1-2 minutes.
- Season with salt and pepper.
- Close the lid and cook on BEANS mode for 10 minutes.
- Transfer to a serving dish and sprinkle chili powder on top.

43. Mango Pudding
(Time: 15 minutes \ Servings: 2)

INGREDIENTS:

1 cup mango, chunks
1 cup orange juice
1 pear, chopped

1 apple, chopped
1 cup milk

DIRECTIONS:

- Place all the ingredients in the Fagor Pressure Cooker and stir well.
- Cook on MANUAL on high pressure for 15 minutes.

44. Brown Sugar and Carrot Shake
(Time: 20 minutes \ Servings: 2)

INGREDIENTS:

4 carrots, peeled, sliced
2 cups milk
1 cup mango juice

½ cup brown sugar
1 cup whipped cream

DIRECTIONS:

- Add all ingredients in the Fagor Pressure Cooker and cover with a lid.
- Cook for 20 minutes on MANUAL on high pressure.
- Transfer to a blender and blend to a puree.
- Top with whipped cream.

45. Peanut Slabs
(Time: 35 minutes \ Servings: 4)

INGREDIENTS:

1 cup peanuts, roughly chopped	1 cup strawberry jam
1 cup all-purpose flour	¼ cup almonds, sliced
¼ cup caster sugar	½ teaspoon baking powder
¼ cup butter	¼ teaspoon salt

DIRECTIONS:

- In a bowl, add the flour, sugar, baking powder, salt, almonds, and peanuts and mix well.
- Beat the butter until fluffy and stir in the flour mixture.
- Take a greased baking dish and spread half of the flour mixture on the bottom and press very well using the back of a spoon. Spread strawberry jam.
- Spread the remaining flour mixture on top and press lightly with spoon.
- Place a trivet in the Fagor Pressure Cooker and place the dish on top.
- Cook on MANUAL on medium pressure for 25 minutes.

46. Blueberries and Cream with Oats
(Time: 20 Minutes \ Servings: 4)

INGREDIENTS

1 tbsp. of coconut oil	1 ½ cups of coconut milk
1 cup of steel cut oats	1 ½ cups of water
2 tbsp. of coconut sugar	¾ cup of dried blueberries
1 tsp. of vanilla	1 tbsp. of chia seeds

FOR THE TOPPING:

Use cream and a little bit of milk.	½ cup of fresh blueberries

DIRECTIONS

- Melt the coconut oil on SAUTÉ mode, and add the oats and keep stirring for 5 minutes.
- Add the rest of the ingredients except for the fresh blueberries. Lock the lid and close tightly the pressure valve. Cook on a high pressure and set the timer to 10 minutes.
- When you hear the timer, release the pressure after 10 minutes and press the quick release.
- Stir the ingredients and serve in bowls. You can add the cream and the fresh blueberries and enjoy!

47. Asian-Style Scotch Eggs
(Time: 20 Minutes \ Servings: 5)

INGREDIENTS

4 large eggs	½ lb. of cauliflower florets
1 lb. of ground sausage	½ cup of oat flour
1 tbsp. of vegetable oil	1 tsp. of ginger
1 tbsp. of coconut oil	1 tsp. of flaxseed powder

DIRECTIONS

- Place the steamer basket in the Fagor Pressure Cooker. Add 1 cup of water and the eggs.
- After that, lock the lid and cook the eggs for 6 minutes on MANUAL mode.
- When the timer goes off, release the pressure naturally for around 5 minutes.
- When the pressure is completely released, carefully remove the lid.
- Chop the sausage into 4 pieces of equal size. Flatten each of the pieces until flat and round.
- Then put the hard boiled eggs in the center and wrap the sausage around each egg.
- Heat the Fagor Pressure Cooker and press SAUTÉ mode for 10 to 15 minutes.
- When the pressure cooker is hot, add the oil and let the scotch eggs get a brown color. Remove them.
- Place the rack in the Fagor Pressure Cooker and line the egg rolls on that rack; then lock the lid and set the timer to 6 minutes. Serve and enjoy.

48.   Cut Oats Breakfast
(Time: 35 Minutes \ Servings: 3-4)

INGREDIENTS

2 cups of cut oats
2 cups of coconut milk
1 cup of yogurt
3 cups of water
4 apples, diced
1 ½ cups of fresh cranberries

3 tbsp. of butter or coconut oil
1 tsp. of fresh lemon juice
½ tsp. of nutmeg
¼ cup of maple syrup
2 tsp. of vanilla
3 strawberries

DIRECTIONS

- Start by greasing the bottom of the Fagor Pressure Cooker container and add butter or coconut oil.
- Soak all ingredients except the maple syrup and the vanilla and leave them overnight in the Fagor Pressure Cooker. The next morning, add the quantity of syrup and cook on MANUAL setting. Seal the valve.
- Set the timer to 15 minutes to reach high pressure, then add 20 more minutes to cook the ingredients.
- Once the timer beeps, open the valve to release the pressure. Serve with milk, vanilla, and strawberries.

49.   Mashed Potatoes with Flax seeds
(Time: 20 Minutes \ Servings: 4)

INGREDIENTS

3 cups of mashed potatoes
2 cups of water
3 tbsp. of cider vinegar
½ lb. of salmon
1 avocado

2 cups of quinoa
1 cup of blueberries
4 tbsp. of coconut oil
3 tsp. of round flax seed

DIRECTIONS

- Start by soaking the quinoa a few hours before cooking the meal. Press the SAUTÉ button on the Fagor Pressure Cooker. Cut the salmon into cubes and add it to the Pressure cooker.
- Cook the salmon for about 5 minutes, then add the soaked quinoa and a cup of water. Stir the ingredients and add the veggies, but do not mix them. Then, lock the lid and adjust the time to 10 minutes on VEGETABLES mode.
- Meanwhile, remove the seed of the avocado and mash it with the cubes of mango. Season the mixture with the chia seed powder and add 1 tbsp. of coconut oil.
- When the Pressure cooker beeps, release the pressure. Open it and add the fruits and 3 tbsp. of coconut oil. Stir the ingredients together and mix well. Serve and enjoy.

50. Oatmeal soaked in Coconut milk

(Time: 5 Minutes \ Servings: 3)

INGREDIENTS

3 cups of rolled oats, soaked
3 cups of water (filtered)
6 tbsp. of kombucha or buttermilk
3 cups of raw coconut milk
1 tbsp. of cinnamon
1 tbsp. lemon juice
¼ tsp. of stevia

2 tbsp. of coconut oil
¼ to ½ cup of organic raisins
¼ cup of pomegranate
¼ cup of unsweetened shredded coconut
¼ cup of chopped nuts
¼ cup of almonds

DIRECTIONS

- The night before mix together the oats, water, and a little bit of lemon juice in a pressure cooker. Cover the pressure cooker and set aside on the counter.
- In the morning, take the soaked oats and pour them into the Fagor Pressure Cooker, add most of the coconut milk and the cinnamon.
- Add the stevia and set to SOUP mode, letting the ingredients simmer.
- Set the timer to 5 minutes or until the mixture thickens.
- Add the coconut oil, raisins, coconut, almonds, and nuts.
- Keep stirring gently. Add the remaining coconut milk, pomegranate, and cream.

51. Eggs Benedict with Asparagus

(Time: 20 Minutes \ Servings: 2-3)

INGREDIENTS

7 stalks of asparagus
5 eggs
2 tsp. of apple cider vinegar
chives for garnishing
2 tbsp. hollandaise sauce

2 egg yolks
¼ cup of coconut oil
2 tsp. of fresh lemon juice
¼ tsp. of paprika
¼ tsp. of sea salt

DIRECTIONS

- Heat the Fagor Pressure Cooker and place the trivet inside it.
- Break each of the eggs into a small ramekin.
- Trim the asparagus stalks from the bottom.
- Slice the asparagus stalks lengthwise. Pour 1 cup of water into a sauce pan and cook the asparagus for 5 minutes.
- Place the asparagus in each ramekin and add the cider vinegar.
- Slide the eggs in the ramekin, then cover the Pressure cooker with a lid and set to SOUP, cooking the ingredients for 8 minutes.
- Prepare the sauce by boiling water in a blender, then cover and set aside for 10 minutes. Blend the egg yolk and add the lemon juice, the salt, and the paprika.
- Add the melted butter and keep mixing for 40 seconds.
- Serve each of the eggs over the dish of asparagus stalks and top with the hollandaise sauce and chives.

52. Coconut Muffins

(Time: 10 Minutes \ Servings: 3-5)

INGREDIENTS

½ cup of almonds
½ cup of walnuts
1 cup of unsweetened coconut flakes
½ cup of flaxseed meal
3 tsp. of cinnamon
1 tsp. of nutmeg

½ tsp. of salt
¼ cup of coconut oil
¼ cup of coconut sugar
1 mashed banana
2 tsp. of vanilla extract

FOR THE TOPPING:

Use Almond milk or Coconut milk

Raspberries, blueberries or blackberries

DIRECTIONS

- Heat the Fagor Pressure Cooker on high heat and pour 1 ½ cups of water inside.
- Coat a muffin tin with coconut oil.
- In a food processor, add the almonds, walnuts, and unsweetened coconuts flakes. Grind the ingredients. Transfer the mixture to another large bowl and add the flaxseed meal, cinnamon, nutmeg, and the salt. Mix very well.
- In another bowl, melt the coconut oil, add the coconut sugar, banana, vanilla extract, and mix well.
- In a bowl, pour and mix the wet ingredients with the dry mixture and blend thoroughly. Using your hands, separate the mixture into even parts and place the cookies in the muffin tins.
- Set to high pressure for 10 minutes. Once the timer goes off, remove the tins from the Pressure cooker after releasing the pressure.
- Serve the cookies with the almond milk or yogurt and the berries.

53. Quinoa with Pomegranate

(Time: 10 minutes \ Servings: 2)

INGREDIENTS

½ cup of uncooked quinoa
1 cup of water
1 cup of milk

½ cup of pomegranate arils
¼ cup of shelled and chopped pistachios
2 tsp. of honey

DIRECTIONS

- Rinse ½ cup of uncooked quinoa. Pour a cup of water in the Fagor Pressure Cooker.
- Set to MANUAL and set the time to 4 minutes. Don't close the lid of the Pressure cooker.
- When the water boils, add the quinoa.
- Add 1 cup of coconut milk with the pomegranate and the honey.
- Close the lid and set the function to STEAM for 10 minutes.
- Once the timer beeps, release the pressure by applying quick release.
- Remove the quinoa from the heat and press Keep Warm for around 10 minutes.
- Serve and enjoy the quinoa with pistachios and honey.

Lunch

54. Cod Fillets
(Time: 20 minutes \ Servings: 3)

INGREDIENTS:

3 cod fillets
2 cups cabbage
1 cup all-purpose flour
½ tbsp. cornstarch
½ tsp. baking powder
Salt to taste

Juice from 1 lemon
1 Jalapeno pepper
½ tsp. oregano
½ tsp. cumin powder
½ tsp. cayenne pepper
2 tbsp. olive oil

DIRECTIONS:

- Put flour, cornstarch, salt, baking powder and lemon juice into a bowl. Mix well.
- If you need to add water, it can be added accordingly as well.
- Mix cayenne powder, cumin powder and oregano in the mixture made in step 1.
- Stir well. Add oil into the Fagor Pressure Cooker and let the ingredients sauté.
- Add the cod fillets, jalapeno and cabbage over it.
- Pour the flour mixture into the cooker and cook for 15 minutes on VEGETABLES mode.

55. Chicken in Mushrooms
(Time: 18 minutes \ Servings: 2)

INGREDIENTS:

2 tomatoes, chopped
½ lb. chicken, cooked and mashed
1 cup broccoli, chopped
1 tbsp. butter

2 tbsp. mayonnaise
½ cup mushroom soup
salt and pepper, to taste
1 onion, sliced

DIRECTIONS:

- Put chicken into a bowl. Mix mayonnaise, mushroom soup, tomatoes, onion, broccoli, salt and pepper.
- Grease a round baking tray with butter. Put the mixture in a tray.
- Cook in the Fagor Pressure Cooker for 15 minutes on VEGETALBES mode. Serve hot!

56. Shrimp with Honey
(Time: 19 minutes \ Servings: 2)

INGREDIENTS:

1 lb. shrimp, tails removed
2 tbsp. ketchup
1 tbsp. soy sauce
2 tbsp. cornstarch
1 tsp. honey

½ tsp. red pepper
½ tsp. ginger powder
½ tsp. vegetable oil.
2 onions
2 garlic cloves

DIRECTIONS:

- Mix honey, red pepper, cornstarch, soy sauce, ketchup, ginger powder and garlic cloves in a bowl.
- Put vegetable oil in the Fagor Pressure Cooker and add the honey mixture. Stir for 3 minutes.
- Add shrimp to it and mix well. Stir-fry for another 10 minutes.
- When ready, serve and enjoy!

57. Halibut Fillets

(Time: 15 minutes \ Servings: 2)

INGREDIENTS:

2 halibut fillets
1 tbsp. dill
1 tbsp. onion powder
1 cup parsley

2 tbsp. paprika
1 tbsp. garlic powder
1 tbsp. lemon pepper
2 tbsp. lemon juice

DIRECTIONS:

- Mix lemon juice, lemon pepper, garlic powder, and paprika, parsley and onion powder in a bowl.
- Add dill to it. Pour the mixture in the Fagor Pressure Cooker and place halibut fish over it.
- Cook for 10 minutes on VEGETABLES mode. When ready, serve and enjoy!

58. Salmon with Soy Sauce

(Time: 15 minutes \ Servings: 3)

INGREDIENTS:

2 Salmon fillets
½ maple syrup
2 tbsp. soy sauce

1 tbsp. garlic powder
salt and pepper, to taste

DIRECTIONS:

- Put maple syrup, soy sauce, salt, pepper and garlic powder into a bowl.
- Dip salmon in the mixture and place it in the Fagor Pressure Cooker.
- Cook on SAUTÉ for 10 minutes, turning it once. Serve immediately.

59. Shrimp with Linguine

(Time: 15 minutes \ Servings: 2)

INGREDIENTS:

1 lb. shrimp, cleaned
1 lb. linguine. cooked
1 tbsp. butter
½ cup white wine

½ cup cheese, shredded
2 garlic cloves, minced
1 cup parsley
salt and pepper, to taste

DIRECTIONS:

- Put butter in the Fagor Pressure Cooker and sauté it.
- Mix in linguine, white wine, cheese, garlic cloves and parsley.
- Cook for 4 minutes. Add shrimp and cook for 5 more minutes.
- When done, serve and enjoy!

60. Corn Kernels with Jicama

(Time: 16 minutes \ Servings: 2)

INGREDIENTS:

2 cups corn kernels
½ onion, minced
½ cup Jicama
½ cup bell pepper
1 cup cilantro leave

½ cup lemon juice
salt and pepper, to taste
1 tbsp. oil
5 corn tortillas
2 tbsp. sour cream

DIRECTIONS:

- Mix onion, corn kernels, bell peppers, cilantro, lemon, salt and pepper into a bowl.
- Out oil in the Fagor Pressure Cooker and let the ingredients sauté.
- Add jicama to the pressure cooker and the mixture. Cook for 10 minutes on SAUTÉ mode.

61. Simple Salmon

(Time: 10 minutes \ Servings: 3)

INGREDIENTS:

1 lb. salmon, cooked, mashed
2 eggs
2 onions
2 stalks celery

1 cup parsley, chopped
1 tbsp. oil
salt and pepper, to taste

DIRECTIONS:

- Mix salmon, onion, celery, parsley, salt and pepper in a bowl.
- Put oil in the Fagor Pressure Cooker and sauté it.
- Meanwhile, make patties out of the mixture and dip them in the whisked eggs.
- Place each patty in the pressure cooker when all are made, and cook for 5 minutes.
- When ready, enjoy the delicious fish patties.

62. Simply Cooked Shrimp

(Time: 13 minutes \ Servings: 2)

INGREDIENTS:

1 lb. shrimp
2 garlic cloves
2 tbsp. oil
1 tbsp. butter.

red pepper, a pinch
salt and pepper, to taste
1 cup parsley, chopped

DIRECTIONS:

- Put the shrimp into the Fagor Pressure Cooker and SAUTÉ them with the oil for 2 minutes.
- Add garlic cloves, butter, red pepper, and salt and pepper. Stir-fry for another 5 minutes.
- When ready, take them out and garnish with parsley.

63. Lemony Scallops with Mushroom

(Time: 24 minutes \ Servings: 2)

INGREDIENTS:

1 lb. scallops
2 onions , chopped
1 tbsp. butter

2 tbsp. oil
1 cup mushrooms, sliced
1 tbsp. lemon juice

DIRECTIONS:

- Put oil into the Fagor Pressure Cooker.
- Add onions, butter, mushrooms, salt and pepper, lemon juice and scallops.
- Cook for 15 minutes on MANUAL on high pressure. When ready, it beeps, so take it out and serve!

64.   Delicious Crab Meat Balls

(Time: 15 minutes \ Servings: 3)

INGREDIENTS:

1 lb. crab meat
½ cup cream cheese
2 tbsp. mayonnaise

salt and pepper, to taste
1 tbsp. lemon juice
1 cup mozzarella cheese, shredded

DIRECTIONS:

- Mix mayonnaise, cream cheese, salt and pepper, and lemon juice in a bowl.
- Add crab meat to it and make small balls.
- Place the balls in the Fagor Pressure Cooker and let them cook for 10 minutes on STEAM setting.
- When done, sprinkle the cheese over it and serve!

65.   Tilapia Delight

(Time: 16 minutes \ Servings: 4)

INGREDIENTS:

4 tilapia fillets
4 tbsp. lemon juice
2 tbsp. butter

2 garlic cloves
½ cup parsley
salt and pepper, to taste

DIRECTIONS:

- Mix tilapia with lemon juice and put it into the Fagor Pressure Cooker.
- Add butter, garlic cloves, parsley, and sprinkle salt and pepper over it.
- Cover it and cook for 10 minutes on STEAM setting.
- When ready, serve and enjoy this simple tilapia recipe.

66.   Salmon with Black Olives

(Time: 14 minutes \ Servings: 2)

INGREDIENTS:

1 lb. salmon fillets
2 tbsp. oil
2 tomatoes
½ cup peas
1 cup basil, chopped

1 onion
½ cup black olives
2 tbsp. lemon Juice
salt and pepper, to taste

DIRECTIONS:

- Mix salmon fillets with lemon juice in a bowl. Set aside.
- Press SAUTÉ and add oil to the Fagor Pressure Cooker.
- Add tomatoes, peas, basil, onion, black olives, and salt and pepper. Mix well.
- Add the salmon fillets and brown them for 7 minutes on each side. When ready, serve and enjoy!

67. Quinoa Stuffed Peppers

(Time: 20 minutes \ Servings: 4)

INGREDIENTS

2 cups of mixed quinoa
2 cups of water
4 red bell peppers
1 cup crumbled feta cheese or chia cheese.
2 seeded, chopped tomatoes
1 finely chopped bunch of fresh cilantro

2 chopped onions
2 garlic cloves
1 tsp. of ginger
1 tsp. of flax seed powder
zest of one lime
1 tbsp. of coconut oil.

DIRECTIONS

- Set the Pressure Cooker to VEGETABLES mode, and pour 1 cup of water. Boil the quinoa for 10 minutes.
- Drain the quinoa and clean the peppers. Scoop out their seeds and line them in a baking dish.
- Mix the quinoa with the tomatoes, cheese, cilantro, ginger, flax seed powder, onion, oil, and lemon juice.
- Season with a pinch of salt and a pinch of pepper. Fill the peppers with the quinoa mixture.
- Sprinkle cheese on the top and place the dish in the steaming basket
- Pour 1 cup of water in the Pressure cooker and place the basket with the baking dish.
- Cook for 10 minutes on MANUAL on high pressure Optionally, you can serve with greek yogurt.

68. Baked Flaxseed Quinoa

(Time: 15 minutes \ Servings: 3)

INGREDIENTS

3 cups of rolled cooked quinoa
½ cup of toasted almond pieces
½ cup of puffed rice
¼ cup of roasted pumpkin seeds
¼ cup of flax seeds
3 tbsp. of brown sugar

½ tsp. of ground cinnamon
¼ tsp. of salt
½ cup of honey
¼ cup of coconut oil
1 tsp. of almond extract

DIRECTIONS

- In a bowl, mix quinoa, almonds, puffed rice, pumpkin seeds, flax seeds, brown sugar, cinnamon, and salt.
- In another bowl, mix together the oil, honey, and almonds.
- Pour it over the dry mixture and combine with the honey mixture.
- Pour 1 cup of water in the Pressure cooker and place the trivet or the steaming basket inside.
- Spread a very thin layer of the mixture on a greased baking dish and cook for around 15 minutes in the Pressure cooker on BEANS mode. When ready, serve and enjoy!

69. Quick Kale

(Time: 12 minutes \ Servings: 3)

INGREDIENTS:

6 cups kale, chopped
2 tbsp. lemon juice
1 tbsp. oil

1 tbsp. garlic, minced
1 tsp. soy sauce
salt and pepper, to taste

DIRECTIONS:

- Add oil into the Fagor Pressure Cooker.
- Sauté garlic, soy sauce, lemon juice for 1-2 minutes. Add the kale, salt and pepper.
- Close the lid and cook for 10 minutes on MANUAL on high pressure.

70. Seashells Spinach Mix

(Time: 15 minutes \ Servings: 3)

INGREDIENTS:

1 lb. seashells, thawed
1 package of 10 oz. fresh spinach, chopped
2 tbsp. oil –

7 cloves garlic , minced
1 tsp. red pepper flakes
Salt

DIRECTIONS:

- Put oil into the Fagor Pressure Cooker, and SAUTÉ it.
- Add garlic, red pepper flakes, spinach and seashells.
- Season with salt, and cook for 10 minutes on VEGETABLES mode.
- When the pressure cooker beeps, serve and enjoy!

71. Cauliflower Special

(Time: 16 minutes \ Servings: 3)

INGREDIENTS:

1 cauliflower, cut in pieces
3 potatoes, peeled and cut in chunks
1 tbsp. oil

1 tbsp. cumin seeds
2 tomatoes , diced
salt to taste

DIRECTIONS:

- Add oil into the Fagor Pressure Cooker. Mix in tomatoes and cumin seeds.
- Add cauliflower and potatoes with the salt.
- Cook for 10 minutes on VEGETABLES mode.
- When ready, serve and enjoy!

72. Sweet Potato with Cheese

(Time: 15 minutes \ Servings: 3)

INGREDIENTS:

2 lb. sweet potatoes, cubed
2 garlic cloves
1 tbsp. sage
1 tbsp. rosemary

2 tbsp. butter
2 cups cheddar cheese, grated
Salt to taste

DIRECTIONS:

- Add garlic cloves into the Fagor Pressure Cooker and sage, butter and rosemary.
- Add sweet potatoes with salt. Cook on MANUAL on high pressure for 10 minutes.
- When ready, enjoy the tasty meal!

73. Spinach and Tomatoes

(Time: 14 minutes \ Servings: 2)

INGREDIENTS:

2 tbsp. butter
1 onion, chopped
2 cloves garlic – 2 cloves
1 tbsp. cumin powder
1 tbsp. paprika

2 tomatoes , chopped
2 cups vegetable broth
1 small bunch of spinach, chopped
cilantro for garnishing

DIRECTIONS:

- Add butter into the Fagor Pressure Cooker. Sauté it.
- Mix onion, garlic, and cumin powder, paprika, and vegetable broth. Stir well.
- Add tomatoes and spinach. Cook on MANUAL on high pressure for 10 minutes.

74. Black Beans with Lentils and Veggies

(Time: 15 minutes \ Servings: 2)

INGREDIENTS:

1 tbsp. olive oil
1 red onion , chopped
2 carrots , chopped
1 tbsp. oregano
2 tbsp. garlic powder

2 tomatoes , chopped
1 cup water
1 cup lentils
4 cups black beans
salt to taste

DIRECTIONS:

- Add oil into the Fagor Pressure Cooker and let it sauté.
- In a bowl, mix together red onion, black beans, lentils, water, tomatoes, garlic powder, oregano and carrots. Add the mixture to the cooker.
- Cook for 15 minutes on BEANS mode. When done, serve!

75. Chicken with Black Beans

(Time: 20 minutes \ Servings: 3)

INGREDIENTS:

1 tbsp. olive oil
2 cups chicken breast, cubed
1 green bell pepper
3 cups black beans
1 tbsp. cumin powder

2 cups cabbage leaves
1 tbsp. garlic powder
1 tbsp. cayenne powder
salt to taste

DIRECTIONS:

- Add oil into the Fagor Pressure Cooker and let it sauté.
- Mix chicken cubes, cumin powder and cayenne powder in a bowl. Mix well.
- Add the chicken mixture to the pressure cooker and the bell pepper, black beans, cabbage leaves and garlic powder. Salt to taste. Cook on BEANS mode for 15 minutes.
- When done, serve and enjoy the meal!

76. Black-Eyed Peas

(Time: 15 minutes \ Servings: 2)

INGREDIENTS:

2 sweet potatoes, sliced
1 tbsp. coriander seeds
1 tbsp. cumin seeds
black-eyed peas

salt to taste
2 garlic cloves
2 cups tomato sauce
1 onion, chopped

DIRECTIONS:

- Add tomato sauce into the Fagor Pressure Cooker. Stir slowly.
- Mix onion, garlic, salt, black-eyed peas, cumin seeds and coriander seeds. Add sweet potatoes.
- Cook for 15 minutes on BEANS mode.

77. Rice and Beans

(Time: 15 minutes \ Servings: 3)

INGREDIENTS:

1 onion , diced
2 garlic cloves
2 cups brown rice
2 cups black beans

3 cups water
salt to taste
1 avocado, cubed

DIRECTIONS:

- Add water into the Fagor Pressure Cooker with the black beans and rice.
- Cook for 4 minutes.
- Add garlic, salt and avocado.
- Cook on MANUAL on high pressure for 10 minutes.

78. Borlotti Beans with Tomato Sauce

(Time: 16 minutes \ Servings: 3)

INGREDIENTS:

2 cups Tomato sauce
2 tbsp. Oregano powder
1 tbsp. Red pepper flakes
1 Carrot, sliced

2 Garlic cloves
1 Onion , chopped
2 cups Borlotti beans
salt to taste

DIRECTIONS:

- Add tomato sauce with oregano powder into the Fagor Pressure Cooker.
- Mix in the carrot, red pepper flakes, garlic, onion, beans and salt.
- Cook for 15 minutes on BEANS mode.
- When ready, serve and enjoy!

79. Simple White Beans

(Time: 15 minutes \ Servings: 3)

INGREDIENTS:

1 tbsp. olive oil
2 tbsp. garlic, minced
2 cups spinach
2 tomatoes

3 cups white beans
salt and pepper, to taste
cheese to garnish

DIRECTIONS:

- Heat oil into the Fagor Pressure Cooker SAUTÉ mode.
- Add garlic, spinach, tomatoes, white beans and salt and pepper. Mix well.
- Cook for 10 minutes on MANUAL on high pressure.
- When ready, garnish with cheese and serve!

80. Black Beans with Tomatoes

(Time: 14 minutes \ Servings: 3)

INGREDIENTS:

2 tbsp. canola oil
1 onion, chopped
1 zucchini, chopped
3 cups black beans

2 tomatoes, diced
salt and pepper, to taste
½ cup corn
parsley to garnish

DIRECTIONS:

- Heat oil into the Fagor Pressure Cooker on SAUTÉ mode.
- Mix onion, black beans, tomatoes, corn, zucchini, and salt and pepper.
- Cook for 10 minutes on MANUAL on high pressure.
- When done, garnish with parsley and serve.

81. Kidney Beans with Chickpeas

(Time: 18 minutes \ Servings: 3)

INGREDIENTS:

3 cups red kidney beans
3 cups chickpeas
1 tbsp. black pepper
1 tbsp. oil

Salt to taste
1 tbsp. mustard seeds
2 cloves garlic, minced
1 cup water

DIRECTIONS:

- Add oil into the Fagor Pressure Cooker. Add chickpeas and stir well.
- Mix in the mustard seeds, kidney beans, garlic, water and black pepper.
- Cook on MANUAL on high pressure for 15 minutes.
- When ready, serve and enjoy!

82. Cheesy Macaroni

(Time: 30 minutes \ Servings: 3)

INGREDIENTS:

1 package macaroni, cooked
half lb. mozzarella cheese
¼ cup cream cheese
1 cup parmesan cheese
2-3 garlic cloves

¼ teaspoon black pepper
¼ teaspoon salt
½ cup vegetable broth
2 tablespoons butter

DIRECTIONS:

- Set the Fagor Pressure Cooker on SAUTÉ mode and melt butter.
- Sauté garlic for 30 seconds and add the vegetable broth.
- Add in the the macaroni, mozzarella cheese, parmesan cheese and cream cheese.
- Season with salt and pepper.
- Cover the pressure cooker with a lid and cook on high pressure on MANUAL mode for 30 minutes.

83. Spaghetti Squash Delight

(Time: 35 minutes \ Servings: 3)

INGREDIENTS:

1 squash, halved
3 tomatoes, chopped
1 onion, sliced
2-3 garlic cloves, minced
4 cups water

1 teaspoon basil, chopped
¼ teaspoon sea salt
2 tablespoons caster sugar
5 tablespoons butter

DIRECTIONS:

- In the Fagor Pressure Cooker, add water and place a trivet.
- Place the squash on the trivet and cover the pressure cooker with a lid.
- Cook on MANUAL on high pressure for 25 minutes.
- When the squash is softened, remove it from the pressure cooker and transfer to a platter.
- Shred it using a fork.
- Melt butter in the Fagor Pressure Cooker and sauté onion and garlic for 1 minute.
- Stir in the shredded squash and fry for 2-3 minutes.
- Season with salt and sugar, and sprinkle basil on top. Serve hot and enjoy.

84. Lentils with Tomato and Cucumber

(Time: 25 minutes \ Servings: 2)

INGREDIENTS:

1 cup lentils, soaked
2 tomatoes, chopped
1 cucumber, chopped
1 onion, chopped
1 teaspoon ginger paste
1 teaspoon garlic paste

1 bay leaf
¼ teaspoon salt
3 cups chicken broth
¼ teaspoon black pepper
2 tablespoons olive oil

DIRECTIONS:

- Heat oil in the Fagor Pressure Cooker on SAUTÉ mode and fry onion, ginger paste, garlic paste and bay leaf for 1 minute. Add the lentils and fry for 4-5 minutes.
- Add the chicken broth, salt, black pepper, and cook on BEANS mode for 20 minutes.
- Add the tomatoes and the cucumber and cook for 5 minutes. Transfer to a serving dish and serve hot.

85. Spinach Tortilla

(Time: 35 minutes \ Servings: 3)

INGREDIENTS:

1 cup gram flour
1 cup spinach, chopped
¼ teaspoon chili flakes

¼ cup mushrooms, sliced
½ teaspoon salt
1 cup cooking oil

DIRECTIONS:

- In a bowl, add the gram flour, the mushrooms, spinach, salt, and chili flakes and mix well.
- Add ¼ cup of water and make a thick batter.
- Heat oil in the Fagor Pressure Cooker on SAUTÉ mode, and drop a spoon of batter.
- Transfer the mixture and cook until golden brown.
- Serve with cilantro sauce and enjoy.

86. Lemony Chicken Pasta

(Time: 35 minutes \ Servings: 3)

INGREDIENTS:

1 package pasta, boiled
¼ lb. chicken, breasts

4 tablespoons lemon juice
2 tablespoons olive oil

DIRECTIONS:

- Heat oil in the Fagor Pressure Cooker and add the chicken. Fry until golden brown.
- Add the pasta and fry for 1-2 minutes.
- Cook for 1-2 minutes. Turn off the heat and transfer to a serving dish.
- Drizzle lemon juice and serve.

87. Lamb with Thyme

(Time: 55 minutes \ Servings: 4)

INGREDIENTS:

½ lb. lamb, pieces
2 carrots, sliced
3 tablespoons thyme springs

1 teaspoon salt
3 cups water
8 oz. boiled rice

DIRECTIONS:

- In the Fagor Pressure Cooker add the lamb pieces, carrots, thyme, salt and water.
- Cover with the lid and cook on MEAT mode for 50-55 minutes. Serve with the boiled rice or bread.

88. Lamb Loin

(Time: 18 minutes \ Servings: 3)

INGREDIENTS:

2 tbsp. butter
4 pieces lamb loin
2 carrots, chopped
2 cups lamb stock

2 cups baby spinach
2 Garlic cloves, minced
salt and pepper, to taste

DIRECTIONS:

- Melt butter into the Fagor Pressure Cooker on SAUTÉ mode.
- Mix in the carrots, lamb stock, baby spinach, garlic cloves, and salt and pepper. Cook for 4 minutes.
- Add lamb loin and cook for another 15 minutes on MEAT mode. When ready, serve and enjoy!

89. White Beans and Broccoli

(Time: 35 minutes \ Servings: 4)

INGREDIENTS:

1 cup white beans, boiled
1 cup broccoli, florets
½ teaspoon salt

3 tablespoons cooking oil
1 cup tomato sauce
3 cups chicken broth

DIRECTIONS:

- In the Fagor Pressure Cooker, add the beans, chicken broth, tomato sauce, broccoli florets, cooking oil and salt.
- Cook on BEANS mode for 30 minutes. Transfer into serving bowls and enjoy.

90. Seasoned Chickpeas

(Time: 35 minutes \ Servings: 4)

INGREDIENTS:

2 cups chickpeas, boiled
2 tomatoes, chopped
¼ cup tomato puree
2 medium onion, chopped
1 teaspoon cumin seeds
1 teaspoon garlic paste

¼ teaspoon salt
1 cup vegetable broth
¼ teaspoon chili powder
¼ teaspoon dry coriander powder
½ teaspoon cinnamon powder
2 tablespoons olive oil

DIRECTIONS:

- Heat oil in the Fagor Pressure Cooker on SAUTÉ mode and add cumin seeds.
- Add onion and fry until lightly golden. Add in garlic, tomatoes, tomato puree, salt, chili powder, and fry for 4-5 minutes. Add the chickpea and stir for 1-2 minutes.
- Transfer the vegetable broth, cover with a lid and cook on MANUAL mode for 30 minutes.
- Sprinkle coriander powder and cinnamon powder.

91. Quick Chickpeas Snack

(Time: 25 minutes \ Servings: 3)

INGREDIENTS:

1 cup chickpeas, soaked
1 carrot, sliced
1 cup mango chunks
½ cup pineapple chunks
1 cucumber, sliced

¼ teaspoon salt
2 tablespoons vinegar
1 tablespoon olive oil
4 cups water

DIRECTIONS:

- Add water and chickpeas in the Fagor Pressure Cooker.
- Cover with a lid and cook on MANUAL on high pressure for 20 minutes.
- Remove the water and add the cucumber, pineapples, mangoes, carrots, salt, pineapple juice, vinegar, and olive oil. Cook for 5 more minutes on high pressure.
- Transfer the snack to a serving bowl before serving.

92. Roasted Turkey

(Time: 50 minutes \ Servings: 4)

INGREDIENTS:

1 white turkey , up to 9 lb.
1 teaspoon garlic paste
¼ teaspoon salt
¼ teaspoon chili powder
½ teaspoon black pepper
¼ teaspoon thyme

¼ teaspoon rosemary
½ teaspoon cinnamon powder
3 tablespoons lemon juice
4 tablespoons orange juice
3 tablespoons olive oil

DIRECTIONS:

- In a bowl combine orange juice, lemon juice, thyme, rosemary, garlic paste salt, pepper, chili powder, olive oil, and cinnamon powder, mix well.
- Pour on the turkey and rub with hands.
- Transfer the turkey to a greased Fagor Pressure Cooker and cover with a lid.
- Cook on MEAT mode for 45-50 minutes.

93. Creamy Broccoli Stew

(Time: 45 minutes \ Servings: 4)

INGREDIENTS:

1 cup heavy cream
3 oz. parmesan cheese
1 cup broccoli florets
2 carrots, sliced
½ teaspoon garlic paste

¼ teaspoon turmeric powder
¼ teaspoon salt
¼ teaspoon black pepper
½ cup vegetable broth
4 tablespoon butter

DIRECTIONS:

- Melt butter in the Fagor Pressure Cooker on SAUTÉ mode.
- Add garlic and sauté for 30 seconds.
- Add the broccoli and the carrots, and cook until softened.
- Stir in the vegetable broth and cover with a lid.
- Cook on SLOW COOK mode for 40 minutes.
- Serve and enjoy.

94. Cellini Beans with Broccoli and Carrots

(Time: 30 minutes \ Servings: 5)

INGREDIENTS:

2 cup Cellini beans, soaked
2 carrots, sliced
1 cup broccoli florets
¼ teaspoon salt

½ teaspoon white pepper
2 tablespoons lemon juice
3 cups chicken broth
3 tablespoons olive oil

DIRECTIONS:

- In the Fagor Pressure Cooker, add the Cellini beans, carrots, broccoli, salt, pepper, lemon juice, chicken broth, and olive oil, stir and cover with a lid.
- Cook on VEGETABLES mode for 25 minutes.

95. Broccoli with Pasta

(Time: 35 minutes \ Servings: 3)

INGREDIENTS:

1 package pasta
1 cup broccoli florets
1 teaspoon garlic paste
¼ teaspoon salt
1 cup vegetable broth

¼ teaspoon white pepper
2 cups chicken broth
2 tablespoons lemon juice
2 tablespoons olive oil

DIRECTIONS:

- In the Fagor Pressure Cooker, add garlic and oil and sauté for 1 minute on SAUTÉ mode.
- Add the broccoli and stir well.
- Pour in the chicken broth with the pasta and mix well.
- Season with salt and pepper.
- Cover with a lid and cook on MANUAL mode for 30 minutes.

96. Spicy Chickpea Stew

(Time: 35 minutes \ Servings: 4)

INGREDIENTS:

2 cups, chickpeas, boiled
3 tomatoes, chopped
3 small onions, chopped
1 teaspoon garlic paste
¼ teaspoon ginger paste
¼ teaspoon turmeric powder
¼ teaspoon salt

¼ teaspoon chili powder
¼ teaspoon cayenne pepper
¼ teaspoon cinnamon powder
½ teaspoon cumin powder
3 cups chicken broth
2 tablespoons olive oil

DIRECTIONS:

- Heat oil in the Fagor Pressure Cooker on SAUTÉ mode. Add the onion and fry until transparent.
- Add in the garlic, ginger, tomatoes, salt, cayenne pepper, chili powder, turmeric powder and fry for 4-5 minutes.
- Add the chickpea and stir fry for 5 minutes.
- Transfer the chicken broth, cover with a lid and cook on CHILI mode for 25 minutes.
- Sprinkle cumin and cinnamon powder before serving.

97. Hot Red Beans

(Time: 50 minutes \ Servings: 5)

INGREDIENTS:

1 cup red beans, soaked overnight
2 tomatoes, chopped
1 medium onion, chopped
1 teaspoon garlic paste
¼ teaspoon salt
¼ teaspoon chili powder

¼ teaspoon cinnamon powder
½ teaspoon cumin powder
2 cups chicken broth
2 cups water
1 green chili
2 tablespoons olive oil

DIRECTIONS:

- Add the water and the red beans and cook for 20 minutes on MANUAL on high pressure.
- Drain the beans and set aside.
- Heat oil in the Fagor Pressure Cooker on SAUTÉ mode and add onion.
- Fry until transparent. Add garlic, tomatoes, salt, chili powder, and fry for 5 minutes.
- Add the red beans and stir fry for 5 minutes.
- Stir in the chicken broth and the green chili.
- Cover with a lid and cook on CHILI mode for 20 minutes.
- Sprinkle cumin powder and cinnamon powder.

98. Black Lentils

(Time: 45 minutes \ Servings: 5)

INGREDIENTS:

1 cup black lentils, soaked overnight
2 tomatoes, chopped
1 teaspoon garlic paste
¼ teaspoon ginger paste
¼ teaspoon turmeric powder
¼ teaspoon salt

¼ teaspoon chili powder
2 cups chicken broth
2 cups water
2 tablespoons olive oil
1 avocado, for garnishing

DIRECTIONS:

- Add the water, lentils, turmeric powder, and chili powder and cook for 30 minutes on MANUAL on high pressure.
- Transfer the lentils and the stew to a bowl and set aside.
- Heat oil in the Fagor Pressure Cooker on SAUTÉ mode and add garlic and ginger.
- Fry for 30 seconds.
- Add the tomatoes, and the salt and fry for 5-6 minutes.
- Stir in the lentils and the chicken broth. Cook on BEANS mode for 15 minutes.

99. Tropical Red Lentils

(Time: 45 minutes \ Servings: 6)

INGREDIENTS:

1 ½ cups red lentils, soaked overnight
2 tomatoes, chopped
¼ teaspoon ginger paste
¼ teaspoon turmeric powder
¼ teaspoon salt

¼ teaspoon chili powder
2 cups chicken broth
1 cup water
2 tablespoons olive oil
½ bunch fresh coriander

DIRECTIONS:

- In the Fagor Pressure Cooker, sauté oil and ginger for 30 seconds.
- Add the tomatoes, salt, turmeric powder, and chili powder and fry for 5-6 minutes.
- Stir in lentils and fry for 5-10 minutes.
- Stir in the chicken broth.
- Cook on BEANS mode for 30 minutes.
- Sprinkle with coriander and serve.

100. Feta and Rice Stuffed Bell Peppers

(Time: 25 minutes \ Servings: 3)

INGREDIENTS:

1 green bell pepper
1 red bell pepper
1 yellow bell pepper
½ cup rice, boiled
1 cup feta cheese
1 onion, sliced

2 tomatoes, chopped
1 teaspoon black pepper
2-3 garlic clove, minced
3 tablespoon lemon juice
3-4 green olives, chopped
3-4 tablespoons olive oil

DIRECTIONS:

- Grease the Fagor Pressure Cooker with olive oil.
- Make a cut at the top of the bell peppers near the stem. Remove top and hollow out the peppers.
- Place the feta cheese, onion, olives, tomatoes, rice, salt, black pepper, garlic powder, and lemon juice into a bowl and mix well.
- Fill up the bell peppers with the feta mixture and insert in the Fagor Pressure Cooker.
- Set the on MANUAL on high pressure for 20 minutes.

101. Orzo with Potatoes and Carrots

(Time: 30 minutes \ Servings: 3)

INGREDIENTS:

1 cup white orzo
3 oz. parmesan cheese, shredded
2 carrots, sliced
2 potatoes, thinly sliced
1 onion, chopped

¼ teaspoon black pepper
½ teaspoon salt
2-3 garlic cloves, chopped
2 cups chicken broth
3 tablespoons cooking oil

DIRECTIONS:

- Set the Fagor Pressure Cooker on SAUTÉ mode. Heat oil and add onion and garlic, sauté until translucent.
- Add the potatoes, carrot, orzo and chicken broth, mix well.
- Season with salt and pepper. Cover with a lid and cook for 30 minutes on MANUAL on high pressure.
- Top with parmesan cheese.

102. Spinach Orzo

(Time: 30 minutes \ Servings: 4)

INGREDIENTS:

1 cup white orzo
1 cup baby spinach, chopped
1 cup cream cheese
¼ teaspoon black pepper

½ teaspoon salt
2-3 garlic cloves, chopped
2 cups vegetable broth
2 tablespoons cooking oil

DIRECTIONS:

- Set the Fagor Pressure Cooker on SAUTÉ mode and heat oil. Sauté garlic for 30 seconds.
- Add the orzo, spinach, salt and pepper and cook for 1-2 minutes.
- Add the chicken broth, stir well.
- Cover with a lid and cook for 30 minutes on SLOW COOK mode.
- Add the cream cheese and cook for another 5 minutes on MANUAL, low pressure.

103. Chili Garlic Eggplant Pasta

(Time: 30 minutes \ Servings: 3)

INGREDIENTS:

16 oz. package of pasta
1 large egg plant, sliced
1 cup chili garlic sauce
2 tablespoons barbecue sauce
½ cup ketchup

¼ teaspoon chili powder
2-3 garlic cloves, chopped
2 cups vegetable broth
2 tablespoons cooking oil

DIRECTIONS:

- Set the Fagor Pressure Cooker on SAUTÉ mode and heat oil. Fry garlic for 30 seconds.
- Add the eggplants and fry until golden.
- Transfer the eggplants to a separate bowl and set aside.
- In the Pressure cooker, add the chili garlic sauce, ketchup, chili powder, barbecue sauce, and vegetable broth, stir well.
- Add the pasta and cook for 35 minutes on SLOW COOK mode.
- Then add the eggplants and mix thoroughly.
- Cook for another minute.

104. Cottage Cheese and Cabbage Macaroni

(Time: 25 minutes \ Servings: 3)

INGREDIENTS:

16 oz. package of macaroni
1 cup cabbage, copped
1 cup cottage cheese, shredded
2-3 garlic cloves, chopped

¼ teaspoon salt
¼ teaspoon white pepper
2 cups vegetable broth
2 tablespoons cooking oil

DIRECTIONS:

- Set the Fagor Pressure Cooker on SAUTÉ mode, heat oil and fry garlic for 30 seconds.
- Add the cabbage and fry for 1-2 minutes.
- Add the vegetable broth, macaroni, salt, pepper, and cheese and cover up with a lid.
- Cook for 20 minutes on MANUAL on high pressure mode.

105. Slow Cooked Spiced Cabbage

(Time: 60 minutes \ Servings: 2)

INGREDIENTS:

1 cabbage, halved
¼ teaspoon salt
½ teaspoon thyme
¼ teaspoon black pepper

1 tablespoon soya sauce
1 teaspoon garlic powder
2 tablespoons olive oil

DIRECTIONS:

- In a bowl, combine the soya sauce, salt, pepper, thyme, garlic powder and olive oil.
- Place the cabbage into the greased Fagor Pressure Cooker.
- Pour the mixture from the bowl over the cabbage.
- Cover the pressure cooker and cook to SLOW COOK mode for 60 minutes.

106. Cauliflower and Asparagus Pasta

(Time: 25 minutes \ Servings: 3)

INGREDIENTS:

16 oz. package of pasta
½ cup peas
¼ cup cauliflower florets
1 cup asparagus, cut, 1-inch slice
1 cup basil pesto

¼ teaspoon black pepper
2-3 garlic cloves, chopped
2 cups vegetable broth
¼ teaspoon salt
2 tablespoons of cooking oil

DIRECTIONS:

- Set the Fagor Pressure Cooker on SAUTÉ mode and heat oil.
- Fry garlic for 30 seconds.
- Add all vegetables and fry for 4-5 minutes.
- Add the pasta and the vegetable broth and stir well.
- Season with salt, basil pesto and pepper.
- Cook on MANUAL on high pressure for 20 minutes.

107. Potato and Zucchini

(Time: 35- 40 minutes \ Servings: 3)

INGREDIENTS:

2 potatoes, peeled, diced
2 zucchinis, sliced
¼ teaspoon chili powder
½ cup tomato puree

1 teaspoon garlic powder
2 cups vegetable broth
¼ teaspoon salt
2 tablespoons cooking oil

DIRECTIONS:

- Set the Fagor Pressure Cooker on SAUTÉ mode and heat oil. Fry garlic for 30 seconds.
- Add the tomatoes, chili powder, and salt and stir-fry for 1-2 minutes.
- Add the potatoes and the zucchinis and fry for 10-15 minutes.
- Add the pasta and the vegetable broth and stir well.
- Cook on VEGETABLES mode for 15 minutes.

Snacks and Appetizers

108. Potatoes and Black Beans

(Time: 16 minutes \ Servings: 3)

INGREDIENTS:

2 tbsp. olive oil
1 sweet potato, sliced
1 onion , diced
2 tbsp. chili powder
1 tbsp. cumin powder

salt to taste
3 cups black beans
cilantro to garnish
2 tbsp. red hot sauce

DIRECTIONS:

- Add oil into the Fagor Pressure Cooker and sauté it. Mix in the onion, red hot sauce, black beans, salt, cumin powder, and chili powder. Stir well.
- Add sweet potatoes and cook on BEANS mode for 15 minutes. When done, garnish with cilantro and serve!

109. Chicken Broth with Dried Cherries

(Time: 14 minutes \ Servings: 3)

INGREDIENTS:

2 tbsp. olive oil
1 Red onion, chopped
3 Garlic, minced
2 cups rice, cooked
2 cups chicken broth
1 tbsp. parsley, chopped

1 tbsp. rosemary, chopped
1 tbsp. sage, chopped
Salt and pepper, to taste
½ cup cherries, dried
hazelnuts for seasoning
thyme, chopped to garnish

DIRECTIONS:

- Add olive oil into the Fagor Pressure Cooker and press the SAUTÉ button.
- Add the onion, chicken broth, parsley, sage, rosemary, salt and pepper, cherries and rice. Mix well.
- Cook for 15 minutes on MANUAL mode.
- When ready, take it out and garnish it with hazelnuts and thyme.

110. Sweet Potatoes with Cheese

(Time: 15 minutes \ Servings: 4)

INGREDIENTS:

4 sweet potatoes, diced
3 garlic cloves, chopped
salt and pepper, to taste
½ cup parsley, chopped
½ cup sage, chopped

½ cup thyme, chopped
½ cup milk
2 tbsp. butter
½ cup mozzarella cheese, shredded

DIRECTIONS:

- Add sweet potatoes, salt and pepper, garlic cloves, sage, parsley, thyme and milk into the Fagor Pressure Cooker. Cook for 10 minutes on MANUAL on high pressure.
- Release the pressure and then add butter and cheese to it.
- Close the lid and cook for another 5 minutes.

111. Simple Rice

(Time: 10 minutes \ Servings: 4)

INGREDIENTS:

4 cups Pink rice, uncooked
5 cups Water

½ tbsp. Salt

DIRECTIONS:

- Add water into the Fagor Pressure Cooker and mix in the rice and salt.
- Cook on MANUAL on high pressure for 5 minutes.
- When ready, perform a quick release.

112. Rice with Saffron

(Time: 11 minutes \ Servings: 3)

INGREDIENTS:

½ tsp. saffron threads
2 tbsp. milk
½ tbsp. olive oil
1 onion, chopped
½ cup rice, uncooked

2 cups vegetable broth
2 cinnamon stick
salt to taste
chopped almonds for seasoning

DIRECTIONS:

- Add onion, vegetable broth, salt, cinnamon stick, olive oil and saffron threads into the pressure cooker, and Cook for 2 minutes.
- Add rice to it and milk. Cook on RICE mode for 5 minutes.
- When ready, serve with chopped almonds on top.

113. Cheesy Plantain Patty

(Time: 12 minutes \ Servings: 2)

INGREDIENTS:

2 large ripe plantains
Oil for frying

8 mozzarella cheese slices

FOR THE BATTER

2 Eggs
4 tbsp. all-purpose flour
2 tbsp. sugar

2 tbsp. milk
a pinch of salt

DIRECTIONS:

- Add oil into the Fagor Pressure Cooker.
- Mix ripe plantain and cheese in a bowl.
- Make round patties out of the mixture. Set aside.
- Prepare the batter: mix eggs, flour, sugar, milk and salt in another bowl.
- Dip the plantain patties into the batter. Place in the cooker.
- Cook for 10 minutes on MANUAL on high pressure.

114. Avocado Snack

(Time: 25 minutes \ Servings: 2)

INGREDIENTS:

2 avocados
¼ cup green bell pepper, diced
2 cup cucumber, diced
salt and pepper, to taste

2 tbsp. lime juice
2 tbsp. cilantro
1 cup water
¼ cup white vinegar

DIRECTIONS:

- Add avocados and green bell pepper into the Pressure cooker. Add in the cucumber and water.
- Cook for 5 minutes on STEAM mode. Transfer to a blender and blend for 2 minutes.
- Put the mixture back into the pressure cooker.
- Sprinkle with lime juice, white vinegar, salt and pepper.
- Cook for 15 minutes on MANUAL on high pressure.
- When ready, garnish with cilantro and serve.

115. Delicious Chorizo Snack

(Time: 12 minutes \ Servings: 2)

INGREDIENTS:

2 cups cornmeal
3 tbsp. oil
2 tbsp. parmesan cheese
2 tbsp. butter

a pinch of salt
1 cup fresco crumbles
2 chorizos, sliced and cooked
cilantro for garnish

DIRECTIONS:

- Mix together cornmeal and parmesan cheese in a bowl. Add butter and salt. Mix well.
- Make small patties out of the mixture. Add oil into the Fagor Pressure Cooker.
- Place patties in pressure cooker and cook for 5 minutes on MANUAL on high pressure.
- When ready, set aside. Place chorizo slices on the plate.
- Add fresco crumbles, then place a patty on top.
- Garnish with cilantro and serve!

116. Minty Cherries

(Time: 9 minutes \ Servings: 4)

INGREDIENTS:

2 tbsp. apple cider vinegar
1 tbsp. lemon juice
2 tbsp. olive oil
salt to taste

½ cup cherries, dried
4 green onions, chopped
½ cup mint leaves, chopped
1 cup fresh cherries

DIRECTIONS:

- Mix apple cider vinegar with lemon juice in a bowl.
- Put the mixture into the Fagor Pressure Cooker and add the dried cherries.
- Add green onions, mint leaves and salt to it and stir.
- Cook on high pressure for 4 minutes.
- When ready, serve with fresh cherries and enjoy!

117. Easy Muffins

(Time: 15 minutes \ Servings: 3)

INGREDIENTS:

1 large package Muffin mix
1 cup Milk

2 Eggs

DIRECTIONS:

- Put muffin mix with milk and eggs in a bowl. Blend well.
- Pour the mixture into the Fagor Pressure Cooker and cook on high pressure for 10 minutes.
- When it beeps, take it out and serve by cutting it into pieces.

118. Eggs with Pecans and Herbs

(Time: 12 minutes \ Servings: 4)

INGREDIENTS:

½ cup breadcrumbs
½ cup pecans, chopped
2 tbsp. butter
1 cup cream cheese

2 eggs
2 tbsp. garlic, minced
2 tbsp. rosemary
a pinch salt and pepper

DIRECTIONS:

- Mix breadcrumbs, butter and pecans in a bowl.
- Add it into the Fagor Pressure Cooker and cook for 2 minutes on SAUTÉ mode.
- Add cream cheese, beaten eggs, garlic, rosemary, salt and pepper.
- Cook for another 5 minutes on MANUAL on high pressure.

119. Delicious Chicken Broth

(Time: 9 minutes \ Servings: 4)

INGREDIENTS:

2 tbsp. butter
2 cups chicken broth

1 6.7 oz. pack of harvest grain blend
a pinch salt and pepper

DIRECTIONS:

- Add chicken broth into the Fagor Pressure Cooker.
- Add harvest grain package, butter, salt and pepper. Set on BROTH mode and cook for 10 minutes.

120. Flavorful Tomatoes

(Time: 10 minutes \ Servings: 3)

INGREDIENTS:

1 tbsp. olive oil
1 onion, chopped
2 garlic cloves, minced
2 cup vegetable stock
2 tomatoes, diced

salt to taste
2 bay leaf
½ tbsp. oregano powder
½ tbsp. rosemary powder.
¼ cup basil

DIRECTIONS:

- Add olive oil in the Fagor Pressure Cooker and press the SAUTÉ button.
- Stir in onion, tomatoes, vegetable stock, bay leaf, rosemary powder, salt, and oregano powder.
- Cook on high pressure for 5 minutes. When ready, top with basil and serve.

121. Sweet Potatoes with Butter and Vanilla

(Time: 15 minutes \ Servings: 4)

INGREDIENTS:

3 sweet potatoes, diced
½ tbsp. sugar
1 tbsp. butter
½ tbsp. vanilla

1 tbsp. cinnamon powder
1 tbsp. nutmeg powder
2 cups heavy cream

DIRECTIONS:

- Add sweet potatoes, sugar, vanilla, butter, nutmeg and cinnamon powder into the Fagor Pressure Cooker.
- Cook on high pressure for 10 minutes. When ready, dress with heavy cream and serve!

122. Rice with Vegetable Broth

(Time: 14 minutes \ Servings: 4)

INGREDIENTS:

2 cups vegetable broth
2 cups rice, cookerd
2 avocado, chopped

½ cup cilantro chopped
½ tbsp. hot sauce
salt and pepper, to taste

DIRECTIONS:

- Add vegetable broth, rice into the Fagor Pressure Cooker.
- Mix avocado, cilantro, hot sauce, and salt and pepper.
- Cook on BROTH mode for 10 minutes. When ready, serve and enjoy!

123. Quinoa with Vegetables

(Time: 10 minutes \ Servings: 4)

INGREDIENTS:

½ cup quinoa, cooked
1 cup water
1 carrot, sliced
1 cucumber, sliced
½ cup frozen edamame

2 onions, sliced
½ cabbage, chopped
½ tbsp. soy sauce
½ tbsp. ginger, minced
salt to taste

DIRECTIONS:

- Add quinoa, salt, water, cucumber, edamame, carrot, cabbage and onion into the Fagor Pressure Cooker.
- Cook for 5 minutes on VEGETALBES mode.
- Mix soy sauce and ginger in a bowl. Pour the sauce over the quinoa and serve.

124. Scotch Eggs

(Time: 20 minutes \ Servings: 4)

INGREDIENTS:

4 eggs
2 cups water

1 lb. ground sausage
4 tbsp. vegetable oil

DIRECTIONS:

- Place the eggs in the Fagor Pressure Cooker.
- Add water and cook them for 10 minutes on SOUP mode.
- When boiled, take them out and peel off the skin.

- Take each egg, cover it with the ground sausage, and shape it into a ball.
- Lightly brush the egg/sausage ball with vegetable oil. Place it in the Fagor Pressure Cooker.
- Do the same with all eggs. Cook in the pressure cooker for 10 minutes on MANUAL mode.

125. Potato with Parsley

(Time: 13 minutes \ Servings: 3)

INGREDIENTS:

4 potatoes, diced
2 cups of water
2 eggs
1 onion, chopped
2 tbsp. mayonnaise

½ cup Parsley, chopped
½ cup dill pickle juice
1 tbsp. mustard
salt and pepper, to taste

DIRECTIONS:

- Add water and potatoes in the Fagor Pressure Cooker. Cook on MANUAL on high pressure for 3 minutes.
- Whisk the eggs and add them to the pot.
- Add onion, parsley, dill pickle juice, mayonnaise, mustard, salt and pepper. Mix well.
- Cook on high pressure for 5 minutes. When ready, serve and enjoy!

126. Creamy Spinach

(Time: 20 minutes \ Servings: 3)

INGREDIENTS:

2 cups milk
½ cup cream
3 minced garlic cloves
1 bay leaf
salt and pepper, to taste
4 slices of bacon

1 cup spinach leaves
1 tsp. butter
2 onions, chopped
½ cup cheese, shredded
1 tsp. lemon juice

DIRECTIONS:

- Mix milk and cream in a bowl. Add garlic, spinach leaves, butter, onions, and cheese and lemon juice.
- Add bay leaf with salt and pepper. Mix well. Grease a round baking tray with butter and add the mixture.
- Cook it in the Fagor Pressure Cooker for 15 minutes on MANUAL mode on high pressure.

127. Cauliflower and Onion

(Time: 15 minutes \ Servings: 3)

INGREDIENTS:

4 cups cauliflower florets
2 tbsp. olive oil
salt and pepper, to taste
2 onion, diced
3 cloves garlic, minced

2 cups chicken broth
1 tbsp. thyme , chopped
1 tbsp. butter
½ bunch parsley, chopped

DIRECTIONS:

- Mix olive oil with salt and pepper into the Fagor Pressure Cooker.
- Add cauliflower florets. Add onion, chicken broth, garlic, thyme and butter.
- Cook it on high pressure for 15 minutes. Release the pressure and take it out.
- Top with parsley and serve.

128. Simple Potatoes

(Time: 15 minutes \ Servings: 4)

INGREDIENTS:

4 potatoes, diced
2 tbsp. olive oil

2 garlic cloves, minced
2 tbsp. rosemary, chopped

DIRECTIONS:

- Add olive oil with potatoes into the Fagor Pressure Cooker.
- Put garlic cloves and rosemary in the cooker, and cook for 10 minutes on high pressure.
- When done, serve in a bowl and enjoy!

129. Simple Fries

(Time: 15 minutes \ Servings: 4)

INGREDIENTS:

2 potatoes, sliced
1 tbsp. flour
½ cup parsley, chopped

2 tbsp. oil
salt and pepper, to taste

DIRECTIONS:

- Put potatoes, flour, parsley, salt and pepper into a bowl. Set it aside.
- Add oil into the Fagor Pressure Cooker.
- Add the potatoes and cook for 15 minutes on MANUAL on high pressure.
- When ready, serve and enjoy!

130. White Rice with Chicken Broth and Vegetables

(Time: 18 minutes \ Servings: 4)

INGREDIENTS:

1 tbsp. butter
1 onion , chopped
2 celery stalk , chopped
½ carrot , chopped
1 cup white rice, boiled
2 cups chicken broth

½ cup water
salt to taste
½ cup frozen peas
½ cup parsley , chopped
sliced almonds for seasoning

DIRECTIONS:

- Add butter into the Fagor Pressure Cooker and cook on SAUTÉ mode.
- Add celery, carrot, onion, chicken broth, water and salt. Cook for 10 minutes.
- Add rice, peas and parsley. Cook for another 5 minutes on MANUAL on high pressure.
- When ready, serve it sprinkled with almonds.

131. Breaded Mozzarella Sticks

(Time: 35 minutes \ Servings: 6)

INGREDIENTS:

¼ lb. mozzarella cheese, cut into 1 inch strips
1 teaspoon onion powder
1 cup bread crumbs
1 egg, whisked
1 teaspoon garlic powder

½ teaspoon salt
½ teaspoon chili powder
½ teaspoon cinnamon powder
1 cup oil, for frying

DIRECTIONS:

- In a bowl, combine bread crumbs, onion powder, salt, chili powder, garlic, cumin powder and toss well.
- Dip each mozzarella stick into the whisked egg and then roll out into the bread crumbs mixture.
- Heat oil in the Fagor Pressure Cooker on SAUTÉ mode. Place the sticks inside the oil and fry until golden.
- Put them on a paper towel to drain out the excess oil. Transfer to a serving dish and serve with any sauce.

132. Mushrooms and Peppers

(Time: 16 minutes \ Servings: 2)

INGREDIENTS:

1 onion, chopped
1 green bell pepper, chopped
5 mushrooms, chopped

2 eggs
salt and pepper, to taste

DIRECTIONS:

- Whisk eggs in a bowl. Mix onion, green bell pepper, mushrooms, salt and pepper with the eggs.
- Blend well. Pour the mixture into a round baking tray.
- Cook in the Fagor Pressure Cooker for 10 minutes on high pressure.
- When done, serve with bread or tortillas.

133. Sweet Potato Wedges

(Time: 25 minutes \ Servings: 4)

INGREDIENTS:

3 medium sweet potatoes, cut into wedges
1 teaspoon garlic powder
½ teaspoon salt
½ teaspoon black pepper

½ teaspoon cinnamon powder
½ teaspoon cumin powder
2 tablespoons lemon juice
1 cup oil, for frying

DIRECTIONS:

- In a bowl, combine salt, garlic, pepper, cumin powder, and cinnamon powder. Toss and set aside.
- Heat oil in the Fagor Pressure Cooker on SAUTÉ mode.
- Transfer the sweet potato into the oil and fry until golden.
- Place on a paper towel. Season with salt and pepper.
- Transfer to a serving dish, drizzle some lemon juice on top and serve.

134. Potato Chips

(Time: 30 minutes \ Servings: 4)

INGREDIENTS:

3 potatoes, sliced
¼ teaspoon salt
1 teaspoon thyme
¼ teaspoon black pepper

¼ garlic powder
2 tablespoons lemon juice
½ cup cooking oil, for frying

DIRECTIONS:

- Heat oil in the Fagor Pressure Cooker on SAUTÉ mode.
- Fry some chips until golden and crisp. Transfer to a paper towel and drain out excess oil.
- Season with thyme, garlic powder, salt and pepper.
- Drizzle lemon juice and serve.

135. Fried Mushrooms

(Time: 15 minutes \ Servings: 4)

INGREDIENTS:

2 oz. mushrooms, sliced
¼ teaspoon salt
¼ teaspoon black pepper

¼ garlic powder
4 tablespoons oil, for frying

DIRECTIONS:

- Heat oil the in Fagor Pressure Cooker on SAUTÉ mode. Fry mushrooms until golden.
- Transfer to a paper towel to drain excess oil. Season with garlic powder, salt and pepper.
- Drizzle lemon juice and enjoy.

136. Spiced Carrots

(Time: 55 minutes \ Servings: 3)

INGREDIENTS:

2 oz. carrots, sliced
¼ teaspoon salt
¼ teaspoon black pepper

2 tablespoons lemon juice
1 cup orange juice
2 tablespoons oil, for frying

DIRECTIONS:

- Heat oil the in Fagor Pressure Cooker on SAUTÉ mode. Add carrots and simmer for 10-15 minutes.
- Season with salt and pepper. Add in orange juice.
- Cover and cook on SLOW COOK mode for 35 minutes. Drizzle lemon juice on top.

137. Greek-style Fried Shrimp

(Time: 25 minutes \ Servings: 3)

INGREDIENTS:

2 oz. carrots, sliced
½ lb. shrimp
¼ teaspoon salt
¼ teaspoon black pepper

2 tablespoons lemon juice
1 teaspoon garlic powder
2 tablespoons oil, for frying

DIRECTIONS:

- Heat oil in the Fagor Pressure Cooker on SAUTÉ mode. Add the shrimp and stir fry for 10 minutes.
- Season with salt, garlic and pepper. Fry for another 5-10 minutes.
- Drizzle lemon juice and toss around.

138. Stir Fried Cherry Tomatoes

(Time: 15 minutes \ Servings: 4)

INGREDIENTS:

2 cups cherry tomatoes, sliced
¼ teaspoon salt
¼ teaspoon black pepper

3 tablespoons vinegar
2 tablespoons oil, for frying

DIRECTIONS:

- Heat oil in the Fagor Pressure Cooker on SAUTÉ mode. Add the shrimp and stir fry for 10-12 minutes.
- Season with salt and pepper. Add vinegar and toss.
- Stir fry for 4 minutes and serve with cherry tomatoes.

139. Easy Rice Smash with Potatoes

(Time: 50 minutes \ Servings: 4)

INGREDIENTS:

1 cup rice, soaked
2 potatoes, peeled, diced
1 pinch salt
¼ teaspoon black pepper

2 cups of water
2 tablespoons olive oil
1 onion, chopped
2 garlic cloves, minced

DIRECTIONS:

- Transfer all ingredients into the Fagor Pressure Cooker and set to MANUAL mode.
- Cook on RICE for 20 minutes. Cool and then mash with a potato masher.
- Serve with meat or fish.

140. Potato Wedges

(Time: 35 minutes \ Servings: 6)

INGREDIENTS:

3 large potatoes, cut into wings
2 tablespoons gram flour
1 teaspoon garlic powder
½ teaspoon salt
½ teaspoon black pepper

½ teaspoon cinnamon powder
½ teaspoon cumin powder
2 tablespoons lemon juice
1 cup oil, for frying

DIRECTIONS:

- In a bowl, combine flour, salt, garlic, pepper, cumin powder, cinnamon powder and toss.
- Add in the potato wings and toss.
- Heat oil in the Fagor Pressure Cooker on SAUTÉ mode.
- Transfer the potatoes into the oil and fry until golden.
- Place on a paper towel to drain excess oil.
- Transfer to a serving dish, drizzle some lemon juice on top and serve.

141. Crispy Okra

(Time: 25 minutes \ Servings: 6)

INGREDIENTS:

½ lb. okra, heads removed
½ teaspoon salt

½ teaspoon black pepper
¼ cup oil, for frying

DIRECTIONS:

- Slice the okra lengthwise.
- Heat oil in the Fagor Pressure Cooker on SAUTÉ mode.
- Transfer the okra into the oil and fry until golden.
- Place on a paper towel then season with salt and pepper.
- Transfer to a serving dish and enjoy.

142. Fried Pumpkin

(Time: 25 minutes \ Servings: 4)

INGREDIENTS:

1 cup pumpkin, chunks
½ teaspoon salt
½ teaspoon black pepper

¼ teaspoon chili powder
2 tablespoons gram flour
¼ cup oil, for frying

DIRECTIONS:

- Combine the flour, chili powder, salt, and pepper.
- Add the pumpkin and mix well.
- Heat oil in the Fagor Pressure Cooker on SAUTÉ mode.
- Transfer the pumpkin chunks into the oil and fry until golden.
- Place on a paper towel to drain. Season with salt and pepper.

143. Crunchy Garlic Bread

(Time: 20 minutes \ Servings: 4)

INGREDIENTS:

1 French baguette
3 garlic cloves, minced
2 tablespoons oil

½ teaspoon salt
½ teaspoon black pepper, freshly ground

DIRECTIONS:

- Cut the baguette to 8 slices. Mix olive oil, garlic, black pepper and salt, in a bowl
- Brush this mixture onto each bread slice and transfer into a baking sheet.
- Put this sheet into the Fagor Pressure Cooker and cook for 15 minutes on high pressure.

144. Crispy Chicken Fritters

(Time: 25 minutes \ Servings: 4)

INGREDIENTS:

6 chicken breasts fillets
½ cup bread crumbs
1 teaspoon garlic powder
1 teaspoon onion powder
1 teaspoon dry coriander powder

1 teaspoon cumin powder
Oil spray
1 egg
1 teaspoon salt
½ teaspoon black pepper

DIRECTIONS:

- In a bowl, mix breadcrumbs with coriander powder, onion powder, cumin powder, salt, and black pepper and toss well.
- Roll each chicken fillet into the breadcrumbs mixture and transfer into a platter.
- Place the chicken fillets into the Fagor Pressure Cooker and set it on MANUAL mode.
- Cook for 20 minutes on high pressure.
- Serve with tomato ketchup and enjoy.

145. Spiced Fried Cauliflower

(Time: 35 minutes \ Servings: 2)

INGREDIENTS:

1 cup cauliflower florets
1 teaspoon onion powder
1 cup all-purpose flour
1 teaspoon garlic powder

½ teaspoon salt
½ teaspoon chili powder
½ teaspoon cinnamon powder
1 cup oil, for frying

DIRECTIONS:

- In a bowl, combine flour, onion powder, salt, chili powder, garlic, and cumin powder, and toss.
- Add in cauliflower and mix well.
- Heat oil in Fagor Pressure Cooker on SAUTÉ mode.
- Transfer the cauliflower into the oil and fry until golden.
- Place on paper towel to drain out excess oil.
- Transfer to serving dish and serve with any sauce.

146. Spiced Chickpea

(Time: 15 minutes \ Servings: 3)

INGREDIENTS:

1 cup chickpeas, boiled
½ teaspoon salt
½ teaspoon black pepper
¼ teaspoon cayenne pepper

2 tablespoons tamarind pulp
1 tablespoon vinegar
¼ cup oil, for frying

DIRECTIONS:

- Heat oil in the Fagor Pressure Cooker on SAUTÉ mode. Fry chickpeas until golden brown.
- Drain out the excess oil and a paper towel.
- Transfer to a serving dish and season with salt, pepper, tamarind pulp, and cayenne pepper.
- Drizzle vinegar on top and serve.

147. Salty Fried Peanuts

(Time: 10 minutes \ Servings: 4)

INGREDIENTS:

2 cups peanuts
1 bay leaf

¼ cup oil, for frying

DIRECTIONS:

- Heat oil in the Fagor Pressure Cooker on SAUTÉ mode.
- Fry the bay leaf for 20 seconds and discard it.
- In the same oil, add peanuts and fry well.
- Place to a paper towel and drain the excess oil.
- Sprinkle salt and toss around.

148. Roasted Nuts

(Time: 10 minutes \ Servings: 12)

INGREDIENTS:

1 cup almonds
1 cup pistachios
1 cup pine nuts

½ cup walnuts
½ cup peanuts
¼ cup oil, for frying

DIRECTIONS:

- Heat oil in the Fagor Pressure Cooker on SAUTÉ mode.
- Transfer all dry fruits in the cooker and stir fry until lightly golden.
- Sprinkle salt and toss. Put on a paper towel and let it cool before serving.

149. Bruschetta with Potato Smash

(Time: 10 minutes \ Servings: 4)

INGREDIENTS:

1 cup potatoes
2 tablespoons lemon juice
1 pinch salt

¼ teaspoon black pepper
2 cups of water
1 French bread

DIRECTIONS:

- Place the potatoes into the Fagor Pressure Cooker, add water and boil on SAUTÉ mode
- Let cool and then mash with a potato masher. Season with salt and pepper.
- Cut the French bread into slices, top each slice with mashed potatoes.
- Place into a serving dish and drizzle lemon juice.

150. Creamy Mashed Potatoes

(Time: 30 minutes \ Servings: 3)

INGREDIENTS:

4 large potatoes, boiled peeled
1 cup sour cream
½ cup heavy cream

1 pinch salt
¼ teaspoon black pepper

DIRECTIONS:

- Place the boiled potatoes, sour cream, and heavy cream into the Fagor Pressure Cooker and cover with a lid. Cook on SLOW COOK mode for 30 minutes. Season with salt and pepper.

151. Chickpea Hummus

(Time: 40 minutes \ Servings: 4)

INGREDIENTS:

1 cup chickpea, soaked
1 pinch salt
¼ teaspoon chili powder

3 cups of water
2 tablespoons olive oil
2 garlic cloves, minced

DIRECTIONS:

- Transfer the water, chickpea, salt and garlic into the Fagor Pressure Cooker.
- Set it on MANUAL mode, low pressure. Cover with a lid and cook for 35 minutes.
- Let it cool a little, then transfer the boiled chickpea into a blender and blend to a puree.
- Add olive oil gradually and keep blending. Put on a serving dish and sprinkle chili powder on top.

152. Zucchini and Potato Hummus

(Time: 40 minutes \ Servings: 4)

INGREDIENTS:

4 large zucchini
2 potatoes, boiled, mashed
1 pinch salt
¼ teaspoon black pepper

2 cups chicken broth
2 tablespoons olive oil
2 garlic cloves, minced

DIRECTIONS:

- Transfer the chicken broth, zucchini, potatoes, salt, and garlic into the Fagor Pressure Cooker.
- Set it on SLOW COOK mode and cook for 35 minutes.
- Let it cool for a while and then blend it to a puree.
- Add olive oil gradually and blend again.
- Put to a serving dish and sprinkle black pepper on top.

153. Easy Cauliflower Hummus

(Time: 50 minutes \ Servings: 4)

INGREDIENTS:

2 cups cauliflower, chunks
1 pinch salt
¼ teaspoon chili powder
3 cups of water

2 tablespoons olive oil
1 onion, chopped
2 garlic cloves, minced

DIRECTIONS:

- Transfer the water, cauliflower, salt, onion and garlic into the Fagor Pressure Cooker.
- Cover with a lid and cook for 45 minutes on SLOW COOK mode.
- Let it cool a little then transfer to a blender and blend to a puree.
- Add olive oil gradually and blend.
- Put to a serving dish and sprinkle chili powder on top.

154. Chicken Bites

(Time: 20 minutes \ Servings: 6)

INGREDIENTS:

2 chicken breast
4 tablespoons breadcrumbs
½ teaspoon salt
1 egg

1 teaspoon black pepper
1 teaspoon red paprika
1 bunch of parsley
2 tablespoons oil

DIRECTIONS:

- Cut the chicken breasts into small chunks.
- Put the chicken breasts an a bowl. Sprinkle salt and pepper, then combine with egg and breadcrumbs.
- Add oil in the Fagor Pressure Cooker and transfer the chicken to it.
- Cook on POULTRY for 15 minutes.

155. Stir Fried Spinach

(Time: 20 minutes \ Servings: 3)

INGREDIENTS:

1 bunch baby spinach leaves
½ teaspoon salt
1 teaspoon black pepper
2 garlic cloves, minced

2 tablespoons soya sauce
1 teaspoon lemon juice
2 tablespoons oil

DIRECTIONS:

- Heat oil in the Fagor Pressure Cooker and stir fry garlic for 1 minute on SAUTÉ mode
- Add spinach and sauté for 10-15 minutes.
- Season with salt, pepper, soya sauce and lemon juice.

156. Ginger Pineapple Slices

(Time: 15 minutes \ Servings: 3)

INGREDIENTS:

2 cups pineapple slices
1 pinch salt
¼ teaspoon black pepper

1-inch ginger slice, chopped
1 teaspoon lemon juice
2 tablespoons oil

DIRECTIONS:

- Heat oil in the Fagor Pressure Cooker and stir fry ginger for 1 minute on SAUTÉ mode.
- Add in pineapple and stir fry well.
- Season with salt, and pepper.
- Drizzle lemon juice and toss well.

Dinner

157. Stir Fried Shrimp
(Time: 25 minutes \ Servings: 2)

INGREDIENTS:

1 cup shrimp
4-5 garlic cloves, chopped
½ teaspoon salt

1 teaspoon black pepper
3 tablespoons olive oil

DIRECTIONS:

- Heat oil in the Fagor Pressure Cooker and add garlic cloves, sauté for 1 minute.
- Add the shrimp and fry until golden brown. Sprinkle salt and black pepper, mix thoroughly.
- Turn off the heat and transfer into a serving dish.

158. Garlicky Roasted Potatoes
(Time: 45 minutes \ Servings: 3)

INGREDIENTS:

3 large potatoes, cut, 1-inch slice
1 teaspoon garlic powder
1 teaspoon black pepper

1 teaspoon salt
4 tablespoons olive oil

DIRECTIONS:

- In a bowl, add olive oil, garlic powder, salt, and black pepper and mix.
- Add the potatoes and toss well. Transfer into the Fagor Pressure Cooker and cook on MANUAL on high pressure for 20 minutes.

159. Cauliflower Carrot Risotto
(Time: 45 minutes \ Servings: 4)

INGREDIENTS:

1 cup cauliflower, florets
2 carrots, sliced
1 oz. tofu
1 onion, thinly sliced
1 teaspoon garlic paste

2 tomatoes, chopped
1 teaspoon black pepper
½ teaspoon salt
1 cup chicken broth
2 tablespoons cooking oil

DIRECTIONS:

- Set the Fagor Pressure Cooker on VEGETABLES mode.
- Combine the cauliflower, carrots, tofu, tomatoes, onion, garlic paste, vegetable broth and cooking oil.
- Season with salt and black pepper. Cover and cook for 30 minutes.

160. Chicken Orzo Soup
(Time: 25 minutes \ Servings: 3)

INGREDIENTS:

1 cup orzo, boiled
1 cup chicken boneless, pieces
1 carrot, sliced
1 asparagus stem

½ cup spinach leaves
black pepper and salt, to taste
3 tablespoons cooking oil
3 cups chicken broth

DIRECTIONS:

- Heat oil in the Fagor Pressure Cooker and add the chicken pieces. Fry on SAUTÉ mode until lightly brown. Add the orzo, spinach, carrots, asparagus, chicken broth and cook on SCUP for 25 minutes.
- Season with salt and black pepper.

161. Carrot Broccoli Stew

(Time: 35 minutes \ Servings: 3)

INGREDIENTS:

1 cup broccoli, florets
1 cup carrots, sliced
½ teaspoon salt

1 teaspoon black pepper
3 cups chicken broth
1 cup cream

DIRECTIONS:

- Add the broccoli florets, cream, carrots, salt, and chicken broth and toss well.
- Cook on BEANS mode for 30 minutes. Transfer into serving bowls and sprinkle black pepper on top.

162. Creamy Pumpkin Puree Soup

(Time: 55 minutes \ Servings: 3)

INGREDIENTS:

1 cup pumpkin puree
2 cups chicken broth
4-5 garlic cloves

salt and black pepper, to taste
1 cup cream
2 tablespoons olive oil

DIRECTIONS:

- In the Fagor Pressure Cooker, add all ingredients and cook on SOUP mode for 30 minutes.
- After that, transfer to a blender and blend well. Pour into a bowl and enjoy.

163. Creamy Mushrooms

(Time: 25 minutes \ Servings: 3)

INGREDIENTS:

1 cup mushrooms, sliced
1 cup cream
½ cup cream cheese

½ teaspoon salt
2 garlic cloves, minced
2 tablespoons olive oil

DIRECTIONS:

- Set the Fagor Pressure Cooker on SAUTÉ mode and fry garlic for a minute. Add oil and sauté mushrooms for 4-5 minutes. Stir in the cream, chicken broth, and cream cheese and season with salt.
- Cook for 20-25 minutes on high pressure mode.

164. Black Lentils Tacos

(Time: 35 minutes \ Servings: 4)

INGREDIENTS:

1 cup black lentils, soaked
½ cup sour cream
2 tomatoes, chopped
¼ cup corn kernels
½ teaspoon chili powder
2-3 garlic cloves, minced

½ teaspoon salt
2 cups water
4 tablespoons cooking oil
¼ cup spinach, chopped
3 tablespoons lemon juice
3-4 corn tortillas

DIRECTIONS:

- Set the Fagor Pressure Cooker on BEANS mode.
- Add all the ingredients except the tortillas. Cook for 20 minutes.
- Place 1-2 tablespoons of the mixture on each tortilla.
- Repeat for all tortillas.
- Drizzle with lemon juice.

165. Potato with Peas

(Time: 40 minutes \ Servings: 5)

INGREDIENTS:

1 cup peas
3 potatoes, peeled, cut into slices
2-3 garlic cloves, minced

½ teaspoon salt
¼ teaspoon black pepper
2 cups water

DIRECTIONS:

- Set the Fagor Pressure Cooker on SAUTÉ mode.
- Heat oil and fry garlic for 30-40 seconds.
- Add the peas and the potatoes, fry until lightly golden.
- Add salt, black pepper, and water and cover the cooker with a lid.
- Cook on MANUAL on high pressure for 30 minutes.

166. Stir-Fried Spinach with Garlic

(Time: 25 minutes \ Servings: 3)

INGREDIENTS:

2 cups baby spinach
3-4 garlic cloves, thinly sliced
¼ teaspoon salt

½ cup chicken stock
4 tablespoons butter

DIRECTIONS:

- Set the Fagor Pressure Cooker on SAUTÉ mode, melt the butter and fry the garlic for 20 seconds.
- Add the spinach and stir fry for 10 minutes.
- Add in the chicken stock and mix well.
- When the water is dried out, season with salt and pepper.

167. Spiced Stir Fried Chickpeas

(Time: 15 minutes \ Servings: 3)

INGREDIENTS:

2 cups chickpeas, boiled
4 tablespoons tamarind pulp
¼ teaspoon salt
¼ teaspoon black pepper

¼ teaspoon cumin powder
½ teaspoon cinnamon powder
1 teaspoon vinegar
1 tablespoon olive oil

DIRECTIONS:

- Heat oil in the Fagor Pressure Cooker on SAUTÉ mode.
- Add in the chickpeas and stir fry for 2-3 minutes.
- Add in the tamarind pulp, salt, pepper, cumin powder, cinnamon powder, vinegar and cook for another 5-10 minutes.

168. Chicken Stock

(Time: 35 minutes \ Servings: 5)

INGREDIENTS:

¼ lb. chicken stock
2 onions, halved
1 cup celery stems
4-5 garlic cloves
½ teaspoon black pepper

1 pinch turmeric powder
½ teaspoon salt
4 cups water
2 tablespoons cooking oil

DIRECTIONS:

- In the Fagor Pressure Cooker, add all ingredients and cook on BROTH mode for 30 minutes.
- Serve hot.

169. Sweet Potato Casserole

(Time: 45 minutes \ Servings: 4)

INGREDIENTS:

4-5 sweet potatoes, boiled
½ teaspoon ginger powder
½ cup brown sugar
1 pinch salt

½ cup milk
3 eggs
4 tablespoons butter, melted

DIRECTIONS:

- Transfer the boiled sweet potatoes, salt, milk, brown sugar, ginger powder and blend until smooth.
- Crack the eggs in a blender and blend for another minute.
- Grease the Fagor Pressure Cooker with butter and transfer the sweet potatoes mixture.
- Cover with a lid and cook for 40 minutes on SLOW COOK mode.

170. Tuna Pasta Braise

(Time: 35 minutes \ Servings: 3)

INGREDIENTS:

½ lb. tuna
16 oz. package of pasta, boiled
½ cup mayonnaise
½ cup sour cream
½ teaspoon salt

1 teaspoon black pepper
4-5 garlic cloves, minced
2 oz. cheddar cheese, shredded
2 tablespoons butter

DIRECTIONS:

- Mmelt butter on SAUTÉ mode. Add in the tuna and stir fry for 4-5 minutes.
- Add in the garlic powder, salt, pepper, mozzarella cheese, sour cream and mayonnaise.
- Add the pasta and cook for 20 minutes on MANUAL.

171. Creamy Spinach Puree

(Time: 25 minutes \ Servings: 3)

INGREDIENTS:

3 cups spinach, chopped
1 cup heavy cream
¼ teaspoon salt
1 teaspoon black pepper

1 onion, chopped
4-5 garlic cloves, minced
1 cup chicken stock
2 tablespoons butter

DIRECTIONS:

- In the Fagor Pressure Cooker, melt butter on SAUTÉ mode.
- Then sauté onion and garlic for 1 minute.
- Add the spinach and simmer until lightly softened.
- Add in the chicken stock, salt, pepper, cream and mix well.
- Transfer this mixture to a blender and blend to a puree.
- Pour the blended spinach back into the cooker and cook for 15 minutes on MANUAL on high pressure.

172. Hot Stir-Fried Peppers with Chile

(Time: 20 minutes \ Servings: 3)

INGREDIENTS:

2 green bell peppers, sliced
2 red bell peppers, fried
1 onion, sliced
½ teaspoon salt

½ teaspoon chili powder
½ teaspoon garlic paste
2 tablespoons olive oil

DIRECTIONS:

- In the Fagor Pressure Cooker, heat oil and fry the onion and the garlic.
- Add the salt, chili powder, bell peppers and keep stirring.
- Stir fry for 10-15 minutes with few splashes of water.
- Transfer to a serving dish and serve.

173. Creamy Sausage Pasta Casserole

(Time: 35 minutes \ Servings: 4)

INGREDIENTS:

¼ lb. sausage, pieces
1 onion, chopped
¼ cup parmesan cheese, grated
¼ cup cheddar cheese
1 package pasta, boiled
½ teaspoon salt

1 teaspoon black pepper
1 teaspoon garlic paste
2 tablespoons olive oil
3 tablespoons tomato ketchup
1 cup milk

DIRECTIONS:

- Heat oil in the Fagor Pressure Cooker on SAUTÉ mode, add onion and sauté for 1 minute.
- Add the garlic and the sausage and stir for 2 minutes.
- Season with salt and black pepper.
- Pour milk and let simmer for 5 minutes.
- Transfer the boiled pasta, ketchup, parmesan cheese, and cheddar cheese, stir and cover with a lid.
- Cook on MANUAL mode for 20-25 minutes.

174. Cheesy Mashed Potatoes

(Time: 45 minutes \ Servings: 4)

INGREDIENTS:

4 potatoes, boiled, peeled
1 cup milk
¼ lb. mozzarella cheese
¼ teaspoon salt

1 teaspoon black pepper
½ cup parmesan cheese, shredded
2 garlic cloves, minced
2 tablespoons butter

DIRECTIONS:

- Set the Fagor Pressure Cooker on SAUTÉ mode.
- Add butter, onion, and garlic and sauté for 1-2 minute.
- In a bowl, add the potatoes, parmesan cheese, cream, mozzarella cheese, salt, and black pepper, mash using a potato masher.
- Transfer this mixture to the Fagor Pressure Cooker and cover with a lid.
- Cook on SLOW COOK mode for 35-40 minutes.

175. Fried Potatoes

(Time: 35 minutes \ Servings: 3)

INGREDIENTS:

4 potatoes, peeled, thinly sliced
½ teaspoon chili flakes
¼ teaspoon salt

¼ teaspoon turmeric powder
2 tablespoons olive oil

DIRECTIONS:

- Set the Fagor Pressure Cooker on SAUTÉ mode.
- Add the potatoes and cook for 15 minutes on VEGETABLES mode.
- Season with turmeric, salt and chili flakes. Cook on for another 10 minutes.
- Transfer to a serving dish and enjoy.

176. Mango Mash with Potatoes

(Time: 35 minutes \ Servings: 3)

INGREDIENTS:

4 potatoes, boiled, peeled
1 cup mango, chunks
1 cup sour cream
1 avocado, pulp
½ cup mango juice

¼ teaspoon salt
1 teaspoon black pepper
2 garlic cloves, minced
2 tablespoons olive oil

DIRECTIONS:

- Set the Fagor Pressure Cooker on SLOW COOK mode.
- Add in the olive oil, avocado, cream, potatoes, salt, black pepper, mango juice, garlic and cover with a lid. Cook for 35 minutes and serve with fish or poultry.

177. Chicken Potato Puffs

(Time: 35 minutes \ Servings: 4)

INGREDIENTS:

2 potatoes, boiled, peeled
1 cup chicken cubes, boiled
¼ teaspoon garlic paste
¼ teaspoon salt
¼ teaspoon cumin powder

½ teaspoon chili flakes
1 onion, chopped
2 puff pastry sheets, cut into 4 small squares
¼ cup water
2 tablespoons cooking oil

DIRECTIONS:

- Set the Fagor Pressure Cooker on SAUTÉ mode. Heat oil and fry the garlic.
- Add in the chicken and the potatoes and cook until lightly golden.
- Season with cumin powder, salt and chili flakes. Transfer this mixture to a bowl.

- Spread the puff pastry squares and top with 3-4 tablespoons of the chicken mixture.
- Lift the sides of the squares and place on top of the stuffing. Repeat.
- Transfer to a greased Fagor Pressure Cooker and cook for 25 minutes on high pressure.
- Serve with chili garlic sauce and enjoy.

178. Chicken Spinach Beef Stew

(Time: 35 minutes \ Servings: 6)

INGREDIENTS:

½ lb. beef, pieces
1 chicken breast, cut into pieces
1 cup spinach, sliced
2 green chilies
1 cup tomato puree
¼ teaspoon garlic paste

1 onion, chopped
¼ teaspoon cumin powder
½ teaspoon black pepper
4 cups water
2 tablespoons cooking oil

DIRECTIONS:

- Set the Fagor Pressure Cooker on MANUAL on high pressure.
- Add all ingredients and cook for 35 minutes. Serve with chili garlic sauce.

179. Stir Fried Garlic Mushroom

(Time: 35 minutes \ Servings: 4)

INGREDIENTS:

2 cups mushrooms, sliced
2 tablespoons soya sauce
2 tablespoons oyster sauce
¼ teaspoon garlic paste
¼ teaspoon salt

1 cup baby corns
½ teaspoons black pepper
2 tablespoons coconut oil
2 tablespoons cilantro, chopped
¼ cup chicken broth

DIRECTIONS:

- Set the Fagor Pressure Cooker on SAUTÉ mode.
- Heat oil and fry the garlic and the mushrooms. Cook for 10 minutes.
- Season with broth, corns, oyster sauce, soya sauce, salt and pepper.
- Cook for 20 minutes on BEANS mode. Sprinkle cilantro on top.

180. Pineapple Lemon Pilaf

(Time: 25 minutes \ Servings: 4)

INGREDIENTS:

1 cup rice, soaked
1 cup pineapple juice
1 cup water
1 teaspoon salt
1 cup pineapple chunks
3 tablespoons lemon juice

½ teaspoon black pepper
1 onion, chopped
2 tablespoons cooking oil
a few pineapple slices
1 lime slice

DIRECTIONS:

- Set the Fagor Pressure Cooker on SAUTÉ mode. Heat oil and fry onion until softened.
- Add the pineapple juice, water, lemon juice, salt and pepper; then boil.
- Add in the rice and boil on WHITE RICE mode for 20 minutes.
- Garnish with pineapple and lime slices.

181. Spiced Zucchini Slices

(Time: 15 minutes \ Servings: 5)

INGREDIENTS:

2 large zucchinis, sliced
1 teaspoon cumin powder
1 teaspoon cinnamon power
¼ teaspoon garlic powder

¼ teaspoon salt
2 tablespoons all-purpose flour
½ teaspoon chili powder
½ cup cooking oil

DIRECTIONS:

- Roll out the zucchini slices into the flour and set aside.
- Set the Fagor Pressure Cooker on SAUTÉ mode.
- Heat oil and deep fry the zucchinis until lightly golden.
- Drain out the excess oil on a piece of paper.
- Sprinkle with salt, chili powder, cinnamon powder, and cumin powder.

Vegetables and Eggs

182. Spinach and Potato Risotto

(Time: 45 minutes \ Servings: 5)

INGREDIENTS:

2 cups spinach, chopped
¼ cup mushrooms, sliced
2 large potatoes, peeled, diced
1 onion, chopped
2-3 cherry tomatoes, halved
½ teaspoon salt

¼ teaspoons turmeric powder
1 teaspoon chili flakes
½ teaspoon garlic paste
3 tablespoons cooking oil
2 cups water

DIRECTIONS:

- Heat oil in the Fagor Pressure Cooker on SAUTÉ mode. Fry the onion until transparent.
- Add the mushrooms, garlic, salt, chili flakes, turmeric powder and fry for 2-3 minutes.
- Add spinach, water, potatoes and cover with a lid. Cook on MANUAL mode for 35 minutes.
- Top with cherry tomatoes and cook for 1-2 minutes.

183. Zucchini Chips

(Time: 15 minutes \ Servings: 4)

INGREDIENTS:

3 large zucchinis, thinly sliced
¼ teaspoon salt

¼ teaspoon black pepper
½ tablespoons cooking oil, for frying

DIRECTIONS:

- Heat oil in the Fagor Pressure Cooker on SAUTÉ mode.
- Put a few slices of zucchini in the Fagor Pressure Cooker and fry until golden and crisp.
- Repeat the same steps for all zucchini chips.
- Then place onto a paper towel to drain out the excess oil.
- Season with salt and pepper.

184. Roasted Fennel with Tomatoes

(Time: 35 minutes \ Servings: 3)

INGREDIENTS:

4-5 fennel bulbs, timed and quartered
3 Cherry tomatoes
1 pinch of caraway seed
1 tablespoon olive oil

¼ teaspoon salt
¼ teaspoon red chili flakes
2 cups vegetable broth

DIRECTIONS:

- Add all ingredients.
- Cook on SLOW COOK mode until funnels become tender.
- Serve and enjoy.

185. Thyme Potatoes

(Time: 35 minutes \ Servings: 5)

INGREDIENTS:

4 baking potatoes
1 teaspoon salt
1 teaspoon black pepper

1 teaspoon garlic paste/powder
4 tablespoons olive oil
3 sprigs of fresh thyme

DIRECTIONS:

- Peel and wash the potatoes. Prick with a fork.
- Drizzle a few drops of oil on the potatoes and place in the Fagor Pressure Cooker.
- Cook for 20-25 minutes on VEGETABLES mode.
- Sprinkle the potatoes with the spices.

186. Asparagus Chowder

(Time: 45 minutes \ Servings: 5)

INGREDIENTS:

1 tablespoon olive oil
2 cups chopped onion
2 teaspoons grated lemon rind
1 cup boiled rice
3 cans fat-free, chicken broth

2 cups sliced asparagus
2 cups chopped spinach
¼ teaspoon ground nutmeg
½ cup grated Parmesan cheese
½ teaspoon salt

DIRECTIONS:

- Heat oil in the Fagor Pressure Cooker on SAUTÉ mode.
- Add onion, stirring for 5 minutes until transparent.
- Add the rice, lemon rind, asparagus, spinach, chicken broth, salt.
- Cover with the lid and cook for 10 minutes on MANUAL mode.
- Turn off the heat and then top with parmesan cheese and ground nutmeg.

187. Slow-Cooked Cabbage

(Time: 45 minutes \ Servings: 5)

INGREDIENTS:

4-5 baby cabbages, halved
1 teaspoon salt
1 cup tomato sauce

2 tablespoons olive oil
¼ teaspoon white pepper
½ teaspoon salt

DIRECTIONS:

- Add all ingredients to the Fagor Pressure Cooker.
- Cook on SLOW COOK mode for 45 minutes.

188. Roasted Fennel with Carrots

(Time: 30 minutes \ Servings: 3)

INGREDIENTS:

4-5 fennel bulbs, timed and quartered

3 carrots, shredded
1 pinch of caraway seed
1 tablespoon olive oil

¼ teaspoon salt
¼ teaspoon red chili flakes

DIRECTIONS:

- Place the fennel bulbs into the Fagor Pressure Cooker and add the tomatoes and the olive oil. Mix well.
- Add all remaining ingredients. Cook on SLOW COOK mode for about 30 minutes until the funnel is tender.

189. Eggplant and Tomatoes

(Time: 25 minutes \ Servings: 4)

INGREDIENTS:

3 eggplants, cut into small pieces
1 onion, chopped
3 large tomatoes, chopped
½ teaspoon salt

1 teaspoon chili powder
½ teaspoon garlic paste
½ teaspoon ginger paste
¼ cup cooking oil

DIRECTIONS:

- Heat oil in the Fagor Pressure Cooker on SAUTÉ mode.
- Add the eggplants and fry until golden, then set aside.
- In the same oil, sauté onion until transparent.
- Add in the tomatoes, salt, chili powder, ginger paste, garlic paste and fry well.
- Add the fried eggplants and cook for 15 minutes on VEGETABLES mode.

190. Chili and Garlic Pumpkin

(Time: 30 minutes \ Servings: 3)

INGREDIENTS:

2 cups pumpkin, cut into small slices
3 green chilies, chopped
¼ teaspoon salt
1 teaspoon chili powder

¼ teaspoon turmeric powder
½ teaspoon garlic paste
2 tablespoons cooking oil

DIRECTIONS:

- Heat oil in the Fagor Pressure Cooker on SAUTÉ mode and fry the garlic and the green chilies for a minute.
- Add in the salt, chili powder, turmeric powder, pumpkin slices and cook for 15 minutes.
- Then cover with a lid and cook on MANUAL for another 15 minutes.

191. Carrot and Pumpkin Stew

(Time: 60 minutes \ Servings: 4)

INGREDIENTS:

1 cup pumpkin, chopped
1 onion, chopped
4 carrots, peeled, chopped
1 teaspoon salt
1 teaspoon black pepper

½ teaspoon cumin powder
3-4 garlic cloves, minced
2 tablespoons olive oil
2 cups chicken broth
1 cup vegetable broth

DIRECTIONS:

- In the Fagor Pressure Cooker, add the pumpkin, carrots, chicken broth, onion, oil, salt, garlic, cumin powder, vegetable broth, black pepper and mix well.
- Cover the cooker with a lid and cook on SLOW COOK mode for 60 minutes.
- Transfer to a blender and blend to a puree.
- Pour the stew into serving bowls and serve hot.

192. Peas and Carrots with Potatoes

(Time: 40 minutes \ Servings: 5)

INGREDIENTS:

1 cup peas
1 cup cauliflower florets
3 potatoes, small cubes
2 carrots, peeled, cut into small cubes
1 onion, chopped
1 teaspoon salt
1 teaspoon chili powder

¼ teaspoon turmeric powder
½ teaspoon cumin powder
2 tomatoes chopped
½ teaspoon cinnamon powder
½ teaspoon garlic paste
2 tablespoons cooking oil
1 cup water

DIRECTIONS:

- Heat oil in the Fagor Pressure Cooker on SAUTÉ mode and sauté onion until transparent.
- Add in the tomatoes, salt, chili powder, turmeric powder, ginger paste, garlic paste and keep frying.
- Add all vegetables and fry for 15 minutes.
- Add the water and cover with a lid. Cook on MANUAL for another 15 minutes.

193. Slow Cooked Honey Glazed Carrots

(Time: 45 minutes \ Servings: 5)

INGREDIENTS:

1 oz. carrots, peeled
1 tablespoon red wine vinegar
2 tablespoons of unsalted butter
1 teaspoon black pepper

1 pinch salt
1 cup water
½ cup brown sugar
2 tablespoons honey

DIRECTIONS:

- Add all ingredients in the Fagor Pressure Cooker except the honey.
- Cook on SLOW COOK mode for 45 minutes.
- Drizzle honey on top and serve.

194. Tropic Cauliflower Manchurian

(Time: 35 minutes \ Servings: 4)

INGREDIENTS:

2 cups cauliflower florets
1 onion, chopped
1 teaspoon salt
1 teaspoon chili flakes
½ teaspoon cumin powder
3 green chilies, sliced

1 cup tomato puree
3 tablespoons tomato ketchup
½ teaspoon cinnamon powder
½ teaspoon garlic paste
¼ teaspoon turmeric powder
¼ cup cooking oil

DIRECTIONS:

- Heat oil in the Fagor Pressure Cooker on SAUTÉ mode.
- Add the cauliflower florets and fry until lightly golden, then set aside.
- In the same pot, sauté onion until transparent.
- Add in the tomato puree, tomato ketchup, salt, chili flakes, turmeric powder, garlic paste and fry for 5-6 minutes.
- Add in the cauliflower and fry again for 4-5 minutes.
- Sprinkle cinnamon powder, cumin powder, and green chilies on top.

195. Garlic-Fried Mushrooms

(Time: 15 minutes \ Servings: 3)

INGREDIENTS:

2 cups mushrooms, sliced
¼ teaspoon salt
1 teaspoon black pepper
½ teaspoon garlic paste

2 tablespoons soya sauce
1 teaspoon basil, chopped
2 tablespoons cooking oil

DIRECTIONS:

- Heat oil on SAUTÉ mode. Fry garlic for 30 seconds. Stir in the mushrooms and fry for 8-10 minutes.
- Add in the soya sauce and season with salt and pepper.
- Cook for 5 more minutes, stirring occasionally. Sprinkle basil on top and serve.

196. Rice with Carrots

(Time: 35 minutes \ Servings: 4)

INGREDIENTS:

2 cups rice, soaked
2 carrots, peeled, chopped
1 potato, peeled, chopped
1 teaspoon cumin seeds
1 black cardamom
2-3 cinnamon sticks

1 tomato, sliced
2 large onions, sliced
1 teaspoon salt
4 tablespoons olive oil
4 cups vegetables broth

DIRECTIONS:

- Heat oil on SAUTÉ mode.
- Cook the onion, cumin seeds, cinnamon sticks and cardamom, until golden.
- Add the carrots, potatoes, salt, chili powder and fry.
- Then add the tomato slices and pour in the vegetable broth, then boil.
- Add the rice and when bubbles appear on the top, cover the pot.
- Cook for 20-25 minutes on MANUAL on low pressure.

197. Tropical Potato Gravy

(Time: 25 minutes \ Servings: 4)

INGREDIENTS:

4 potatoes, boiled, peeled, cut into cubes
1 onion, chopped
1 teaspoon cumin seeds
1 teaspoon chili powder
½ teaspoon cumin powder
1 cup tomato puree

½ teaspoon cinnamon powder
½ teaspoon garlic paste
½ teaspoon thyme
¼ teaspoon turmeric powder
2 tablespoons cooking oil
½ cup chicken broth

DIRECTIONS:

- Heat oil in the Fagor Pressure Cooker on SAUTÉ mode and sauté onion, cumin seeds and garlic for 1 minute.
- Add in the tomato puree, salt, chili powder, turmeric powder, garlic paste and fry for 5-6 minutes.
- Add the potatoes and mix thoroughly.
- Stir in the chicken broth and cook for 10 minutes on WHITE RICE mode.
- Sprinkle cinnamon powder, thyme and cumin powder on top.

198. Crispy Kale Chips

(Time: 10 minutes \ Servings: 4)

INGREDIENTS:

2 cups kale leaves, halved
¼ teaspoon salt
¼ teaspoon black pepper

½ teaspoon garlic powder
½ tablespoons cooking oil, for frying

DIRECTIONS:

- Heat oil in the Fagor Pressure Cooker on SAUTÉ mode.
- Deep fry some the kale leaves until golden and crisp.
- Repeat the steps for all kale leaves.
- Set on paper towel and let the excess oil drain out.
- Season with garlic powder, salt and pepper.

199. Ground Beef Zucchini Zoodles

(Time: 35 minutes \ Servings: 4)

INGREDIENTS:

¼ lb. beef mince
1 large zucchini, spiralled
1 onion, chopped
2 tablespoons olive oil
2 tomatoes, chopped
2-3 garlic cloves, minced

½ teaspoon black pepper
¼ teaspoon chili powder
2 tablespoons soya sauce
1 oz. parmesan cheese, grated
¼ teaspoon salt

DIRECTIONS:

- Heat oil on SAUTÉ mode. Fry onion and garlic for a minute.
- Add the beef and fry until brown.
- Add in the tomatoes, salt, chili powder, soya sauce and black pepper.
- Transfer the fried ground beef to a bowl and set aside.
- In the same pot, add the zucchini zoodles and fry for 5-10 minutes.
- Add in the fried ground beef and mix well. Sprinkle cheese on top and serve.

200. Spinach Black Beans Chili

(Time: 45 minutes \ Servings: 4)

INGREDIENTS:

2 cans of black beans
2 tomatoes, chopped
1 cup spinach, chopped
1 cup red bell pepper, chopped
2 large onions, chopped
1 teaspoon salt
3 garlic cloves, minced

2 tablespoons olive oil
4 cups vegetables broth
½ teaspoon black pepper
1 teaspoon red chili powder
1 bunch coriander, chopped
2 tablespoons sour cream
2 green chilies, chopped

DIRECTIONS:

- In the Fagor Pressure Cooker, add all ingredients, stir well and cover with a lid.
- Cook on SLOW COOK mode for 40-45 minutes.
- Transfer to a serving dish and sprinkle coriander. Top with sour cream.

201. Mashed Potato Pilaf

(Time: 45 minutes \ Servings: 5)

INGREDIENTS:

2 cups rice, soaked
3 potatoes, boiled, mashed
1 teaspoon cumin seeds
1 carrot, peeled, chopped
1 bay leaf
2 garlic cloves, minced

2 cloves
1 tomato, chopped
2 large onions, sliced
1 teaspoon salt
4 tablespoons olive oil
4 cups vegetables broth

DIRECTIONS:

- Heat oil in the Fagor Pressure Cooker on SAUTÉ mode.
- Fry onion and the cumin seeds, bay leaf and cloves until brown.
- Add in the potatoes, carrots, salt, chili powder, garlic and fry. Add in the tomatoes and stir fry until the potatoes are softened. Pour in vegetable broth and boil.
- Add the rice and cover the cooker when bubbles appear on the surface.
- Cook for 20 minutes on WHITE RICE mode.

202. Stir Fried Vegetables

(Time: 15 minutes \ Servings: 4)

INGREDIENTS:

2 green bell peppers
1 yellow bell pepper
1 zucchini, sliced
1 onion, sliced
½ cup mushrooms, sliced
¼ teaspoon salt

¼ teaspoon chili powder
½ teaspoon garlic paste
2 tablespoons soya sauce
2 tablespoons vinegar
2 tablespoons oil

DIRECTIONS:

- Heat oil in the Fagor Pressure Cooker on SAUTÉ mode and stir fry all vegetables.
- Season with salt, pepper and soya sauce. Cover with a lid and stir-fry for 5-10 minutes.

203. Peas Pilaf

(Time: 45 minutes \ Servings: 5)

INGREDIENTS:

2 cups rice, soaked
1 cup peas
1 teaspoon cumin seeds
1 bay leaf
2 garlic cloves, minced
1 pinch turmeric powder
1 teaspoon cumin powder

1 teaspoon cinnamon powder
2 tomatoes, chopped
2 medium onions, sliced
1 teaspoon salt
3 tablespoons olive oil
4 cups chicken broth

DIRECTIONS:

- Heat oil in the Fagor Pressure Cooker on SAUTÉ mode and fry the onion, the cumin seeds and bay leaf.
- Add the peas, salt, turmeric powder, chili powder, garlic, tomatoes and stir fry.
- Pour in and boil the vegetable broth. Add the cumin and the cinnamon powder.
- Add the rice and simmer until you see bubbles, then cover the pot.
- Cook for 20 minutes on BEANS mode.

204. Eggplant and Potato Gravy

(Time: 55 minutes \ Servings: 5)

INGREDIENTS:

2 eggplants, sliced
2 potatoes, peeled, diced
1 onion, chopped
3 large tomatoes, chopped
½ teaspoon salt

1 teaspoon chili powder
¼ teaspoon dry coriander powder
¼ teaspoon turmeric powder
½ teaspoon garlic paste
2 tablespoons cooking oil

DIRECTIONS:

- Heat oil in the Fagor Pressure Cooker on SAUTÉ mode and sauté onion until transparent.
- Add in the tomatoes, salt, chili powder, turmeric powder, garlic paste and fry well.
- Add the eggplants and fry for 15 minutes. Add the potatoes, stirring continuously.
- Add a few splashes of water while frying. Cover with a lid and cook on BEANS mode for 15 minutes.
- Sprinkle cumin powder and mix thoroughly.

205. Cabbage with Potatoes

(Time: 35 minutes \ Servings: 5)

INGREDIENTS:

1 cup cabbage, chopped
2 potatoes, sliced
1 onion, chopped
2 tomatoes, chopped
½ teaspoon salt

1 teaspoon chili powder
¼ teaspoon turmeric powder
½ teaspoon garlic paste
2-3 green chilies, chopped
2 tablespoons cooking oil

DIRECTIONS:

- Heat oil in the Fagor Pressure Cooker on SAUTÉ mode, sauté onion until transparent.
- Add in the tomatoes, salt, chili powder, turmeric powder, garlic paste and fry for 5-10 minutes.
- Add the cabbage and fry well. Add the potatoes and stir well until the potatoes are softened.
- Cook on MANUAL mode on high pressure for 10 minutes.

206. Cauliflower with Carrot Stew

(Time: 35 minutes \ Servings: 4)

INGREDIENTS:

2 cups cauliflower florets
1 cup green beans
2 carrots, sliced
1 onion, chopped
1 cup spinach
1 teaspoon salt

1 teaspoon black pepper
1 bay leaf
½ teaspoon cumin powder
½ teaspoon garlic paste
1 ginger slice
2 tablespoons cooking oil

DIRECTIONS:

- In the Fagor Pressure Cooker, add all ingredients and stir, then cover with a lid.
- Set on BEANS mode and cook for 20 minutes. Serve hot.

Soups and Stews

207. Pumpkin and Potato Soup

(Time: 35 minutes \ Servings: 4)

INGREDIENTS:

1 cup pumpkin chunks, peeled
2 potatoes, cut into small cubes
2 cups vegetable broth
1 cup milk
2 tablespoons fish sauce

¼ teaspoon turmeric powder
½ teaspoon chili powder
4-5 garlic cloves, minced
¼ teaspoon salt
1 tablespoon oil

DIRECTIONS:

- Heat oil in the Fagor Pressure Cooker and add the garlic cloves, cook for 1 minute.
- Add the pumpkin and the potatoes and stir-fry for 5 minutes.
- Stir in the vegetable broth, salt, chili powder, turmeric powder, fish sauce and mix.
- Cook for 20 minutes on SOUP mode. Add the milk and cook for another 5 minutes.
- Turn off the heat and ladle the soup into serving bowls.

208. Mushroom Soup

(Time: 35 minutes \ Servings: 3)

INGREDIENTS:

1 cup mushrooms, sliced
1 onion, sliced
1 cup chicken broth
3 garlic cloves, minced

¼ teaspoon ginger paste
½ teaspoon black pepper
¼ teaspoon salt
1 tablespoon oil

DIRECTIONS:

- Heat oil in the Fagor Pressure Cooker.
- Add onion and garlic cloves, sauté for 1 minute on SAUTÉ mode.
- Add the mushrooms with ginger paste and stir fry for 5 minutes.
- Pour in the chicken broth, salt, pepper and mix well. Cook for 25 minutes on SOUP mode.

209. Tomato Soup

(Time: 45 minutes \ Servings: 4)

INGREDIENTS:

1 cup tomato puree
2 tablespoons chili garlic sauce
2 cups chicken broth
1 garlic clove minced

1 red chili
¼ teaspoon salt
¼ teaspoon black pepper
2 tablespoons cooking oil

DIRECTIONS:

- In the Fagor Pressure Cooker, add the tomato puree, chicken broth, salt, pepper, garlic, chili, chili garlic sauce, oil, and stir well.
- Cover with a lid and cook on SOUP mode for 40 minutes.
- Transfer the soup to a blender and blend it. Transfer to the cooker again and let it simmer for 5 minutes.

210. Cauliflower Soup

(Time: 35 minutes \ Servings: 4)

INGREDIENTS:

1 cup cauliflower florets
1 teaspoon ginger paste
1 red bell pepper chopped
2 cups vegetable broth
2 tablespoons vinegar
1 lemon, sliced

1 green chili, chopped
4-5 garlic cloves, minced
½ teaspoon black pepper
¼ teaspoon salt
1 tablespoon oil

DIRECTIONS:

- Heat oil in the Fagor Pressure Cooker, add the ginger paste and cook for 1 minute on SAUTÉ mode.
- Add the cauliflower and fry well for 5-10 minutes.
- Add the bell pepper, salt, pepper, vinegar, green chilies, lemon slices and mix well.
- Add the vegetable broth and cook for 15 minutes on SOUP mode.

211. Peas and Spinach Soup

(Time: 15 minutes \ Servings: 4)

INGREDIENTS:

1 cup baby spinach
1 cup peas
2 cups vegetable broth
½ cup milk
4-5 garlic cloves, minced

1 cup cream
½ cup tofu
½ teaspoon chili flakes
¼ teaspoon salt
2 tablespoons oil

DIRECTIONS:

- Heat oil in the saucepan and add the garlic cloves, cook for 1 minute on SAUTÉ mode.
- Add the vegetable broth, spinach, peas, tofu, cream, chili flake and salt, mix well.
- Cook for 15 minutes on SOUP mode. Pour in the milk and cook for another 5 minutes.

212. Coriander and Spinach Soup

(Time: 20 minutes \ Servings: 4)

INGREDIENTS:

1 cup baby spinach
1 bunch coriander, puree
2 cups vegetable broth
1 cup heavy cream
½ cup milk

4-5 garlic cloves, minced
½ teaspoon chili flakes
¼ teaspoon salt
2 tablespoons oil

DIRECTIONS:

- Heat oil in the saucepan and add garlic cloves, cook for 1 minute on SAUTÉ mode.
- Add vegetable broth, spinach, coriander puree, cream, chili flake, and salt, mix well.
- Cook for 10 minutes on SOUP mode. Pour in milk and cook for another 5 minutes.

213. Shrimp Soup

(Time: 25 minutes \ Servings: 4)

INGREDIENTS:

2 oz. shrimp
2 cups chicken broth
¼ cup apple cider vinegar
4-5 garlic cloves, minced

½ teaspoon black pepper
¼ teaspoon salt
1 tablespoon oil
2 tomatoes, sliced

DIRECTIONS:

- Heat oil on SAUTÉ mode and add garlic cloves, fry for 1 minute.
- Add the shrimp and fry for 10 minutes. Season with salt and pepper.
- Add chicken broth, tomatoes, vinegar and stir well.
- Cook for 10 minutes on SOUP mode.

214. Chicken Corn Soup

(Time: 25 minutes \ Servings: 3)

INGREDIENTS:

1 cup chicken, boiled, shredded
¼ cup water
2 tablespoons corn flour
3 cups chicken broth

1 garlic clove minced
¼ teaspoon salt
¼ teaspoon black pepper
2 tablespoons cooking oil

DIRECTIONS:

- Heat oil in the Fagor Pressure Cooker and fry garlic for 30 seconds.
- Add shredded chicken and stir fry. Add chicken broth and cook for 20 minutes on SOUP mode.
- Combine the corn flour with water and pour gradually into the soup until it thickens.
- Season the soup with salt and pepper. Ladle to a serving dish and serve.

215. Chickpea and Basil Soup

(Time: 35 minutes \ Servings: 3)

INGREDIENTS:

1 cup chickpeas, boiled
2-3 basil leaves
3 cups vegetable broth
1 garlic clove minced

¼ teaspoon salt
¼ teaspoon chili powder
¼ teaspoon black pepper
2 tablespoons cooking oil

DIRECTIONS:

- In the Fagor Pressure Cooker, add all ingredients and cook on SOUP mode for 35 minutes.
- Transfer to serving bowls and serve hot.

216. Quinoa with Chicken Broth

(Time: 15 minutes \ Servings: 3)

INGREDIENTS:

2 tbsp. butter
1 onion, chopped
2 celery stalk
½ cup quinoa
½ cup chicken broth

½ cup water
salt to taste
sliced almonds for seasoning
chopped parsley for seasoning

DIRECTIONS:

- Add butter into the Fagor Pressure Cooker and press the SAUTÉ button.
- Mix in onion, quinoa, water, celery, salt and chicken broth.
- Cook for 10 minutes on BROTH mode.
- When ready, dress it with almonds and parsley.

217. Chicken and Mushroom Soup

(Time: 15 minutes \ Servings: 2)

INGREDIENTS:

¼ cup oil
¼ cup all-purpose flour
1 bell pepper, sliced
1 onion, chopped
2 cups chicken breast, chopped
4 oz. mushrooms

2 tomatoes , diced
3 garlic cloves
1 tsp. soy sauce
1 tsp. sugar
salt and pepper, to taste
3 drops hot sauce

DIRECTIONS:

- Add oil into the Fagor Pressure Cooker and let it sauté.
- Mix bell pepper, chicken, mushrooms, tomatoes, onion, soy sauce, garlic, sugar and hot sauce.
- Season with salt and pepper. Add flour and stir well.
- Cook on MANUAL on high pressure for 10 minutes.

218. Chicken Broth with Broccoli

(Time: 11 minutes \ Servings: 3)

INGREDIENTS:

½ cup butter
1 onion , chopped
1 package broccoli, frozen
2 cans chicken broth

1 tbsp. garlic powder
½ cup cornstarch
1 cup water

DIRECTIONS:

- Sauté butter and onion into the Fagor Pressure Cooker.
- Mix onion, cornstarch, water, garlic powder, broccoli and chicken broth.
- Cook on MANUAL on high pressure for 5 minutes.

219. Pumpkin Seed Soup

(Time: 16 minutes \ Servings: 3)

INGREDIENTS:

2 tbsp. olive oil
1 onion, chopped
1 carrot, chopped
2 cloves garlic, minced

4 cups vegetable broth
2 tbsp. pumpkin seeds
salt to taste
parsley to garnish

DIRECTIONS:

- Add oil into the Fagor Pressure Cooker and let it sauté.
- Mix vegetable broth, pumpkin seeds, salt, garlic, carrots and onion.
- Cook on MANUAL on high pressure for 10 minutes.

220. Turkey Soup

(Time: 20 minutes \ Servings: 2)

INGREDIENTS:

3 cups turkey, cubed
2 cups water
3 stalks celery, chopped
2 garlic cloves

2 onions, chopped
salt and pepper, to taste
2 cups green onion chopped

DIRECTIONS:

- Add water and turkey cubes into the Fagor Pressure Cooker.
- Add celery, garlic, salt and pepper, onion and green onion. Stir well.
- Cook it on MANUAL on high pressure for 15 minutes.

221. Cheesy Chicken

(Time: 16 minutes \ Servings: 2)

INGREDIENTS:

1 tbsp. sour cream
1 tbsp. ranch dressing
4 bacon slices

1 lb. chicken breast, cubed
1 cup cheddar cheese, cubed
3 cups chicken broth

DIRECTIONS:

- Mix sour cream, ranch dressing, bacon slices, chicken and cheddar cheese in a bowl.
- Add the mixture into the Fagor Pressure Cooker. Cook for 10 minutes on MANUAL on high pressure.
- Mix in the chicken broth and cook for 4 more minutes.

222. Mushroom Soup

(Time: 16 minutes \ Servings: 3)

INGREDIENTS:

2 tbsp. butter
1 onion, chopped
3 cups mushrooms, chopped
2 garlic cloves

2 cups thyme, chopped
2 tbsp. flour
3 cups chicken stock
2 cups parmesan cheese, shredded

DIRECTIONS:

- Add butter and onion into the Fagor Pressure Cooker. Stir in mushrooms, garlic cloves, thyme, chicken stock, flour, and salt. Cook on MANUAL on high pressure for 10 minutes.
- When done, sprinkle shredded cheese on it and serve.

223. Chicken and Green Onion Soup

(Time: 15 minutes \ Servings: 3)

INGREDIENTS:

1 lb. chicken breast, shredded
2 cups chicken stock
1 tbsp. ginger

2 tbsp. sesame oil
salt to taste
green onions, chopped

DIRECTIONS:

- Sauté sesame oil into the Fagor Pressure Cooker.
- Mix in the chicken stock, chicken breast, ginger, salt and green onions.
- Cook on MANUAL on high pressure for 10 minutes.

224. Vegetable Broth with Veggies Soup

(Time: 20 minutes \ Servings: 3)

INGREDIENTS:

2 tbsp. olive oil
1 onion, chopped
2 cups vegetable broth
3 potatoes, diced

1 tsp. thyme
2 tbsp. apple cider vinegar
2 carrots, sliced
parsley to garnish

DIRECTIONS:

- Sauté oil into the Fagor Pressure Cooker.
- Mix in the vegetable broth, thyme, apple cider vinegar, carrots, potatoes and onion.
- Cook for 14 minutes on MANUAL on high pressure.
- When done, garnish with chopped parsley and serve.

225. Chicken and Lettuce Soup

(Time: 12 minutes \ Servings: 2)

INGREDIENTS:

1 lb. boneless chicken, cubed
½ cup oil
2 eggs
1 cup breadcrumbs
2 tbsp. flour
2 tsp. garlic powder

salt and pepper, to taste
1 head green leaf lettuce
1 mango, cubed
1 cucumber, diced
1 cup cilantro, chopped

DIRECTIONS:

- Add eggs, flour and garlic powder in a bowl. Season with salt and pepper, and mix well.
- Add oil into the Fagor Pressure Cooker.
- Dip the chicken cubes into the mixture and cook for 10 minutes on SAUTÉ mode.
- Add green leaf lettuce, mangoes, cucumbers, cilantro and cooked chicken.
- Cook for 4 minutes on MANUAL on high pressure.

226. Black Bean Soup

(Time: 16 minutes \ Servings: 2)

INGREDIENTS:

4 cups black beans
3 onions , chopped
2 tbsp. olive oil
1 tbsp. oregano

1 tbsp. chili powder
½ cup green chilies
cilantro leaves to garnish
salt to taste

DIRECTIONS:

- Sauté oil into the Fagor Pressure Cooker.
- Mix in the onions, salt, oregano, green chilies, chili powder and black beans.
- Cook on on MANUAL high pressure for 10 minutes.
- When done, serve and enjoy the meal.

227. Corn and Potato Soup

(Time: 15 minutes \ Servings: 3)

INGREDIENTS:

1 tbsp. butter
2 cups chicken broth
2 tbsp. cornstarch
2 tbsp. red pepper flakes
4 slices bacon, chopped, cooked

1 onion , chopped
2 potatoes, cubed
1 cup corn

DIRECTIONS:

- Sauté butter into the Fagor Pressure Cooker.
- Mix in the chicken broth with cornstarch, red pepper flakes, onion, potatoes, corn and bacon.
- Cook for 10 minutes on high pressure.

228. Delicious Chicken Soup

(Time: 15 minutes \ Servings: 2)

INGREDIENTS:

2 lb. chicken breast fillet, strips
1 tbsp. canola oil
1 tsp. oregano powder
2 red bell peppers, sliced

2 green bell peppers, sliced
2 onions, sliced
4 cups chicken broth
salt and pepper, to taste

DIRECTIONS:

- Add canola oil into the Fagor Pressure Cooker and brown the chicken fillets on SAUTÉ mode.
- Mix in the oregano powder, salt and pepper, red bell pepper, green bell pepper and onion.
- Cook on POULTRY for 10 minutes.
- Add chicken broth. Cook for another 5 minutes.

229. Chicken Tomato Sauce

(Time: 16 minutes \ Servings: 2)

INGREDIENTS:

2 cups chicken broth
1 lb. chicken breast, chopped
2 cups squash, chopped

2 tbsp. tomato sauce
2 cups beans
1 tbsp. cumin powder

DIRECTIONS:

- Add chicken broth into the Fagor Pressure Cooker.
- Mix in the squash, chicken breast, tomato sauce, beans, cumin powder, and salt.
- Cook on high pressure for 10 minutes.

230. Baby Spinach Soup

(Time: 19 minutes \ Servings: 3)

INGREDIENTS:

2 tbsp. ginger, minced
4 garlic cloves, minced
1 tbsp. mustard seeds
1 tbsp. vegetable oil
2 cups vegetable broth

½ tbsp. fenugreek
1 tbsp. coriander powder
1 tbsp. cumin powder
4 cups baby spinach

DIRECTIONS:

- Sauté oil into the Fagor Pressure Cooker.
- Mix in the mustard seeds, garlic, fenugreek, cumin powder, coriander powder and vegetable broth.
- Add chopped spinach and cook for 15 minutes on SOUP mode.

231. Bacon Vegetable Broth

(Time: 15 minutes \ Servings: 3)

INGREDIENTS:

2 cups corn
1 onion, chopped
1 tbsp. cornstarch
4 pieces bacon, sliced

2 cups vegetable broth
1 potato, sliced
½ tsp. red pepper

DIRECTIONS:

- Add onion, corn, cornstarch, bacon, potato, vegetable broth and red pepper into the Fagor Pressure Cooker. Cook it on high pressure for 10 minutes.

232. Ham Hock

(Time: 10 minutes \ Servings: 3)

INGREDIENTS:

2 lbs. ham hock
1 onion, chopped
2 garlic cloves , minced
2 cups black beans

2 bay leaves
2 cups chicken stock
2 tbsp. oregano powder

DIRECTIONS:

- Add onion and bay leaves into the Fagor Pressure Cooker.
- Mix in the ham hock, garlic, black beans, oregano powder and chicken stock.
- Cook on high pressure for 10 minutes.

233. Broccoli Soup

(Time: 10 minutes \ Servings: 2)

INGREDIENTS:

2 cups vegetable broth
3 cups broccoli
1 tbsp. cumin powder

1 tbsp. cayenne powder
3 green onion
salt to taste

DIRECTIONS:

- Add vegetable broth into the pressure cooker.
- Mix broccoli, cumin powder, green onion and cayenne powder with salt.
- Cook on high pressure for 5 minutes.

234. Chicken Noodle Soup

(Time: 15 minutes \ Servings: 3)

INGREDIENTS:

1 lb. chicken breast, cubed
1 12oz. package of egg noodles
1 lb. Bok Choy

4 cups chicken stock
2 cups hot water
2 carrots

DIRECTIONS:

- Add chicken stock into the Fagor Pressure Cooker. Cook for 5 minutes on SAUTÉ mode.
- Mix chicken, Bok Choy, carrots, noodles, salt and hot water into the pot.
- Cook on high pressure for 10 minutes.

235. Beef Soup

(Time: 14 minutes \ Servings: 3)

INGREDIENTS:

1 lb. ground beef
1 onion , diced
2 garlic cloves , minced
2 cups beans, any
1 potato, cubed

2 tomatoes, cubed
2 celery stalks, chopped
2 tbsp. cumin powder
salt and pepper, to taste

DIRECTIONS:

- Add onion and potato in the Fagor Pressure Cooker. Mix well.
- Mix in the ground beef, garlic, beans, tomatoes, celery stalks and cumin powder. Stir well.
- Cook for 10 minutes in high pressure.

236. Sweet Potato Soup

(Time: 16 minutes \ Servings: 2)

INGREDIENTS:

2 tbsp. butter
1 onion
2 sweet potatoes
2 cups corn

2 cups chicken broth
1 tbsp. cornstarch
1 tbsp. red pepper flakes
salt and pepper, to taste

DIRECTIONS:

- Add butter and onion into the Fagor Pressure Cooker.
- Mix chicken broth into it and stir well.
- Add sweet potatoes, corn, salt and pepper, cornstarch and red pepper flakes.
- Cook for 10 minutes on high pressure.

237. Squash Soup

(Time: 15 minutes \ Servings: 3)

INGREDIENTS:

1 lb. squash
2 tbsp. butter
1 onion, chopped
2 garlic cloves, minced

3 cups chicken broth
2 tbsp. nutmeg powder
½ cup half and half
1 lb. chicken breast, cubed

DIRECTIONS:

- Add butter into the Fagor Pressure Cooker and sauté it.
- Mix squash, chicken broth, garlic, onion, nutmeg powder, chicken cubes and half and half.
- Cook for 10 minutes on SOUP mode.

238. Kale and Chicken Soup

(Time: 10 minutes \ Servings: 3)

INGREDIENTS:

2 tbsp. olive oil
2 lb. chicken thighs, cubed
2 cups chicken broth

2 tomatoes , chopped
2 potatoes , chopped
2 cups kale, chopped

DIRECTIONS:

- Add oil into the Fagor Pressure Cooker.
- Add chicken broth, potatoes, tomatoes, salt and pepper, kale and chicken cubes.
- Cook on high pressure for 10 minutes.

239. Sweet and Sour Tomato Soup

(Time: 35 minutes \ Servings: 3)

INGREDIENTS:

1 cup tomato sauce
½ cup tomato ketchup
2 cups vegetable broth
¼ cup water
3 tablespoons of corn flour
2 tablespoons vinegar

2 garlic cloves, minced
4 tablespoons brown sugar
½ teaspoon black pepper
¼ teaspoon salt
1 tablespoon oil

DIRECTIONS:

- Set the Fagor Pressure Cooker on SAUTÉ mode.
- Heat oil inside it and add garlic cloves, sauté for 1 minute.
- Add tomato puree, tomato ketchup, vinegar and fry for 1-2 minutes.
- Add in vegetable broth, and season with salt, sugar and pepper.
- Let it simmer for 20 minutes on SOUP mode. Combine water with corn flour and mix well.
- Gradually add this mixture into the soup and stir continuously for 1-2 minutes.
- Pour into serving bowls and enjoy.

240. Vegetable Soup

(Time: 30 minutes \ Servings: 3)

INGREDIENTS:

1 cup broccoli florets
1 green bell pepper, sliced
1 red bell pepper, sliced
1 carrot, sliced
1 onion, sliced
2 cups vegetable broth

1 tablespoon lemon juice
4-5 garlic cloves, minced
½ teaspoon black pepper
¼ teaspoon salt
1 tablespoon cooking oil

DIRECTIONS:

- Set the Fagor Pressure Cooker on SAUTÉ mode.
- Heat oil, add onion and garlic cloves, sauté for 1 minute.
- Add all vegetables, stir fry and cook for 5-10 minutes.
- Add vegetable broth, salt, and pepper and mix well.
- Cook on SOUP mode for 15 minutes. Drizzle lemon juice.

241. Spicy Chicken Noodle Soup

(Time: 25 minutes \ Servings: 4)

INGREDIENTS:

3 oz. chicken, boiled, cubes
1 onion, sliced
1 12 oz. package egg noodles, cooked
3 cups chicken broth
2 tablespoons vinegar

4-5 garlic cloves, minced
½ teaspoon black pepper
¼ teaspoon salt
1 tablespoon oil

DIRECTIONS:

- Heat oil in the Fagor Pressure Cooker and add garlic cloves and onion; cook for 1 minute on SAUTÉ mode. Add the chicken and the carrots and fry for 5 minutes.
- Stir in the chicken broth, vinegar, salt, and pepper.
- Add the noodles and cook on 15 minutes on SOUP mode. Ladle into serving bowls.

242. Garlic Chicken and Egg Soup

(Time: 35 minutes \ Servings: 3)

INGREDIENTS:

¼ lb. chicken, cut into small pieces
1 onion, chopped
2 eggs, whisked
2 cups chicken broth
¼ cup water

3 tablespoons of corn flour
4-5 garlic cloves, minced
½ teaspoon black pepper
¼ teaspoon salt
1 tablespoon oil

DIRECTIONS:

- Heat oil in the Fagor Pressure Cooker on SAUTÉ mode, sauté garlic and onion for 1 minute.
- Add the chicken and fry for 10 minutes.
- Shred chicken and transfer it to the Fagor Pressure Cooker again. Season with black pepper and salt.
- Add the chicken broth, simmer for 15 minutes on SOUP mode.
- In a bowl, combine water with corn flour and mix well.
- Gradually pour this mixture into soup and stir continuously for 2 minutes.
- Add the eggs by gradually. Cook for another 2 minutes.

243. Pumpkin Purée Soup

(Time: 35 minutes \ Servings: 3)

INGREDIENTS:

2 cups pumpkin puree
2 cups vegetable broth
1 cup milk
2 tablespoons soya sauce
¼ teaspoon turmeric powder

½ teaspoon black pepper
4-5 garlic cloves, minced
¼ teaspoon salt
1 tablespoon oil

DIRECTIONS:

- Heat oil in the Fagor Pressure Cooker and add garlic cloves, cook for 1 minute on SAUTÉ mode.
- Add pumpkin and fry for 5 minutes.
- Stir in vegetable broth, salt, pepper, turmeric powder, soya sauce and mix, cook for 20 minutes on SOUP mode. Add milk and cook for another 5 minutes.

244. Bell Pepper and Cabbage Soup

(Time: 55 minutes \ Servings: 4)

INGREDIENTS:

1 cup cabbages, shredded
1 red bell pepper, sliced
1 onion, sliced
2 cups chicken broth
1 tablespoon fish sauce

4-5 garlic cloves, minced
½ teaspoon black pepper
¼ teaspoon salt
1 tablespoon oil

DIRECTIONS:

- Heat oil in the Fagor Pressure Cooker, add onion and cook for 1 minute on SAUTÉ mode.
- Add the garlic, bell pepper, cabbage and cook for 5 minutes.
- Add chicken broth, fish sauce, salt, and pepper and mix well.
- Cook for 15 minutes on SOUP mode. Add cream and cook for 5 minutes.

245. Spinach Soup

(Time: 35 minutes \ Servings: 3)

INGREDIENTS:

1 cup baby spinach
2 cups vegetable broth
½ cup milk
2 garlic cloves, minced

½ teaspoon chili flakes
¼ teaspoon salt
¼ cup sour cream
2 tablespoons oil

DIRECTIONS:

- In the Fagor Pressure Cooker, add all ingredients and cover with a lid.
- Set the cooker on SOUP mode, cook for 25 minutes.
- Transfer to a blender and blend until creamy.
- Pour the spinach soup back into the cooker and cook for another 6 minutes.
- Top with sour cream.

246. Cabbage Soup

(Time: 35 minutes \ Servings: 3)

INGREDIENTS:

1 cup cabbage, chopped
2 cups chicken broth
2 garlic cloves, minced
½ teaspoon black pepper

2 tablespoons soya sauce
1 tablespoon vinegar
¼ teaspoon salt
2 tablespoons oil

DIRECTIONS:

- In the Fagor Pressure Cooker, add all ingredients and cover with a lid.
- Set the cooker on SOUP mode and cook for 35 minutes. Serve hot.

247. Onion and Carrot Soup

(Time: 35 minutes \ Servings: 3)

INGREDIENTS:

1 onion, sliced
2 carrots, chopped
1 tablespoon fish sauce
2 cups chicken broth
1 egg, whisked
2 tablespoons vinegar

1 cup tomato puree
4-5 garlic cloves, minced
½ teaspoon black pepper
¼ teaspoon salt
1 tablespoon oil

DIRECTIONS:

- Heat oil in the Fagor Pressure Cooker and add garlic cloves and onion.
- Cook for 1 minute on SAUTÉ mode.
- Stir in the carrots and cook for 2 minutes. Add salt, pepper, and fish sauce and stir.
- Add chicken broth, and tomato puree and cook for 15 minutes on SOUP mode.
- Add the egg and stir continuously.

248. Chickpea Broccoli Soup

(Time: 35 minutes \ Servings: 3)

INGREDIENTS:

1 cup broccoli florets
1 cup chickpea, boiled
1medium onion, chopped
2 cups chicken broth
3 garlic cloves, minced

½ teaspoon black pepper
¼ teaspoon salt
2 tablespoons white rice vinegar
1 tablespoon oil

DIRECTIONS:

- Heat oil in the Fagor Pressure Cooker and sauté garlic cloves for 1 minute on SAUTÉ mode.
- Stir in chickpeas, broccoli, onion, salt, pepper and sauté well.
- Pour in chicken broth, and vinegar, cook for 25 minutes on SOUP mode.
- Transfer to a blender and blend to a puree.

249. Rice Soup with Broccoli

(Time: 35 minutes \ Servings: 3)

INGREDIENTS:

1 cup broccoli florets
1 cup rice, boiled
1 onion, sliced
2 cups vegetable broth
1 cup chicken broth

1 tablespoon lemon juice
2 garlic cloves, minced
½ teaspoon black pepper
¼ teaspoon salt
1 tablespoon oil

DIRECTIONS:

- In the Fagor Pressure Cooker, add all ingredients and stir.
- Cover up with a lid.
- Cook for 30 on SOUP mode. Blend the soup in a blender.
- Ladle the soup to bowls and serve hot.

250. Yellow Lentils Hot Soup

(Time: 60 minutes \ Servings: 3)

INGREDIENTS:

1 cup yellow lentils, soaked
1 cup water
¼ teaspoon turmeric powder
½ teaspoon ginger paste
1 onion, chopped

3 cups chicken broth
4-5 garlic cloves, minced
½ teaspoon chili powder
¼ teaspoon salt
2 tablespoons butter

DIRECTIONS:

- In the Fagor Pressure Cooker, add all ingredients and stir.
- Set the pressure cooker on SLOW COOK mode and cover up with a lid. Cook for 60 minutes.

251. Red Beans Soup

(Time: 35 minutes \ Servings: 3)

INGREDIENTS:

2 cups red beans, boiled
1 onion, sliced
1 tomato chopped
2 cups chicken broth
1 tablespoon lemon juice

4-5 garlic cloves, minced
½ teaspoon black pepper
¼ teaspoon salt
1 green chili, chopped
1 tablespoon oil

DIRECTIONS:

- Heat oil in the Fagor Pressure Cooker and sauté garlic with onion for 1 minute on SAUTÉ mode.
- Stir in the beans, chicken broth, salt, pepper, and green chili.
- Cook on MANUAL mode for 30 minutes. Ladle into serving bowls and drizzle lemon juice.

252. Potato Cream Soup

(Time: 35 minutes \ Servings: 3)

INGREDIENTS:

4 large potatoes, boiled, mashed
1 onion, sliced
2 cups chicken broth
1 cup heavy cream

3 garlic cloves, minced
½ teaspoon black pepper
¼ teaspoon salt
1 tablespoon oil

DIRECTIONS:

- Heat oil in the Fagor Pressure Cooker, add onion and garlic cloves, cook for 1 minute on SAUTÉ mode.
- Add the boiled potatoes and stir well.
- Stir in cream, chicken broth, salt, and pepper. Cook for 20 minutes on CHILI mode.
- Remove from the heat and let cool a little bit. Transfer into a food processor and blend to a puree.
- Pour into the Fagor Pressure Cooker and cook for 5 minutes.

253. Spinach and Chickpea Soup

(Time: 65 minutes \ Servings: 4)

INGREDIENTS:

1 cup chickpea
1 cup spinach, chopped
2 cups chicken broth
4-5 garlic cloves, minced

½ teaspoon black pepper
¼ teaspoon chili powder
¼ teaspoon salt
1 tablespoon oil

DIRECTIONS:

- Transfer all ingredients into the Fagor Pressure Cooker and stir.
- Set on SLOW COOK mode and cover with a lid. Cook for 60-65 minutes.
- Ladle the soup to bowls and serve.

254. Chicken Spaghetti Soup

(Time: 35 minutes \ Servings: 3)

INGREDIENTS:

1 onion, sliced
4 tablespoons tomato puree
1 cup chicken, boneless, cubed, boiled
1 package spaghetti, boiled
2 cups chicken broth

3 garlic cloves, minced
½ teaspoon chili powder
1 carrot, sliced
¼ teaspoon salt
1 tablespoon oil

DIRECTIONS:

- Heat oil in the Fagor Pressure Cooker, sauté onion and garlic for 1 minute on SAUTÉ mode.
- Stir in tomato puree and fry for 1 minute.
- Add the chicken pieces, carrot, spaghetti, chicken broth and cook for 20 minutes on CHILI mode.
- Season with salt and chili powder.

255. Butternut Squash Soup

(Time: 25 Minutes \ Servings: 6)

INGREDIENTS

1 peeled and diced butternut squash.
1 peeled and diced apple
1 tbsp. of ginger powder or pureed ginger

4 cups of chicken broth
2 tbsp. of coconut oil to taste

DIRECTIONS

- Start by hitting the SAUTÉ button on the Fagor Pressure Cooker to preheat it.
- Add the coconut oil and add some of the butternut squash cubes to it. Brown it lightly for approximately 5 minutes.
- Add the remaining squash and add the rest of the ingredients.
- Close and lock the Pressure cooker. Press (+) button so 10 more minutes are added on high pressure.
- When the time is over, open the Pressure cooker by using the Quick Release.
- Puree the mixture in a blender. Serve and enjoy the delicious, healthy soup.

256. Quinoa Soup

(Time: 30 Minutes \ Servings: 5)

INGREDIENTS

3 tbsp. of olive oil
1 small chopped white onion
3 peeled, chopped carrots
2 stalks of chopped celery
2 cups of chopped vegetables: yellow squash,
   zucchini, sweet potatoes, and bell pepper
5 minced garlic cloves.
½ tsp. of dried thyme

1 can cubed and drained tomatoes
1 cup of rinsed quinoa
4 cups of vegetable broth
1 tsp. of salt and Leaves of bay
1 pinch of red pepper
1 pinch of fresh black pepper
1 can rinsed chickpeas or beans
1 cup of chopped kale.

DIRECTIONS

- Rinse the quinoa well and soak it for a night in a filtered water. Add to it 1 tbsp. of lemon or vinegar; then strain.
- Place all the ingredients in the preheated Fagor Pressure Cooker; close and lock the lid.
- Press the MANUAL button and use the (-) button in order to choose 2 minutes of pressure cooking time.
- When the time is up, let the soup simmer for another 10 minutes.

257. Cream of Asparagus Soup

(Time: 20 Minutes \ Servings: 4)

INGREDIENTS

½ lb. of fresh asparagus, cut into pieces
1 sliced yellow onion
3 chopped or minced cloves of garlic cloves
3 tbsp. of coconuts oil
½ tsp. of dried thyme

5 cups of bone broth
1 tbsp. lemon juice and zest
1 tsp. of sea salt
2 cups of organic sour cream

DIRECTIONS

- Prepare the asparagus, onion, and garlic. Remove the woody ends from the asparagus stalks and discard it. Chop the asparagus into 1-inch pieces.
- Slice the onion into halves and chop it. Smash the garlic cloves. Then set the ingredients aside and place the stainless-steel bowl inside the Fagor Pressure Cooker without putting the lid on.
- Set to SAUTÉ and add the coconut oil; then add the onions and the garlic.
- Cook the mixture for 5 minutes and stir occasionally; add the thyme and cook for 1 more minute.
- Add the broth, asparagus, and lemon zest with the salt.
- Then lock the lid of the Pressure cooker and press MANUAL on high pressure for 5 minutes.
- When the timer goes off, add the sour cream and stir after the pressure cooker releases the steam.

258. Lentils Soup with Coconut Milk

(Time: 40 Minutes \ Servings: 6)

INGREDIENTS

1 diced onion
3 minced garlic cloves
2 tbsp. of red curry paste
¼ tsp. of ginger powder
1 tbsp. of red pepper flakes

6 oz. canned coconut milk
6 oz. canned cut tomatoes
2 cups of vegetable broth
1 ½ cups of lentils

DIRECTIONS:

- In the Fagor Pressure Cooker cooker, click the SAUTÉ button and wait a couple minutes until it becomes warm. Add the diced onion and garlic; then sauté altogether until brown. Add a 1/4 cup of broth.
- Once the ingredients start to brown, press the cancel button to stop the sautéing.
- Add the paste of the red curry, ginger powder, and red pepper flakes and keep stirring.
- Add the coconut milk, diced tomatoes, vegetable broth, and lentils and stir again.
- Lock the lid and press the MANUAL button then reduce the timer to around 7 minutes.

259. Roasted Tomato and Avocado Soup

(Time: 40 Minutes \ Servings: 6)

INGREDIENTS

2 tbsp. of coconut oil
½ can cut fire roasted tomatoes
1 cut sweet onion
5 diced carrots
1 diced sweet potato
5 minced garlic cloves

4 cups of bone broth or chicken stock
1 pinch of salt
1 pinch of pepper
2 avocado chunks
1 lemon

DIRECTIONS

- Press the SAUTÉ button function on the Fagor Pressure Cooker.
- Add the coconut oil to a stainless-steel bowl and add the onions until they soften and become translucent.
- Add 1 pinch of salt and stir; add the ingredients starting with the sweet potato, minced garlic, and carrots.
- Continue sautéing the mixture for 10 more minutes. Then pour in the tomatoes and bone broth.
- Press Keep Warm/ Cancel in order to stop the mode SAUTÉ; keep stirring, place the lid and lock it.
- Set the timer to 20 minutes using the (+) and the (−).
- Blend the soup after the steam is released and serve it with avocado chunks, fresh cracked pepper, and fresh lemon wedges.

260. Creamy Cauliflower Soup

(Time: 20 Minutes \ Servings: 5)

INGREDIENTS

4 cups of vegetable broth
1 head of cubed and chopped cauliflower
3 cups of potatoes, cubed
4 cups of onion, chopped

2 large carrots, cubed
½ cup of celery, diced
2 tbsp. of raw coconut amino
1 tbsp. of coconut oil

DIRECTIONS

- Pour the coconut oil in the Fagor Pressure Cooker and add all ingredients inside.
- Lock the lid and seal the vent of the steam. Press MANUAL and adjust the timer to 9 minutes.
- Once the pressure is reached, the countdown starts.
- Add 2 tsp. of cashew butter. Use a blender to mash the soup.

261. Broccoli Soup with Cheese

(Time: 20 Minutes \ Servings: 4)

INGREDIENTS

2 tbsp. of coconuts oil
2 minced cloves of garlic

1 head of broccoli, into florets
2 lb. of peeled, diced Yukon Gold Potatoes

4 cups of vegetable or chicken broth
1 pinch of salt
1 pinch of pepper

½ cup of shredded cheddar cheese
6 bacon slices
1 cut green onion for garnish

DIRECTIONS

- Press the SAUTÉ on the Fagor Pressure Cooker.
- Once hot, add the coconut oil and minced garlic and sauté the ingredients for one to two minutes. Add in the broccoli, potatoes, and broth.
- Season the ingredients with salt and pepper before securing the lid of the Pressure cooker.
- Select MANUAL to cancel the SAUTÉ mode and cook the rest of the ingredients for 5 minutes at a high pressure.
- Once the cooking process is finished, use the natural release for 10 minutes; then remove the remaining steam. Once you open the lid; blend the ingredients in batches and add a little more broth with the cheddar cheese.
- Add salt and pepper with ½ cup cheddar cheese.

262. Carrot Soup
(Time: 15 Minutes \ Servings: 5)

INGREDIENTS

1 tbsp. of avocado oil or coconut oil
1 large, roughly chopped yellow onion
1¼ lb. of chopped carrots
1 roughly chopped serrano pepper with
  seeds
2 tsp. of grated ginger
4 cups of chicken broth

1 tsp. of sea salt
1 tsp. of garlic powder
¼ tsp. of cayenne pepper
chopped cilantro
½ cup of coconut milk
10 drops of liquid stevia

DIRECTIONS

- Use the SAUTÉ mode and heat the oil; then add the onion. Sauté the mixture for about 2 minutes until they soften but be careful not to brown the ingredients.
- Add the carrots and peppers and sauté for a few minutes. Pour in the type of broth you prefer with all the spices and keep stirring.
- Seal the lid of the Pressure cooker and the set the MANUAL high pressure for 13 minutes. When the time is up, try a fast release and unlock the lid.
- Add the puree and the cilantro to the soup and process the ingredients into a food processor. Return the ingredients to the Pressure cooker and pour the cream with the stevia.

263. Spinach Soup with Asparagus
(Time: 30 Minutes \ Servings: 5)

INGREDIENTS

2 courgettes
1 handful of kale
2 celery sticks
4 asparagus spears
¼ lb. of baby spinach
1 small onion
¼ quarter of deseeded chili

2 minced garlic cloves
2 tbsp. of coconut oil
1 pinch of salt
1 pinch of ground black pepper
1 cube of vegetable stock
2 tsp. of spirulina
½ cup of fresh parsley

DIRECTIONS

- Start by peeling and chopping the onion, garlic, and chili and set it aside for 5 to 10 minutes. Finely chop the parsley and the vegetables.

- Add 2 tbsp. of oil into a preheated Fagor Pressure Cooker; then add the onion and press SAUTÉ for 3 minutes. Once the onion softens, cancel the sauté. Add the garlic and chili.
- Add the chopped vegetables and leaves, except the parsley. Add the stock, salt, and pepper; then lock the lid and set the timer to 10 minutes.
- Once the timer goes off, release the pressure and blend the ingredients. Add the spirulina and cook for 5 more minutes, then serve and enjoy the soup.

264. Coconut Lime Soup

(Time: 20 Minutes \ Servings: 3-4)

INGREDIENTS

½ tbsp. of coconut Oil
1 finely chopped onion
1 tsp. of ground coriander powder
1 cauliflower, into florets

3 cups of vegetable broth
½ cup of coconut milk
2-3 tbsp. of lime juice
1 pinch of salt to taste

DIRECTIONS

- Start by heating the Fagor Pressure Cooker and set to SAUTÉ mode. Sauté the onion for 6 minutes. Add the coriander and stir for a couple of minutes. Add the rest of the ingredients and stir to combine them.
- Lock the lid and set the timer to 10 minutes on SOUP.
- Once the timer goes off, press the Warm button and release the pressure.
- Blend the ingredients until soft. Add the lime juice and adjust the salt to taste.

265. Black Bean Soup with Flax seeds

(Time: 10 Minutes \ Servings: 5)

INGREDIENTS

1 ½ cups of dry black beans, soaked
1 tbsp. of coconut oil
1 cup of chopped onion
3 minced cloves of garlic
1 tbsp. of ground cumin
¼ tsp. of chipotle powder

6 cups of vegetable broth
1 bay leaf
2 tsp. of dried oregano leaves
1 tsp. of salt, or just to taste
2 tsp. of ground flax seeds.
1 cup of soy yogurt or sour cream

FOR GARNISH

chopped cilantro

1 Avocado

DIRECTIONS

- Drain the soaking beans and set them aside. Heat the oil in the Fagor Pressure Cooker using the SAUTÉ button. Add the onion and keep sautéing for 2 more minutes.
- Add garlic, cumin, chipotle powder, beans, broth, bay leaf, ground flax seeds, and oregano. Keep stirring.
- Set the heat up to its highest degree. Seal the lid and set the steam valve to "Sealed".
- Click the MANUAL button and set the timer to 8 minutes.
- When the timer goes off and the pressure is released, blend the ingredients.
- Finally garnish with cilantro and avocado, serve and enjoy the soup!

266. Garlic and Almond Soup

(Time: 15 Minutes \ Servings: 7-8)

INGREDIENTS

3 ¼ cups of freezing water
2 ¼ cups of blanched almonds
5 peeled and minced cloves of garlic
1 baguette, cut in pieces
½ cup of coconut oil

2 ½ tbsp. of sherry vinegar
2 drops of almond extract
1 pinch of Kosher salt
10 halved almonds

DIRECTIONS:

- In the Fagor Pressure Cooker, combine the 2 cups of water with the almonds, garlic, and bread.
- Set to SAUTÉ mode and cook the ingredients until softened, around 5 minutes.
- Add the remaining quantity of water, coconut oil, vinegar, extract, and salt. Cancel the Sauté feature and set the timer to 10 minutes on SOUP mode.
- Once the timer goes off, release the pressure and blend the ingredients.
- Garnish the soup with the halves of almonds, serve and enjoy!

267. Beef Noodle Soup

(Time: 50 Minutes \ Servings:5)

INGREDIENTS

½ lb. of beef shoulder
1 tbsp. of kosher salt
¼ cup of fresh ground black pepper
½ tsp. of allspice
¼ tsp. of ground ginger
1 tbsp. of coconut oil
1-inch of fresh ginger
4 cups of chicken broth

¼ cups of fish sauce
1 head of bok Choy
1 head of cabbage
2 packages of 7 oz. of Shriataki noodles
2 scallions
¼ cup of cilantro
1 cup of bean sprouts

DIRECTIONS

- Cut the beef into small cubes of 1 inch each. Season with the salt, pepper, allspice powder, and ginger.
- Press SAUTÉ, and once it's hot, stir in the beef and sauté it. Then, add the chicken broth with the fish sauce and the ginger. Lock the lid and set to CHILI; cook for around 30 minutes.
- Meanwhile, cut the bok Choy, the Napa cabbage and the scallions.
- When the cooking process is complete, vent the steam and remove the lid. Then set to SAUTÉ mode.
- Add the Napa cabbage, bok Choy, and scallion; then simmer for around 5 minutes.
- Drain and rinse the noodles and add them to the Pressure cooker.
- Let the ingredients simmer for around 2 minutes; then garnish with cilantro and serve.

268. Lamb Stew With Carrots

(Time: 35 Minutes \ Servings: 3)

INGREDIENTS

2 lb. of diced lamb stew meat
1 large acorn squash
4 carrots
2 yellow onions
2 rosemary sprigs

1 bay leaf
6 sliced or minced cloves of garlic
3 tbsp. of broth or water
2-3 pinches of salt

DIRECTIONS

- Start by peeling, seeding, then cubing the acorn squash. A quick trick - microwave the squash for 2 minutes.
- Slice the carrots into thick circles.
- Peel the onions and cut in half; then slice them into half-moon shape.
- Place all the ingredients in the Fagor Pressure Cooker and set SOUP button.
- Lock the lid and set the timer to 35 minutes.
- When the timer goes off, release the steam pressure before opening the lid. Serve and enjoy the stew.

269. Beef and Broccoli Stew

(Time: 35 Minutes \ Servings: 4-5)

INGREDIENTS

1 lb. of beef stew meat	2 large minced cloves of garlic
1 large quartered onion	1 tsp. of ground ginger
½ cup of beef or bone broth	½ tsp. of salt
¼ cup of coconut aminos	1 tbsp. of coconuts oil
2 tbsp. of fish sauce	¼ lb. of frozen broccoli

DIRECTIONS

- In the Fagor Pressure Cooker, place all ingredients except the broccoli.
- Lock the lid. Press the MEAT button and cook for 35 minutes.
- When the timer goes off, carefully release the pressure and open the lid.
- Add the broccoli to the inner pot. Place the lid loosely.
- Let the ingredients simmer for around 15 minutes. Serve and enjoy the stew.

270. Coconut Fish Stew with Garlic

(Time: 15 Minutes \ Servings: 6)

INGREDIENTS

2 to 4 Pieces of study or monkfish (or white fish)	3 minced garlic cloves
1 juiced lime	2 cups of halved grapes or cherry tomatoes
2 tbsp. of coconut oil	1 pinch of cayenne
1 sliced leek	1 tsp. of chia powder
1 seeded and thinly sliced jalapeño	1 medium can of light coconut milk (13.5 oz.)
	Quinoa, cooked, for garnish

DIRECTIONS

- Start by chopping and marinating the fish; then cut it into cubes and place it inside the fridge after adding lime juice. In the Fagor Pressure Cooker, press SAUTÉ and sauté the veggies for 5 minutes.
- Add the coconut oil, jalapeños, and leeks. When the timer goes off, press to cancel the sauté button.
- Add the garlic and the tomatoes and season with salt.
- Add the marinated fish and the lime juice; then pour the coconut milk and a little bit of water.
- Stir and add the cayenne and chia power.
- Press the CHILI button. Lock the lid and set the timer to 10 minutes. Serve the stew with quinoa.

271. Guinness Stew with Green Beans

(Time: 35 Minutes \ Servings: 4)

INGREDIENTS

¼ cup of oat flour
1 lb. of beef diced into small pieces
¼ cup of coconut oil
3 peeled and coarsely cut carrots
1 Large, halved, and coarsely cut brown
   onion
2 minced garlic cloves
2 tbsp. of tomato paste

1 cup of Guinness beer
1 cup of Campbell's Stock Beef
2 Sprigs of fresh thyme
2 Bay leaves, dried
¼ cup of coarsely chopped parsley
¼ lb. of green beans
2 tsp. of grated lemon rind

DIRECTIONS

- Preheat the Fagor Pressure Cooker and pour the coconut oil into it.
- Put the flour in a large bowl and season it with salt and pepper; then add the beef to coat it in the mixture.
- Press SAUTÉ for 5 minutes. Add the beef and cook it for the designated time.
- After the timer goes off, cancel SAUTÉ and add the carrots, green beans, onion, and garlic.
- After 2 minutes or when the ingredients soften, add the tomato paste.
- Pour the beer and the stock with the thyme and the bay; make sure there is enough water.
- Lock the lid and set on MANUAL for 35 minutes. Garnish with parsley.

272. Lentils, Indian Dal, and Spinach Stew

(Time: 25 Minutes \ Servings: 5)

INGREDIENTS

2 tbsp. of coconut oil
2 red chopped onions
3 minced garlic cloves
1 tsp. of ground cumin
1 tsp. of ground coriander
1 tsp. of ground turmeric
¼ tsp. of dried cayenne pepper
¼ tsp. of flax seeds
1 cup of red lentils

½ cup of yellow peas
3 cups of warm water
½ tsp. of salt
2 diced medium tomatoes
4 cups of spinach
¼ cup of chopped fresh cilantro
2 tsp. of butter
Yogurt and fresh cilantro for garnish

DIRECTIONS

- Pour the coconut oil into the Fagor Pressure Cooker and cook on SAUTÉ mode.
- When the oil heats up, add the cut onions and keep cooking until softened. Add the garlic and cook for around 3 minutes.
- Cancel the SAUTÉ mode. Add the flax seeds, coriander, turmeric, and cayenne; then mix well.
- Add the lentils, water, salt, and tomato wedges.
- Stir them into the onion mixture. Cover the Fagor Pressure Cooker with its lid, press MANUAL and cook for 10 minutes.
- Press Cancel and release the pressure.
- Add the spinach with the cilantro and serve with brown rice.

273. Ginger and Sesame Asparagus Stew

(Time: 40 Minutes \ Servings: 3)

INGREDIENTS

8 oz. of diagonally sliced asparagus
2 tbsp. of hoisin sauce
1 ½ tsp. of rice wine
1 tsp. of sesame oil
1 tbsp. of coconut oil
1 tsp. of sesame seeds

1 tsp. of chia powder
2 tsp. of minced and peeled ginger
2 minced garlic cloves
3 coarsely cut carrots
½ tsp. of coarse salt
½ cup of coconut milk.

DIRECTIONS

- In the Fagor Pressure Cooker, pour the coconut oil with ½ cup of water and add the asparagus. Press SAUTÉ and set the timer to 5 minutes.
- When the timer goes off, cancel Sauté and add the rest of the ingredients. Lock the lid and set the timer to 35 minutes on MANUAL mode.
- Let the ingredients boil, and when the timer goes off, release the pressure.

274. Tuna and Avocado Stew

(Time: 15 Minutes \ Servings: 5)

INGREDIENTS

1 ½ lb. tuna steak, cubed into 1-inch
2 Diced avocados
¼ cup of red diced onion
¼ cup of thinly sliced scallions
1 Diced large potato
2 Cut carrots
4 tbsp. of Coconut oil

1 tbsp. of sesame oil
2 zested and juiced limes
1 tsp. of sriracha
2 tsp. of soy sauce
1 pinch of sea salt and black pepper
1 ½ cups of cooked quinoa

DIRECTIONS

- Pour 1 tbsp. of coconut oil and press the SAUTÉ.
- After 2 minutes, press the cancel button and sprinkle the ingredients with salt and ground pepper.
- Add the onions and slices of scallions, potatoes, and carrots with 2 cups of coconut milk. Set the timer to 20 minutes on high pressure.
- Meanwhile, cut the avocados and add 2 tbsp. of coconut oil, 1 tbsp. of olive oil, sesame oil, lime zest, soy sauce, and sriracha.
- Release the pressure and add the avocado with the red onions and pour the stew on the cooked quinoa.

Poultry

275. Spicy Chicken Nuggets
(Time: 35 minutes \ Servings: 5)

INGREDIENTS:

3 chicken breasts, cut into 2 inch pieces
1 teaspoon garlic powder
1 cup all-purpose flour
2 tablespoons coriander, chopped

½ teaspoon chili pepper
½ teaspoon cinnamon powder
1 cup oil, for frying
¼ cup water

DIRECTIONS:

- In a bowl, combine flour, salt, chili powder, cumin powder, coriander and toss well.
- Add water and make a thick paste. Heat oil in the Fagor Pressure Cooker on SAUTÉ mode.
- Dip each chicken piece into the flour mixture and then put into the oil.
- Fry each chicken wing until golden and place on a paper towel to drain out the excess oil.
- Transfer to a serving dish and serve with mint sauce.

276. Hot Chicken Fingers
(Time: 40 minutes \ Servings: 8)

INGREDIENTS:

3 chicken breasts, cut into 1-inch thick strips
1 teaspoon garlic powder
½ cup flour
½ cup bread crumbs

2 eggs, whisked
½ teaspoon black pepper
½ teaspoon cinnamon powder
1 cup oil, for frying

DIRECTIONS:

- In a platter, combine flour, bread crumbs, salt, pepper, garlic powder and cinnamon powder, mix well.
- Dip each chicken strip into the eggs and roll them out in the flour mixture. Set aside.
- Set the Fagor Pressure Cooker on SAUTÉ mode and heat oil.
- Fry each chicken finger until golden and place on a paper towel. Drain out the excess oil.
- Transfer to a serving dish and serve with ketchup.

277. Whole Chicken
(Time: 70 minutes \ Servings: 6)

INGREDIENTS:

1 whole white chicken, 3-4 lb.
1 teaspoon garlic paste
1 teaspoon ginger paste
1 teaspoon salt
1 teaspoon cayenne pepper
¼ teaspoon chili powder

½ teaspoon cinnamon powder
½ teaspoon cumin powder
3 tablespoons lemon juice
2 tablespoons apple cider vinegar
2 tablespoons soya sauce
3 tablespoons olive oil

DIRECTIONS:

- In a bowl, combine vinegar, cayenne pepper, lemon juice, ginger garlic paste, salt, pepper, chili powder, olive oil, cumin powder and cinnamon powder, mix well. Pour over the chicken and rub with all over hands.
- Put the chicken in a greased Fagor Pressure Cooker and cover up with a lid. Cook on SLOW COOK mode for 65-70 minutes.

278. Chicken and Beans Stew

(Time: 45 minutes \ Servings: 5)

INGREDIENTS:

1 tablespoon olive oil
1 medium onion, chopped
4 garlic cloves, minced
1 tablespoon chopped fresh thyme
1 cup red beans, boiled
½ cup water
4 canned plum tomatoes, drained

1 can fat-free, less-sodium chicken broth
3 oz. baby spinach leaves, coarsely chopped
2 cups shredded skinless, boneless rotisserie chicken breast
½ teaspoon salt
½ teaspoon black pepper

DIRECTIONS:

- Heat oil in the Fagor Pressure Cooker, add onion and stir for 2 minutes until soften.
- Add the chicken and garlic and stir for another minute.
- Add thyme, red beans, tomatoes, salt, water and chicken broth.
- Cover and cook on POULTRY mode until the stew bubbles.
- Add spinach and cook it for another 5 minutes.
- Sprinkle with black pepper and serve hot.

279. Chicken Nuggets

(Time: 25 minutes \ Servings: 6)

INGREDIENTS:

2 chicken breasts, cut into small pieces
1 teaspoon garlic powder
1 teaspoon onion powder
½ cup bread crumbs
1 teaspoon salt

½ teaspoon black pepper
½ teaspoon cinnamon powder
½ teaspoon cumin powder
1 egg, whisked
1 cup oil, for frying

DIRECTIONS:

- In a bowl mix garlic powder, bread crumbs, onion powder, cinnamon powder, salt, pepper and cumin powder.
- Dip the chicken pieces into the whisked egg and roll out onto the bread crumbs mixture.
- Set the Fagor Pressure Cooker on SAUTÉ mode and heat oil.
- Deep fry each chicken nugget until golden. Transfer to a paper towel.

280. Delicious Chicken Breasts

(Time: 30 minutes \ Servings: 4)

INGREDIENTS:

2 chicken breasts
2 tablespoons rice vinegar
2 tablespoons lemon juice
1 teaspoon rosemary

1 teaspoon garlic paste
1 teaspoon salt
½ teaspoon black pepper
3 tablespoons olive oil

DIRECTIONS:

- Combine vinegar, oil, black pepper, salt, rosemary, garlic paste and lemon juice, mix well.
- Drizzle over the chicken and toss well.
- Set the pressure cooker on POULTRY and transfer in the chicken breasts. Cook for 30 minutes.

281. Pepper Chicken with Noodles

(Time: 35 minutes \ Servings: 4)

INGREDIENTS:

¼ lb. chicken, boneless, cut into small pieces
1 12 oz. package egg noodles, boiled
1 red bell pepper, chopped
1 green bell pepper, chopped
1 cup sour cream

1 teaspoon rosemary
2-3 garlic cloves garlic, minced
1 teaspoon salt
½ teaspoon black pepper
3 tablespoons butter

DIRECTIONS:

- Melt butter in the Fagor Pressure Cooker on SAUTÉ mode and fry garlic for 1 minute.
- Add the chicken and stir fry until lightly golden. Season with salt and pepper.
- Stir in the bell peppers and sauté for 3-4 minutes. Add noodles and cream, toss well.
- Cook for 5-8 minutes and then turn off the heat. Transfer to a serving dish and serve hot.

282. Chicken with Green Chilies

(Time: 35 minutes \ Servings: 4)

INGREDIENTS:

¼ lb. chicken, boneless, cut into small pieces
1 bunch green coriander
2 green chilies

2-3 garlic cloves garlic, minced
½ teaspoon black pepper
3 tablespoons butter

DIRECTIONS:

- In a blender, add coriander, green chili, and tomatoes, blend to a puree.
- Melt butter in the Fagor Pressure Cooker on SAUTÉ mode and fry garlic for 1 minute.
- Add the chicken and stir fry until lightly golden. Season with salt and pepper.
- Add in coriander, sauce and mix well. Let it simmer for 10-15 minutes. Serve hot.

283. Chicken Shashlik

(Time: 35 minutes \ Servings: 4)

INGREDIENTS:

¼ lb. chicken, boneless, cut into small pieces
2 green bell peppers, chopped
1 cup tomato ketchup
½ cup tomato sauce

1 teaspoon salt
½ teaspoon black pepper
3 tablespoons butter

DIRECTIONS:

- Melt butter in the Fagor Pressure Cooker on SAUTÉ mode and fry garlic for 1 minute.
- Add the chicken and stir fry until lightly golden. Season with salt and pepper.
- Add tomato ketchup and tomato sauce, stir well. Let it simmer for 10-15 minutes.

284. Broccoli Chicken

(Time: 45 minutes \ Servings: 3)

INGREDIENTS:

¼ lb. chicken, boneless, cut into small pieces
1 cup broccoli florets
2-3 garlic cloves garlic, minced
1 teaspoon salt

½ teaspoon black pepper
3 tablespoons butter
1 cup chicken broth
2 cup cream

DIRECTIONS:

- Melt butter in the Fagor Pressure Cooker on SAUTÉ mode and fry garlic for 1 minute.
- Add the chicken and stir fry until golden. Season with salt and pepper.
- Add broccoli and cream and pour in the chicken broth. Cook on MANUAL mode for 10 minutes.

285. Veggie Broth Chicken

(Time: 16 minutes \ Servings: 2)

INGREDIENTS:

1 lb. chicken, cubed
2 carrots, sliced
2 cups vegetable broth
4 cups cauliflower florets

2 tbsp. garlic, minced
2 tbsp. thyme, dried
4 celery stalks
1 tbsp. cornstarch

DIRECTIONS:

- Add vegetable broth into the Fagor Pressure Cooker.
- Add celery stalks, cornstarch, thyme, garlic, cauliflower, chicken, salt and carrots. Stir well.
- Cook on BROTH for 15 minutes. When ready, serve and enjoy!

286. Cauliflower with Chicken Broth

(Time: 15 minutes \ Servings: 4)

INGREDIENTS:

1 tbsp. Butter
3 cloves Garlic cloves
6 cups Cauliflower florets
2 cups Chicken broth

1 cup Spinach , chopped
4 Green onion , chopped
½ lb. Fettuccine pasta
Salt to taste

DIRECTIONS:

- Add butter into the Fagor Pressure Cooker. Press the SAUTÉ button and then add garlic.
- When garlic turns light brown, mix in the cauliflower, spinach and green onion.
- Cook for 5 minutes on high pressure. When ready, add chicken broth, salt and fettuccine pasta.
- Cover it and cook for 10 minutes.

287. Saffron Chicken

(Time: 19 minutes \ Servings: 4)

INGREDIENTS:

2 tbsp. saffron threads
2 tbsp. water
1 lb. chicken thighs, diced
salt to taste
3 garlic cloves, minced
2 tbsp. vegetable oil

½ bell pepper, diced
1 onion, diced
1 tsp. cumin powder
2 cups chicken broth
1 tbsp. oregano powder
sweet peas for garnishing

DIRECTIONS:

- Add vegetable oil into the Fagor Pressure Cooker and press SAUTÉ.
- Mix in the garlic cloves and chicken. Cook for 10 minutes.
- Add bell pepper, saffron threads, onion, cumin powder and oregano powder.
- Add chicken broth and water. Cook on POULTRY mode for 15 minutes.
- When ready, dress it with sweet peas and enjoy!

288. Simple Chicken Wings
(Time: 20 minutes \ Servings: 4)

INGREDIENTS:

2 lb. chicken wings –

1 cup BBQ sauce –

DIRECTIONS:

- Put the chicken wings in the Fagor Pressure Cooker and cover them with the BBQ sauce.
- Cover the lid and cook on POULTRY for 20 minutes.

289. Delicious Chicken
(Time: 15 minutes \ Servings: 3)

INGREDIENTS:

2 cups chicken broth
2 chicken breasts, diced
4 green chilies, chopped
1 onion, chopped
4 potatoes, diced

1 bell pepper, sliced
2 garlic cloves minced
½ tbsp. cumin powder
½ cup tomato sauce
Taco seasoning

DIRECTIONS:

- Add chicken broth into the Fagor Pressure Cooker and cook for 5 minutes on SAUTÉ mode.
- Mix in the green chilies, onion, potatoes, garlic cloves, bell pepper and salt.
- Add cumin powder with chicken breasts and cook for 10 minutes on POULTRY mode.
- Mix in the tomato sauce and stir well. Serve with the taco seasoning and enjoy!

290. Chicken Thighs with Sauce
(Time: 20 minutes \ Servings: 4)

INGREDIENTS:

1 tbsp. vegetable oil
1 lb. chicken thighs
1 onion , chopped
2 tbsp. ginger, minced
2 tbsp. garlic, mince

2 cups chicken broth
½ cup ketchup
½ cup Mirin (sweet rice wine)
2 tbsp. wine vinegar

DIRECTIONS:

- Add vegetable oil into the Fagor Pressure Cooker with ginger and garlic. Press the SAUTÉ button and when it beeps, add the chicken thighs. Cook for 10 minutes. Add onion and chicken broth.
- Cook for 10 minutes on POULTRY mode. Meanwhile, mix ketchup, mirin and wine vinegar in a bowl.
- Serve the chicken with this sauce.

291. Chicken Meatballs in Broth
(Time: 15 minutes \ Servings: 4)

INGREDIENTS:

2 lb. ground chicken
½ cup breadcrumbs
½ cup mozzarella cheese, shredded
1 onion, chopped
salt and pepper, to taste
3 garlic cloves, minced

½ bunch parsley, chopped
1 egg
2 cups chicken broth
2 tbsp. vegetable oil
2 tbsp. lemon juice
½ cup sour cream

DIRECTIONS:

- Mix ground chicken with onion, salt, garlic, parsley and lemon juice in a bowl. Mix it well with a spoon or your hand. Whisk the egg in another bowl.
- Add vegetable oil in the Fagor Pressure Cooker and press the SAUTÉ button. Meanwhile, make the balls out of the mixture made in step 1.
- Dip them into the egg and then roll them in the breadcrumbs. Place each ball into the pressure cooker.
- When all ready, sprinkle the cheese over them and cook for 10 minutes on high pressure.
- Add chicken broth in the pressure cooker and cook for another 5 minutes. Serve with sour cream.

292. Chicken Breast with Green Onions

(Time: 25 minutes \ Servings: 4)

INGREDIENTS:

4 chicken breast, diced
½ tbsp. soy sauce
2 cups water
½ tbsp. brown sugar
2 tbsp. rice wine vinegar

1 tbsp. sesame oil
2 tbsp. chili garlic sauce
1 tbsp. cornstarch
2 green onions, chopped
½ tbsp. red pepper flakes

DIRECTIONS:

- Add water, soy sauce and rice wine vinegar into the pressure cooker. Cook for 10 minutes on SAUTÉ mode. Add the chicken pieces. Mix well.
- Add sesame oil, chili garlic sauce, green onions, flakes and cornstarch. Cook on POULTRY for 10 minutes.

293. Chicken with Egg Noodles

(Time: 12 minutes \ Servings: 2)

INGREDIENTS:

2 carrots, sliced
4 stalks celery, sliced
1 onion, sliced
1 cup thyme
1 bay leaf

1 lb. chicken thighs
4 cups egg noodles
2 tbsp. lemon juice
½ cup chicken broth
salt and pepper, to taste

DIRECTIONS:

- Add chicken broth into the Fagor Pressure Cooker. Mix in the carrots, celery, onion, thyme, bay leaf, lemon juice and chicken thighs.
- Cook for 10 minutes on high pressure. Add egg noodles and cook for another 10 minutes.

294. Chicken with Shallot

(Time: 20 minutes \ Servings: 3)

INGREDIENTS:

1 lb. chicken breast, pieces
2 lemongrass stalks
2 tbsp. ginger, minced
1 carrot, pieces
2 celery stalks, pieces

1 bay leaf
1 shallot, pieces
1 tbsp. chili powder
2 cups baby spinach
salt and pepper, to taste

DIRECTIONS:

- Add chicken breast into the Fagor Pressure Cooker. Mix in the lemongrass, ginger, carrot, celery stalks, bay leaf and shallots. Add chili powder, baby spinach, salt and pepper. Cook for 20 minutes on MANUAL on high pressure.

295. Chicken and Beans

(Time: 20 minutes \ Servings: 3)

INGREDIENTS:

1 lb. chicken breast, pieces
1 tsp. chili powder
2 tomatoes, diced
2 cups chicken broth
1 tbsp. cumin powder
1 cup black beans

1 red bell pepper, chopped
2 tbsp. chipotle sauce
1 tbsp. lime juice
cilantro leaves for garnishing
salt and pepper, to taste

DIRECTIONS:

- Add lime juice into the Fagor Pressure Cooker.
- Mix in the chicken breast, chili powder, tomatoes, chicken broth, cumin powder, red bell pepper chipotle sauce. Toss well. Add black beans, salt and pepper. Cook for 20 minutes on MANUAL on high pressure.

296. Chicken with Sesame oil

(Time: 20 minutes \ Servings: 3)

INGREDIENTS:

1 tbsp. cornstarch
2 egg whites
1 lb. chicken, sliced
1 tbsp. soy sauce
1 tbsp. sesame oil

1 tbsp. wine vinegar
1 tbsp. ginger, grated
2 tbsp. garlic cloves, minced
salt and pepper, to taste

DIRECTIONS:

- Mix cornstarch and egg whites in a bowl. Add the mixture into the Fagor Pressure Cooker.
- Mix in the chicken, soy sauce, sesame oil, wine vinegar, ginger, garlic, and salt and pepper.
- Cook for 20 minutes on high pressure.

297. Chicken Breasts with Black Beans

(Time: 18 minutes \ Servings: 3)

INGREDIENTS:

2 tbsp. vegetable oil
2 large sweet onions
3 garlic cloves , minced
1 tbsp. cumin powder
2 tbsp. oregano powder

2 tomatoes , diced
3 chicken breasts , diced
2 cups black beans
2 cups cheddar cheese, grated
Salt to taste

DIRECTIONS:

- Heat the Fagor Pressure Cooker and add vegetable oil.
- Add garlic with the chicken breast pieces. Cook for 5 minutes on SAUTÉ mode.
- Add cumin powder, sweet onion, oregano powder, salt and black beans.
- Mix well. Cook it on POULTRY for 5 minutes.
- When ready, serve by spreading cheddar cheese over it.

298. Boneless Chicken with Peanut Butter

(Time: 18 minutes \ Servings: 3)

INGREDIENTS:

½ tbsp. canola oil
1 lb. boneless chicken, cut into small pieces
1 cup chicken broth
1 tbsp. peanut butter
2 tbsp. soy sauce

½ cup cilantro , chopped
1 tbsp. lime juice
1 tbsp. red pepper flakes
2 tbsp. cornstarch
green onions for garnishing

DIRECTIONS:

- Add canola oil into the Fagor Pressure Cooker and press the SAUTÉ button.
- Mix in the chicken broth with the boneless chicken pieces.
- Cook for 10 minutes on POULTRY mode. Meanwhile, put the peanut butter, cilantro, lime juice, soy sauce, red pepper flakes and cornstarch in a bowl. Stir well.
- Add peanut butter mixture into the pressure cooker and cook for another 5 minutes.
- When done, garnish with green onion!

299. Mushrooms with Chicken Broth

(Time: 20 minutes \ Servings: 3)

INGREDIENTS:

2 ½ tsp. butter
1 onion, chopped
2 cloves garlic, chopped
½ cup oats
2 cups chicken broth

1 cup water
thyme for garnishing
salt to taste
1 tbsp. olive oil
½ cup mushrooms, sliced

DIRECTIONS:

- Add the butter into the Fagor Pressure Cooker and cover the lid. Set timer for 1 minute.
- When the butter melts, add onion, garlic, oats, chicken broth, thyme, salt and water.
- Cook on high pressure for 10 minutes.
- Meanwhile, in a pan, add olive oil and lightly cook the mushrooms.
- When ready, add them to the pressure cooker and set timer for 5 minutes on MANUAL mode.

300. Chicken Mushroom Mix

(Time: 14 minutes \ Servings: 2)

INGREDIENTS:

3 cups chicken, shredded
1 tbsp. oil
1 onion, chopped
6 small mushrooms, chopped
2 minced garlic cloves

1 cup spinach
½ cup parsley, chopped
2 cups milk
Salt and pepper, to taste
Almonds for seasoning

DIRECTIONS:

- Place chicken into a bowl. Mix in the onion, mushrooms, garlic, spinach and parsley.
- Blend well. Add milk and salt and pepper.
- Get a round baking tray. Grease it with oil. Add the mixture.
- Cook it in the Fagor Pressure Cooker for 10 minutes on high pressure. Serve with almond seasoning.

301. Chicken Tenders with Garlic

(Time: 13 minutes \ Servings: 2)

INGREDIENTS:

1 lb. chicken tenders
2 garlic cloves, minced
2 tbsp. paprika
2 tbsp. oregano powder
2 tbsp. oil
1 onion, chopped

2 cups peas, frozen
1 cup all-purpose, flour
1 cup chicken stock
1 Egg, raw
Salt and pepper, to taste

DIRECTIONS:

- Add oil into the Fagor Pressure Cooker.
- Mix in the chicken tenders, garlic, paprika, oregano, onion, peas, flour and chicken stock.
- Add egg with salt and pepper. Cook for 10 minutes on high pressure.

302. Creamy Chicken Noodles

(Time: 30 minutes \ Servings: 5)

INGREDIENTS:

¼ lb. chicken, boneless, pieces, boiled
1 package 12 oz. egg noodles, boiled
1 teaspoon tarragon
1 cup cream
¼ cup all-purpose flour
½ cup milk

1 teaspoon rosemary
2-3 garlic cloves garlic, minced
1 teaspoon salt
½ teaspoon black pepper
3 tablespoons butter

DIRECTIONS:

- Melt butter in the Fagor Pressure Cooker on SAUTÉ mode and fry garlic for 1 minute.
- Add in cream and flour, stir continuously. Pour milk by continuously stirring.
- Transfer the chicken and combine well. Season with salt and pepper.
- Spread noodles into a platter and top with the creamy chicken. Sprinkle tarragon and serve.

303. Chicken Pilaf

(Time: 45 minutes \ Servings: 5)

INGREDIENTS:

2 cups rice, soaked
1 cup chicken, pieces
1 teaspoon cumin seeds
1 bay leaf
2 garlic cloves, minced
1 teaspoon black pepper

1 pinch turmeric powder
1 teaspoon cumin powder
2 medium onions, sliced
1 teaspoon salt
3 tablespoons olive oil
4 cups chicken broth

DIRECTIONS:

- Heat oil in the Fagor Pressure Cooker on SAUTÉ mode, fry onion, cumin seeds and bay leaf until golden.
- Add the chicken and brown it for around 5 mintues on each side.
- Season with salt, turmeric powder, pepper, garlic and fry well.
- Pour in the vegetable broth, cumin powder, cinnamon powder and boil.
- Add rice, simmer until bubbles appear on the top, cover the cooker with a lid.
- Cook for 20 minutes on WHITE RICE mode. Transfer to a serving dish and enjoy.

304. Hot Chicken Chili
(Time: 25 minutes \ Servings: 3)

INGREDIENTS:

2 chicken breasts
1 cup chili garlic sauce
¼ cup tomato ketchup
4 tablespoons honey
2 tablespoons soya sauce

2 tomatoes, chopped
¼ teaspoon salt
¼ teaspoon cayenne pepper
3 tablespoons olive oil

DIRECTIONS:

- Combine the chili garlic sauce, tomato ketchup, soya sauce, honey, salt, pepper and mix.
- Pour the sauce over the chicken and toss well. Heat oil in the Fagor Pressure Cooker on SAUTÉ mode.
- Add in the chicken breasts, cover and cook on CHILI mode for 20 minutes.

305. Garlic Chicken Breasts
(Time: 35 minutes \ Servings: 5)

INGREDIENTS:

2 chicken breasts
2 tablespoons apple cider vinegar
1 cup tomato ketchup
1 teaspoon garlic powder

¼ teaspoon salt
½ teaspoon chili powder
3 tablespoons olive oil

DIRECTIONS:

- Combine the vinegar, ketchup, chili powder, salt, and garlic powder.
- Drizzle over the chicken and toss well. Set the Fagor Pressure Cooker on SAUTÉ mode and heat oil.
- Transfer the chicken breasts in the cooker. Cook for 30 minutes on POULTRY mode.

306. Tropical Chicken Masala
(Time: 30 minutes \ Servings: 4)

INGREDIENTS:

2 chicken breasts, cut into small piece
1 cup tomato ketchup
¼ cup cream
1 teaspoon garlic paste

1 teaspoon salt
½ teaspoon black pepper
2 tablespoons olive oil

DIRECTIONS:

- Heat oil in the Fagor Pressure Cooker on SAUTÉ mode and fry garlic for 1 minute.
- Add the chicken and stir fry until lightly golden. Season with salt and pepper.
- Add ketchup and cream, simmer for 10 minutes. Transfer to a serving dish and serve hot.

307. Stir-Fried Ground Chicken
(Time: 35 minutes \ Servings: 4)

INGREDIENTS:

1 cup ground chicken
1 onion, chopped
2-3 garlic cloves, minced
¼ teaspoon cumin powder
¼ teaspoon cinnamon powder

2 tomatoes, chopped
1 teaspoon salt
½ teaspoon black pepper
2 tablespoons olive oil

DIRECTIONS:

- Heat oil in the Fagor Pressure Cooker on SAUTÉ mode and fry garlic and onion for 1 minute.
- Add the ground chicken and stir fry until its color changes. Season with salt and pepper.
- Stir in the tomatoes and sauté for 3-4 minutes. Cook for another 5-8 minutes, then turn off the heat.
- Sprinkle cumin powder and cinnamon powder., and serve hot.

308. Chicken with Chickpeas

(Time: 45 minutes \ Servings: 6)

INGREDIENTS:

1 onion, sliced
2 tomatoes, chopped
1 cup chickpea, boiled
1 cup chicken, cubed
2 cups chicken broth
½ teaspoon garlic paste
½ teaspoon ginger paste

½ teaspoon cumin powder
½ teaspoon cinnamon power
½ teaspoon chili powder
¼ teaspoon salt
¼ teaspoon turmeric powder
3 tablespoons oil

DIRECTIONS:

- Heat oil in the Fagor Pressure Cooker, sauté onion for 1 minute on SAUTÉ mode.
- Stir in the tomatoes, ginger paste, garlic paste, salt, chili powder, turmeric powder and fry for 1 minute.
- Add the chicken cubes and cook until lightly golden.
- Add the chickpea, chicken broth and cook for 20 minutes on POULTRY mode.
- Sprinkle cinnamon and cumin powder.

309. Chicken and Turnip Stew

(Time: 45 minutes \ Servings: 7)

INGREDIENTS:

1 onion, chopped
2 tomatoes, chopped
1 cup chicken pieces
2-3 turnips, peeled, diced
2 cups chicken broth
1 carrot, sliced
1 tablespoon coriander, chopped
½ teaspoon garlic paste

½ teaspoon ginger paste
½ teaspoon cumin powder
½ teaspoon cinnamon power
½ teaspoon chili powder
¼ teaspoon salt
¼ teaspoon turmeric powder
3 tablespoons oil
2 green chilies, whole

DIRECTIONS:

- Heat oil, sauté onion for 1 minute on SAUTÉ mode.
- Stir in the tomatoes, ginger garlic paste, salt, chili powder, turmeric powder and fry for 1 minute.
- Add the chicken pieces and cook until lightly golden. Add the turnips and fry with chicken until tender.
- Add the chicken broth, coriander, carrots, and green chili and cook for 30 minutes on POULTRY mode.
- Add cinnamon and cumin powder and stir.

310. Spinach Chicken

(Time: 55 minutes \ Servings: 6)

INGREDIENTS:

1 cup chicken pieces
1 cup spinach, chopped, boiled
1 onion, chopped
2 tomatoes, chopped
2-3 turnips, peeled, diced

2 cups chicken broth
½ teaspoon garlic paste
½ teaspoon chili powder
¼ teaspoon salt
3 tablespoons oil

DIRECTIONS:

- Heat oil in Fagor Pressure Cooker, sauté onion for 1 minute on SAUTÉ mode.
- Stir in tomatoes, garlic paste, salt, chili powder, and fry for 1 minute.
- Add the chicken pieces and cook until golden.
- Add spinach and cook the chicken for 5 minutes.
- Add the chicken broth, green chili and cook on POULTRY mode for 30 minutes.

311. Creamy Chicken Korma

(Time: 30 minutes \ Servings: 4)

INGREDIENTS:

¼ lb. chicken, boneless, pieces
1 cup cream
¼ teaspoon aniseeds, crushed
½ teaspoon garlic paste

1 teaspoon salt
½ teaspoon black pepper
3 tablespoons butter

DIRECTIONS:

- Melt butter in the Fagor Pressure Cooker on SAUTÉ mode and fry garlic for 1 minute.
- Add the chicken and fry until lightly golden. Season with salt and pepper.
- Add the cream and mix well. Let simmer for 10 minutes.
- Sprinkle aniseeds and mix well.

312. Chicken and Garlic

(Time: 15 minutes \ Servings: 2)

INGREDIENTS:

1 lb. chicken, chopped
2 minced garlic cloves
1 cup parmesan cheese
1 tbsp. oil
1 cup breadcrumbs

½ cup basil , chopped
4 buns
¼ bunch of parsley
salt and pepper, to taste

DIRECTIONS:

- In a bowl, mix garlic, cheese, salt, pepper, basil, parsley with the chicken.
- Grease the Fagor Pressure Cooker grill.
- Make small patties out of the chicken mixture and cover them with breadcrumbs.
- Place them in the pressure cooker to cook for 15 minutes on POULTRY mode.
- When done, serve by placing each patty in a bun.

313. Buttery Chicken

(Time: 40 minutes \ Servings: 4)

INGREDIENTS:

¼ lb. chicken, boneless, pieces
1 cup tomato puree
1-inch ginger slice
1-2 red chilies

½ teaspoon garlic paste
1 teaspoon salt
¼ teaspoon black pepper
4 tablespoons butter

DIRECTIONS:

- In a blender, add tomato puree, chilies, ginger, garlic, salt, pepper and blend well.
- Melt butter in the Fagor Pressure Cooker on SAUTÉ mode and fry the chicken for 5-10 minute.
- Transfer the tomato mixture and combine. Cook for 10-15 minutes until the chicken tenders.

314. Tropical Shredded Chicken

(Time: 30 minutes \ Servings: 4)

INGREDIENTS:

3 chicken breasts, shredded, boiled
½ teaspoon garlic paste
½ teaspoon salt
½ teaspoon soya sauce

2 tablespoons barbecue sauce
½ teaspoon chili powder
2 tablespoons oil

DIRECTIONS:

- Heat oil in the Fagor Pressure Cooker on SAUTÉ mode and fry garlic for 1 minute.
- Add chicken breasts and fry brown them. Add soya sauce, barbecue sauce, salt, chili powder and fry well.

315. Chicken and Lentils

(Time: 70 minutes \ Servings: 5)

INGREDIENTS:

2 chicken breasts, boiled, shredded
1 cup yellow lentil, soaked
1 cup split gram, soaked overnight
¼ teaspoon garlic paste
½ teaspoon salt
1 onion, sliced

1 tomato, chopped
¼ teaspoon turmeric powder
½ teaspoon chili powder
2 tablespoons oil
¼ cup olive oil, for frying
3 cups water

DIRECTIONS:

- Heat the oil in the Fagor Pressure Cooker on SAUTÉ mode and fry onion until golden.
- Spread the onion on paper towel and set aside.
- In the same cooker, add lentils, water, turmeric powder and boil on MANUAL mode for 30 minutes.
- Transfer the shredded chicken and the boiled lentils into a blender and blend to a puree.
- In the Pressure cooker, add 2 tablespoons of cooking oil and fry garlic for 30 seconds until lightly golden.
- Add tomatoes, chili powder, salt and stir fry for 5-6 minutes. Add in the chicken lentils' puree and let simmer for 10 minutes.

316. Ground Chicken and Peas

(Time: 35 minutes \ Servings: 5)

INGREDIENTS:

1 cup chicken mince
1 cup peas
1 onion, chopped
2-3 garlic cloves, minced
¼ teaspoon cumin powder
¼ teaspoon cinnamon powder

2 tomatoes, chopped
1 teaspoon salt
½ teaspoon chili powder
2 tablespoons olive oil
1 bunch coriander, chopped
½ cup chicken broth

DIRECTIONS:

- Heat oil in the Fagor Pressure Cooker on SAUTÉ mode; fry garlic and onion for 1 minute.
- Add the ground chicken and stir fry until its color is slightly changed. Season with salt and chili powder.
- Stir in tomatoes and sauté for 3-4 minutes. Add the peas and fry until soft.
- Add the chicken broth and cook on MANUAL mode for 10 minutes. Sprinkle cumin powder and cinnamon powder. Place on a serving dish and top with coriander.

317. Chicken and Yellow Lentils

(Time: 35 minutes \ Servings: 5)

INGREDIENTS:

1 cup chicken mince
1 cup yellow lentils, cooked
2-3 garlic cloves, minced
2 tomatoes, chopped

½ teaspoon chili powder
2 tablespoons olive oil
1 bunch coriander, chopped
½ cup chicken broth

DIRECTIONS:

- Heat oil in the Fagor Pressure Cooker on SAUTÉ mode and fry garlic for 1 minute.
- Add ground chicken and stir fry until its color is slightly changed. Season with salt and chili powder.
- Stir in tomatoes and sauté for 3-4 minutes. Add the lentils and fry until softened, for 10-15 minutes.
- Sprinkle with coriander and serve.

318. Chicken with Avocado Cream

(Time: 35 minutes \ Servings: 6)

INGREDIENTS

4 lb. of organic chicken
1 tbsp. of coconut Oil
1 tsp. of paprika
1 ½ cups of Pacific Chicken Bone Broth
1 tsp. of dried thyme

¼ tsp. of freshly ground black pepper
1 tsp. of ginger
2 tbsp. of lemon juice
6 cloves of peeled garlic
1 Avocado

DIRECTIONS

- In a medium bowl, combine the paprika, thyme, salt, dried ginger, and pepper. Then rub the seasoning over the outer parts of the chicken.
- Heat the oil in the Fagor Pressure Cooker and let it simmer. Add the chicken breast side down and cook it for 6 minutes. Flip the chicken and add the broth, lemon juice, and garlic cloves. Lock the lid and set the timer to 30 minutes on high pressure.
- Prepare the avocado cream by whisking the contents of the avocado with 2 tbsp. of coconut oil and ½ tsp. of salt. Once the timer beeps, naturally release the pressure.
- Remove the chicken from the Pressure cooker and set it aside for 5 minutes before serving it.

319. Chicken with Sweet Potatoes

(Time: 30 minutes \ Servings: 4)

INGREDIENTS

2 cups of cubed and peeled sweet potatoes
2 tbsp. of coconut oil
1 lb. of skinless and boneless cubed chicken breast halves
3 minced cloves of garlic
6 tbsp. of tamari soy sauce
1 cup of water

3 tbsp. of honey
3 tbsp. of hot sauce
1 peeled and diced mango
¼ tsp. of smashed red pepper flakes
1 tsp. of cornstarch
1 tsp. of ginger
1 cup of warm water

DIRECTIONS

- Start by placing the sweet potatoes in the Fagor Pressure Cooker and pour enough water so the potatoes are covered. Press MANUAL and set the timer to 10 minutes on high pressure.
- Seal the lid, and when the timer goes off, quickly release the pressure and drain the potatoes.
- Place 2 tbsp. of coconut oil in the Pressure cooker and add the chicken. Sauté for 5 minutes. Sprinkle the ginger and garlic and cook for several more minutes. Add the tamari, a cup of warm water, and the honey with the hot sauce. Add the cornstarch to the mixture and set on STEAM feature for 10 minutes.

320. Steamed Chicken with Raspberry

(Time: 5 minutes \ Servings: 3)

INGREDIENTS

2 boneless chicken breasts, cubed
¼ tsp. of salt and pepper
½ tsp. of ginger powder
2 tbsp. of coconut oil
1 sliced onion

1 cup of chicken broth
3 tbsp. of raspberry vinegar
¾ cup of quick cooking rice
½ cup of fresh raspberries

DIRECTIONS

- Sprinkle the chicken with the salt, ginger, and pepper.
- Heat the oil in the Fagor Pressure Cooker and brown the chicken cubes on SAUTÉ mode.
- Add the onions, chicken, and vinegar. Then pour chicken broth.
- Close the lid of the Fagor Pressure Cooker and set to MANUAL on high pressure.
- Cook the chicken for 5 minutes, and once the timer beeps, release the pressure and press keep warm.
- Bring the liquid to boil and add the rice.
- Remove the Fagor Pressure cooker from the heat and set it aside for 4 minutes.
- Add the cooked chicken and the raspberries, and serve.

321. Green Chicken with Carrots and Spinach

(Time: 25 minutes \ Servings: 4)

INGREDIENTS

2 tsp. of coconut oil
3 crushed garlic cloves garlic
3 halved green chilies
¼ piece of peeled and sliced fresh ginger
¼ tsp. of ground coriander
¼ tsp. of ground cumin
2 tbsp. of green curry paste
1 can of 13.5 oz. coconut milk
6 cups of cubed kabocha squash
2 carrots

1 cubed eggplant
1 lb. of chicken cut in small cubes
1 pinch of kosher salt
1 tbsp. of fish sauce
4 oz. of chopped asparagus stalks
½ cup of fresh cilantro leaves
½ cup of loosely fresh basil leaves
1 pinch of ground black pepper
Cooked quinoa or rice, for 4 servings
a few lime wedges

DIRECTIONS

- Heat the oil on SAUTÉ mode.
- Add the garlic, chili, ginger, coriander, and cumin.
- Add the curry paste and stir until the paste becomes slightly brown, for about 3 minutes.
- Add the coconut milk and let it simmer; then cook it for around a minute.
- Season the chicken pieces with salt. Add half squash and the eggplant with the carrots.
- Add the chicken and top it with the remaining squash and eggplant. Season with salt.
- Seal the Fagor Pressure cooker and cook on high pressure for 20 minutes.
- Add the fish sauce and the spinach with ¼ cup of the cilantro and the basil.
- Serve in bowls with the rice and lime wedges.

322. Mediterranean Chicken Masala

(Time: 10 minutes \ Servings: 3)

INGREDIENTS

1 chicken breast, cut in cubes
2 tsp. of chopped garlic
2 tsp. of chopped ginger
1 tsp. of Garam Masala
1 pinch of Salt
1 tbsp. of lemon juice
1 Packet of 1.4 oz of Saffola Masala Oats

1 tbsp. of Saffola oil
1 tbsp. of coconut oil
½ cup of sliced onions
1 tsp. of green chili
1 cup of chopped tomatoes
3 tbsp. of tomato puree
2 cups of chicken stock

DIRECTIONS

- Heat 1 tbsp. of coconut oil in the Fagor Pressure cooker and press SAUTÉ. Add the chicken, garlic, ginger, Garam Masala, salt, lemon juice and add it to the bowl. Mix well.
- After 5 minutes, add the Saffola Masala Oats Classic Masala and mix again.
- To prepare the curry - heat a little bit of oil in a separate pan and sauté the onions until translucent.
- Add the green chili and tomatoes, the tomato puree and the chicken stock.
- Cook for 6 more minutes, serve and enjoy the Masala.

323. Roasted Chicken and Vegetables Almonds

(Time: 40 minutes \ Servings: 4)

INGREDIENTS

1 ½ lb. of chicken, cut into 8 pieces
2 halved onions
4 halved carrots
¼ cup of coconut oil
1 pinch of salt

1 pinch of pepper
1 ½ cups of rinsed rice
½ cup of toasted almond slivers
¼ cup of chopped parsley

DIRECTIONS

- Heat a tbsp. of coconut oil in the Fagor Pressure cooker.
- Arrange the chicken, onions, and carrots in one even layer.
- Toss the coconut oil and sprinkle salt and pepper.
- Press Sauté and roast the ingredients for 5 minutes.
- Stir in the chicken juices and keep cooking for 15 minutes.
- Meanwhile, take a separate pan and boil 1 ½ cups of salted water.
- Boil the rice for 15 minutes. Season with salt and pepper.
- Once perfectly cooked, remove the rice from the heat and transfer it to a serving dish.
- Top it with the vegetables and chicken and sprinkle the almonds.

324. Cheese Omelette

(Time: 15 minutes \ Servings: 2)

INGREDIENTS:

2 eggs, whisked
1 teaspoon garlic powder
¼ teaspoons slat
½ teaspoon black pepper

½ cup parmesan cheese, shredded
½ cup mozzarella cheese, shredded
3 tablespoons butter

DIRECTIONS:

- In a bowl, add the eggs, mozzarella,parmesan cheese, salt, garlic and pepper.
- Melt butter in the Fagor Pressure cooker on SAUTÉ mode.
- Pour the eggs' mixture and spread evenly all over.
- Cook for 2-3 minutes from one each side. Serve hot and enjoy.

325. Egg Scramble

(Time: 10 minutes \ Servings: 3)

INGREDIENTS:

4 eggs
1 pinch of salt
½ teaspoon black pepper

1 cup milk
3 tablespoons butter

DIRECTIONS:

- Melt butter in the cooker on SAUTÉ mode. Crack the eggs and add milk, stir continuously for 5 minutes.
- Transfer to a serving platter and scramble again with a fork.

326. Egg and Onion Frittata

(Time: 25 minutes \ Servings: 3)

INGREDIENTS:

4 eggs, whisked
1 onion, chopped
1 green chili, chopped

¼ teaspoons slat
½ teaspoon black pepper
3 tablespoons butter

DIRECTIONS:

- In a bowl, add eggs, onion, green chilies, salt, and pepper, mix well. Melt butter in the Fagor Pressure cooker on SAUTÉ mode.
- Transfer the eggs mixture and spread all over. Cook for 2-3 minutes from on each side.

327. Egg and Carrot Spread

(Time: 25 minutes \ Servings: 3)

INGREDIENTS:

4 eggs, whisked
3 carrots, shredded, boiled
¼ teaspoons slat

½ teaspoon black pepper
3 tablespoons butter

DIRECTIONS:

- In a blender, add the carrots and blend them to a puree.
- Add them to the Fagor Pressure cooker and let simmer for 2 minutes.
- Add the eggs, butter, salt, and pepper, stir continually for 10-15 minutes. Cook for 5 minutes.
- Serve on top of french toast or corn tortilla.

328. Eggs and Carrots

(Time: 15 minutes \ Servings: 3)

INGREDIENTS:

4 eggs
1 carrot, sliced
1 potato, boiled, diced
1 green chili, chopped

1 pinch of salt
½ teaspoon black pepper
1 cup cream
3 tablespoons butter

DIRECTIONS:

- Melt butter in the Fagor Pressure cooker on SAUTÉ mode.
- Crack eggs in the cooker and add milk, stir continuously for 5 minutes.
- Transfer to a serving platter and scramble with a fork for 1 minute. Combine with the cream, chilies, potatoes, and carrots, and toss well.

329. Egg and Carrots Crumb

(Time: 25 minutes \ Servings: 3)

INGREDIENTS:

4 eggs
1 carrot, shredded

½ teaspoon black pepper
3 tablespoons butter

DIRECTIONS:

- Melt butter on SAUTÉ mode. Sauté carrots for 5-10 minutes until the water evaporates.
- Add the eggs, salt and pepper, stir continuously. Cook for 5 minutes.

330. Half Fry Eggs

(Time: 5 minutes \ Servings: 2)

INGREDIENTS:

2 eggs
1 pinch of salt

½ teaspoon black pepper
3 tablespoons oil

DIRECTIONS:

- Heat oil in the Fagor Pressure cooker on SAUTÉ mode.
- Crack eggs in the cooker and cook for 2-3 minutes.
- Transfer to a platter and season with salt and pepper.

331. Bell Pepper and Eggs

(Time: 25 minutes \ Servings: 3)

INGREDIENTS:

4 eggs, whisked
1 red bell pepper, chopped
1 onion, chopped

¼ teaspoons slat
½ teaspoon black pepper
3 tablespoons butter

DIRECTIONS:

- In a bowl, add the eggs, onion, bell peppers, salt, pepper, mix well.
- Melt butter in the cooker on SAUTÉ mode.
- Pour the eggs mixture and spread all over. Cover the cooker with a lid.
- Cook for 15 minutes on MANUAL mode. Serve hot and enjoy.

332. Hard Boiled Eggs

(Time: 15 minutes \ Servings: 4)

INGREDIENTS:

4 eggs
2 tablespoons salt

3 cups water

DIRECTIONS:

- Fill the Fagor Pressure cooker with water and add salt.
- Place the eggs in the water and cover up with a lid.
- Boil them on BEANS mode for 15 minutes.
- Remove from the cooker and transfer to cold water.

333. Avocado eggs

(Time: 20 minutes \ Servings: 2)

INGREDIENTS:

2 eggs
1 avocado, pitted, halved
1 pinch salt

1 pinch black pepper
2 tablespoons olive oil

DIRECTIONS:

- Spray the Pressure cooker with oil. Place the avocados in the Fagor Pressure Cooker and crack the eggs into each avocado half. Season with salt and pepper.
- Cover and cook for 15 minutes on high pressure.

334. Roasted Eggs Gravy

(Time: 30 minutes \ Servings: 4)

INGREDIENTS:

4 eggs
1 onion, chopped
2 tomatoes, chopped
¼ teaspoon pinch salt
½ teaspoon chili powder

¼ teaspoon turmeric powder
1/3 teaspoon cumin powder
1-2 garlic cloves, minced
2 tablespoons olive oil

DIRECTIONS:

- Heat oil in the Fagor Pressure Cooker on SAUTÉ mode and fry the eggs until lightly golden. Set aside.
- In the same oil, fry onion until lightly golden.
- Add tomatoes, garlic, salt, chili powder, turmeric powder and fry until the tomatoes soften.
- Transfer to a blender and blend well. Return the mixture to the cooker again and fry with a few splashes of water. Add in the roasted eggs and toss around.

335. Squash with Eggs

(Time: 30 minutes \ Servings: 4)

INGREDIENTS:

4 eggs
1 squash, cut into 1-inch thick rings
1 pinch salt

1 pinch chili powder
2 tablespoons olive oil

DIRECTIONS:

- Spray the Fagor Pressure Cooker with oil.
- Place the squash rings in the cooker and crack an egg into each ring.
- Sprinkle with salt and pepper. Cover with a lid and cook for 15 minutes on high pressure.

336. Veggie Eggs

(Time: 25 minutes \ Servings: 5)

INGREDIENTS:

4 eggs, hard boiled, sliced
1 onion, chopped
2 tomatoes, chopped
¼ teaspoon pinch salt
½ teaspoon chili powder

¼ teaspoon turmeric powder
1/3 teaspoon cumin powder
1-2 garlic cloves, minced
2 tablespoons olive oil

DIRECTIONS:

- Heat oil in the Fagor Pressure Cooker on SAUTÉ mode and fry onion for 1 minute.
- Add tomatoes, garlic, salt, chili powder, turmeric powder and fry until the tomatoes soften.
- Transfer the gravy into a blender and blend well.
- Place back everything in the cooker and cook for 10 more minutes.

337. Egg in the Hole

(Time: 10 minutes \ Servings: 3)

INGREDIENTS:

3 bread slices
3 eggs

1 pinch salt
2 tablespoons olive oil

DIRECTIONS:

- Cut a round hole in the center of the bread slices.
- Spray the Fagor Pressure Cooker with oil.
- Place the bread slices inside and crack the eggs in. Repeat for all slices. Sprinkle salt.
- Cover with a lid and cook for 5 minutes on high pressure on MANUAL mode.

338. Traditional Egg Bahaji

(Time: 20 minutes \ Servings: 3)

INGREDIENTS:

2 eggs, whisked
1 onion, chopped
2 tomatoes, chopped

½ teaspoons chili powder
¼ teaspoon salt
2 tablespoons olive oil

DIRECTIONS:

- Heat oil in the Fagor Pressure Cooker on SAUTÉ mode, fry onion until transparent.
- Add the tomatoes and stir fry well. Season with salt and pepper.
- Pour the whisked eggs and stir consciously for 2 minutes.

339. Pepper Egg

(Time: 5 minutes \ Servings: 1)

INGREDIENTS:

1 egg
1 large yellow bell pepper sliced
1 pinch salt

1 pinch black pepper
2 tablespoons olive oil

DIRECTIONS:

- Spray the Fagor Pressure Cooker with oil.
- Place the bell pepper in the Pressure cooker and crack the egg in the center.
- Season with salt and pepper. Cover with a lid and cook for 5 minutes on high pressure.

340. Tomato Eggs

(Time: 10 minutes \ Servings: 2)

INGREDIENTS:

2 eggs, whisked
2 tomatoes, sliced
1 teaspoon garlic powder

¼ teaspoon salt
½ teaspoon chili powder
3 tablespoons butter

DIRECTIONS:

- Melt butter on SAUTÉ mode. Add the eggs and spread all over. Cook for 1-2 minutes then flip.
- Place the tomato slices and in the Fagor Pressure Cooker and cover the cooker with a lid.
- Cook on high pressure for 10 minutes. Season with salt and chili powder.

341. Zucchini Egg

(Time: 15 minutes \ Servings: 2)

INGREDIENTS:

2 eggs, whisked
1 large zucchini, sliced
1 teaspoon garlic powder

¼ teaspoon salt
¼ teaspoon black pepper
3 tablespoons butter

DIRECTIONS:

- Melt butter in the Fagor Pressure Cooker on SAUTÉ mode. Fry zucchini for 3-4 minutes.
- Pour the eggs mixture and spread evenly. Cook for 2-3 minutes on one side then flip over.
- Season with salt and pepper.

342. Pepperoni Pizza Egg

(Time: 15 minutes \ Servings: 2)

INGREDIENTS:

2 eggs, whisked
1 teaspoon garlic powder
¼ teaspoon salt
½ teaspoon black pepper

1 onion, chopped
4-5 pepperoni slices
3 tablespoons butter

DIRECTIONS:

- In the whisked eggs, add in the onion, pepperoni, salt, garlic and pepper.
- Melt butter in the Fagor Pressure Cooker on SAUTÉ mode. Pour the eggs mixture and stir continuously.
- Cook for 1-2 minutes and then transfer to a serving platter.

343. Egg Mac

(Time: 25 minutes \ Servings: 2)

INGREDIENTS:

2 eggs, whisked
1 teaspoon garlic powder
¼ teaspoons slat
½ teaspoon black pepper

1 onion chopped
1 cup macaroni, boiled
1 tomato, chopped
3 tablespoons oil

DIRECTIONS:

- Combine the eggs with the macaroni, onion, salt, pepper, and garlic powder, mix well.
- Heat oil in the Fagor Pressure Cooker on SAUTÉ mode. Pour the eggs mixture and stir.
- Cook for 1-2 minutes.

344. Poached Eggs

(Time: 10 minutes \ Servings: 3)

INGREDIENTS:

3 eggs
3 cups water

2 tablespoons vinegar
1 pinch salt

DIRECTIONS:

- Set the Fagor Pressure Cooker on MANUAL on high pressure. Add water and let it boil.
- Crack 1 egg into a bowl and pour it in the boiled water. Repeat for all eggs.
- Cover with a lid and cook for 5 minutes on MANUAL on high pressure.

345. Coated Eggs

(Time: 45 minutes \ Servings: 4)

INGREDIENTS:

4 hardboiled eggs, peeled
1 teaspoon garlic powder
¼ teaspoon salt
½ teaspoon black pepper

1 cup chicken mince
2 tablespoons gram flour
1 cup oil, for frying

DIRECTIONS:

- Combine the gram flour, mince, garlic powder, salt and pepper, mix well. Take 2-3 tablespoons of this mixture and coat in an egg. Repeat for all eggs.
- Heat oil in the Fagor Pressure Cooker on SAUTÉ mode. Fry the eggs until golden. Place to a paper towel.

346. Cabbage Egg

(Time: 15 minutes \ Servings: 2)

INGREDIENTS:

2 eggs, whisked
1 teaspoon garlic powder
¼ teaspoons slat
½ teaspoon black pepper

½ cup parmesan cheese, shredded
1 cup cabbage, chopped
3 tablespoons butter

DIRECTIONS:

- Add the cabbage and parmesan cheese. Season the whisked eggs with salt, garlic and pepper.
- Melt butter in the Fagor Pressure Cooker on SAUTÉ mode.
- Pour the eggs mixture and spread evenly.
- Cook for 4-5 minutes on one side then flip. Serve hot.

347. Spinach Egg Frittata

(Time: 25 minutes \ Servings: 2)

INGREDIENTS:

2 eggs, whisked
1 cup spinach, chopped
1 cup cherry tomatoes, sliced

¼ teaspoons salt
½ teaspoon black pepper
3 tablespoons butter

DIRECTIONS:

- Add the spinach and tomatoes to the whisked eggs. Season with salt, garlic and pepper.
- Melt butter in the Fagor Pressure Cooker on SAUTÉ mode.
- Pour the eggs mixture and spread all over. Cook each side for 4 minutes.

348. Ginger Zest Cauliflower Egg Soup

(Time: 25 minutes \ Servings: 3)

INGREDIENTS:

1 cup cauliflower florets
1 teaspoon ginger paste
1 red bell pepper chopped
2 cups vegetable broth
2 tablespoons vinegar
1 lemon, sliced

2 eggs, whisked
1 green chili, chopped
4-5 garlic cloves, minced
½ teaspoon black pepper
1 pinch turmeric powder
1 tablespoon oil

DIRECTIONS:

- Heat oil in the Fagor Pressure Cooker, add the ginger paste and cook for 1 minute on SAUTÉ mode.
- Add the cauliflower and fry for 5-10 minutes.
- Add the bell pepper, salt, pepper, vinegar, turmeric powder, green chilies, lemon slices and mix well.
- Add the vegetable broth and cook for 15 minutes on SOUP mode.
- Pour the eggs and stir continuously for 1 minute. Ladle into a serving bowl.

349. Asian Style Steamed Eggs

(Time: 10 Minutes \ Servings: 2)

INGREDIENTS

2 large eggs
⅓ cup of cold water
2 stem of scallions, chopped
1 pinch of sesame seeds
1 pinch of fine garlic powder
pinch of salt and black pepper

1 pinch of flax seeds powder
2 avocados
1 tsp. of ginger
1 tsp. of flax seed powder
1 tbsp. of coconut oil

DIRECTIONS

- Start by placing the eggs into the water in a small bowl.
- Strain the eggs mixture above a mesh strainer above a heat proof bowl.
- Add what is left of the ingredients, except for the avocados.
- Mix very well and set aside. Pour water in the inner pot of the Pressure Cooker and place the trivet or the steamer basket. Place the bowl with the above mixture inside the trivet or the steamer basket.
- Seal the lid of the Pressure cooker tightly and make sure to close the vent valve.
- Press MANUAL and set the to high pressure. Set the timer to 5 minutes.
- And when you hear the beep, open the lid and serve the eggs with cooked quinoa and the avocado.

350. Eggs Steamed in Avocado

(Time: 10 Minutes \ Servings: 4)

INGREDIENTS

2 avocados, ripened
4 large eggs
¼ tsp. of black pepper

¼ tsp. of ground ginger
1 tbsp. of chopped chives

DIRECTIONS

- Halve the avocados and take the pit out. Scoop two tablespoons from its center so enough space is created for the eggs.
- Pour a cup of water inside the Fagor Pressure Cooker and place a trivet or a steamer basket inside.
- Line the avocados into the steamer basket and crack each egg into each avocado half; then let the white spill into the avocado gradually.
- Repeat the same procedure with the rest of the avocado halves. Close the lid tightly and seal the vent valve. Press MANUAL and set to high pressure for 10 minutes.
- Once the timer goes off, release the pressure. Season the eggs with, salt, pepper, ginger, and chives

Red Meat

351. Pork Steaks

(Time: 50 minutes \ Servings: 5)

INGREDIENTS:

2 pork fillets
1 teaspoon garlic powder
½ teaspoon chili powder
2 tablespoons soya sauce

4 tablespoons barbecue sauce
¼ teaspoon turmeric powder
2 tablespoons vinegar
4 tablespoons olive oil

DIRECTIONS:

- In a bowl, add vinegar, soya sauce, barbecue sauce, chili powder, salt, garlic powder and oil.
- Transfer to the Fagor Pressure Cooker, and place the pork fillets on top.
- Cook on MEAT mode for 45 minutes.

352. Mutton Pilaf

(Time: 45 minutes \ Servings: 5)

INGREDIENTS:

2 cups rice, soaked
1 cup broccoli florets
½ lb. mutton, boiled, pieces
1 teaspoon cumin seeds
1 bay leaf
2 garlic cloves, minced
1 teaspoon black pepper

1 pinch turmeric powder
1 teaspoon cumin powder
2 tomatoes, chopped
2 medium onions, sliced
1 teaspoon salt
3 tablespoons olive oil
4 cups chicken broth

DIRECTIONS:

- Heat oil in the Fagor Pressure Cooker on SAUTÉ mode. Fry onion, cumin seeds and bay leaf until golden.
- Add tomatoes and fry well. Add the mutton and stir-fry for a few minutes.
- Season with salt, turmeric powder, pepper, and garlic and fry well.
- Pour in vegetable broth and add cumin powder, and cinnamon powder, then boil.
- Add rice and simmer until bubbles appear on surface, cover with a lid.
- Cook for 20 minutes on WHITE RICE mode.

353. Mutton Gravy

(Time: 45 minutes \ Servings: 4)

INGREDIENTS:

½ lb mutton, boiled
1 cup tomato puree
1-inch ginger slice
½ teaspoon garlic paste
1 teaspoon salt

¼ teaspoon chili powder
1 cup water
½ teaspoon cumin powder
4 tablespoons oil

DIRECTIONS:

- Heat oil in the Fagor Pressure Cooker on SAUTÉ mode and fry tomatoes with chili powder, ginger, garlic and salt, for 5-10 minute. Add mutton and fry well.
- Add in water and cook on CHILI mode for 20 minutes. Sprinkle cumin powder and serve.

354. Ground Beef Risotto

(Time: 25 minutes \ Servings: 3)

INGREDIENTS:

1 cup ground beef
1 cup tomato ketchup
1-inch ginger slice, chopped
2 tablespoons brown sugar

1 teaspoon salt
¼ teaspoon chili powder
4 tablespoons oil

DIRECTIONS:

- Heat oil on SAUTÉ mode and fry the ground beef with ginger for 10 minutes.
- Add tomato ketchup, salt, chili powder, brown sugar and toss around.
- Cook for 20 minutes on MEAT mode. Serve with noodles and enjoy.

355. Tomato Chili Meat

(Time: 45 minutes \ Servings: 3)

INGREDIENTS:

½ lb. beef, pieces
¼ cup tomato ketchup
1 cup chili garlic sauce
1 teaspoon salt
1 cup white beans, soaked

½ cup tomato puree
3 cups chicken broth
2-3 garlic cloves
4 tablespoons oil

DIRECTIONS:

- In the Fagor Pressure Cooker, add all ingredients and cook for 45 minutes on MEAT mode.

356. Ground Beef with Lemon

(Time: 40 minutes \ Servings: 3)

INGREDIENTS:

2 cups beef mince
1 teaspoon salt
2 tablespoons lemon juice
¼ teaspoon chili powder

2 tomatoes, chopped
2-3 garlic cloves, minced
4 tablespoons oil

DIRECTIONS:

- Heat oil in the Fagor Pressure Cooker and fry garlic for 30 seconds on SAUTÉ mode.
- Add the mince and fry well until its color changes. Season with salt and pepper.
- Add tomatoes and stir fry for 10-15 minutes with a few splashes of water. Drizzle lemon juice on top.

357. Beef with Brown Sugar

(Time: 23 minutes \ Servings: 2)

INGREDIENTS:

1 cup thyme
2 garlic cloves, minced
1 lb. ground beef

2 tbsp. balsamic vinegar
1 tbsp. brown sugar
2 tbsp. ketchup

DIRECTIONS:

- Add garlic into the Fagor Pressure Cooker.
- Mix in the thyme, beef, ketchup, brown sugar and balsamic vinegar.
- Cook for 20 minutes on high pressure. When ready, serve and enjoy!

358. Beef with Peas

(Time: 17 minutes \ Servings: 2)

INGREDIENTS:

1 lb. ground beef
1 tbsp. lemon juice
2 tbsp. butter
2 cups peas, frozen

1 onion, chopped
2 garlic cloves, minced
salt and pepper, to taste

DIRECTIONS:

- Add garlic into the Fagor Pressure Cooker.
- Mix in the lemon juice, butter, peas, onion, beef with salt and pepper.
- Cook for 15 minutes on high pressure.

359. Diced Meat with Potatoes

(Time: 22 minutes \ Servings: 3)

INGREDIENTS:

2 tbsp. oil
2 tbsp. soy sauce
1 lb. meat , diced
2 garlic cloves, minced
2 jalapeno peppers, chopped

2 cups potatoes diced
1 cup broth, any
salt and pepper, to taste
cilantro and peanuts for garnishing

DIRECTIONS:

- Add oil into the Fagor Pressure Cooker.
- Mix in the soy sauce, meat, garlic, jalapeno peppers and potatoes.
- Add broth with salt and pepper. Cook for 20 minutes on MEAT mode.
- When ready, serve with cilantro and peanuts dressing.

360. Simple Meatballs

(Time: 17 minutes \ Servings: 3)

INGREDIENTS:

1 lb. beef
½ onion, diced
1 carrot, diced
2 sticks celery, diced
3 garlic cloves, minced

1 cup marsala wine
2 cups beef broth
2 tomatoes, diced
½ tbsp. tomato paste
salt and pepper, to taste

DIRECTIONS:

- Press SAUTÉ and add carrot, onion, and celery. Stir-fry for 2-3 minutes.
- Remove from cooker and set aside in a bowl.
- Add garlic, Marsala wine, tomatoes, beef, salt and pepper.
- Mix well and make small balls out of it.
- Add beef broth and tomato paste into the Fagor Pressure Cooker.
- Place the meat balls in the cooker.
- Cook for 10 minutes on high pressure.

361. Sweet Potatoes with Meat

(Time: 24 minutes \ Servings: 4)

INGREDIENTS:

2 tbsp. olive oil
2 sweet potatoes, diced
2 onion, diced
2 carrots, diced
1 lb. red meat, in chunks
3 garlic cloves, minced

1 tbsp. chili powder
1 tbsp. chipotle powder
1 tsp. cumin powder
2 tomatoes , diced
2 tbsp. lime juice
salt to taste

DIRECTIONS:

- Add oil into the Fagor Pressure Cooker and press SAUTÉ button.
- When it heats up lightly, add onion, garlic cloves, lime juice and red meat.
- Cook for 10 minutes on MEAT mode.
- Add chili powder, carrots, cumin powder, chipotle powder and salt.
- Add sweet potatoes and cook for 10 more minutes. When it beeps, take it out and serve.

362. Diced Meat with Onions

(Time: 15 minutes \ Servings: 2)

INGREDIENTS:

1 large onion, sliced
1 tbsp. olive oil
1 lb. red meat , diced

2 tomatoes, chopped
½ tbsp. chili powder
salt and pepper, to taste

DIRECTIONS:

- Add onion and olive oil into the Fagor Pressure Cooker and press the SAUTÉ button.
- Mix in the tomatoes, red meat, chili powder, salt and pepper. Cook for 10 minutes.

363. Slice Beef with Mushrooms

(Time: 13 minutes \ Servings: 3)

INGREDIENTS:

1 lb. beef meat, sliced
2 tbsp. onion powder
1 cup tomato paste
½ cup thyme, chopped

½ cup mozzarella cheese, shredded
3 cups mushrooms, chopped
½ large onion, chopped
parsley to garnish

DIRECTIONS:

- Mix tomato paste with onion powder in a bowl.
- Put the tomato paste mixture in the Fagor Pressure Cooker and then add meat.
- Cover the meat with thyme, mushrooms and cheese. Cook on MEAT mode for 10 minutes.
- When ready, garnish it with chopped parsley and enjoy!

364. Meat Quiche

(Time: 40 minutes \ Servings: 4)

INGREDIENTS:

1 cup cheddar cheese, grated
2 scallions, choppedr
6 eggs
1 ½ cups water
4 bacon slices, cooked, crumbled

½ cup milk
½ cup ground sausage, cooked
½ ham, diced
½ tsp salt
1 pinch of black pepper

DIRECTIONS:

- Pour the water in the Instant Pot. In a bowl, whisk the eggs. Add salt, pepper and milk.
- Place the bacon, sausages and ham in a 1-qt. bakins dish. Mix well.
- Pour the eggs oveer and stir well. Spinkle with chopped scallions and grated cheese.
- Cover with foil and transfer to the pressure cooker. Cook on MANUAL, high pressure for 30 minutes.

365. Meat with Peppers

(Time: 15 minutes \ Servings: 2)

INGREDIENTS:

1 tbsp. vegetable oil
½ cup tomato sauce
1 lb. ground meat
2 green peppers, sliced
2 red peppers, sliced

1 onion , chopped
2 garlic cloves, chopped
½ tbsp. chili powder
salt and pepper, to taste

DIRECTIONS:

- Add garlic, onion and vegetable oil into the Fagor Pressure Cooker. Press the SAUTÉ button.
- Mix in the ground meat, green peppers and red peppers.
- Sprinkle salt, pepper and chili powder on the meat. Cook on MEAT mode for 15 minutes.

366. Meat with Onion Sauce

(Time: 16 minutes \ Servings: 2)

INGREDIENTS:

1 lb. meat steaks
2 cups meat broth
2 cloves garlic, chopped
2 cups vegetable broth

1 cup tomato paste
salt and pepper, to taste
1 Bay leaf
parsley, chopped to garnish

DIRECTIONS:

- Add vegetable broth into the Fagor Pressure Cooker and cook for 2 minutes.
- Mix in the meat broth, bay leaf, salt and pepper, meat steak, garlic and onion.
- Cook on MEAT mode for 10 minutes. Release the pressure when the cooker beeps.
- Sprinkle with parsley before serving.

367. Simple Bacon Burgers

(Time: 20 minutes \ Servings: 2)

INGREDIENTS:

8 strips of bacon
½ tsp. Paprika
1 tbsp. Garlic powder
1 tbsp. Cayenne powder
4 Hamburger patties

4 Hamburger buns
1 tomato , chopped
½ cup Cheddar cheese
Salt and pepper, to taste

DIRECTIONS:

- Place the hamburger patties on the bottom layer of a round baking tray.
- Add paprika, salt and pepper, garlic powder, tomato, cayenne powder, and cover with cheese.
- Cook in the Fagor Pressure Cooker for 20 minutes on high pressure.
- Heat the buns in the pressure cooker as well for 2 minutes.
- Fry the bacon strips for 2 minutes, or until crispy.
- When done, place patties, and bacon in the buns and serve!

368. Bruschetta Meat

(Time: 45 minutes \ Servings: 3)

INGREDIENTS:

½ lb. beef, pieces
1 cup tomato sauce
1 teaspoon salt

3 cups chicken broth
2-3 garlic cloves
4 tablespoons oil

DIRECTIONS:

- In the Fagor Pressure Cooker, add all ingredients and cook for 45 minutes on MEAT mode.
- Serve on french toast or corn tortillas.

369. Carrot and Pork Stew

(Time: 45 minutes \ Servings: 7)

INGREDIENTS:

1 onion, chopped
2 tomatoes, chopped
2 carrots, sliced
½ lb. pork meat, pieces, boiled
2 cups chicken broth
½ teaspoon garlic paste
½ teaspoon ginger paste

½ teaspoon cumin powder
½ teaspoon cinnamon powder
½ teaspoon chili powder
¼ teaspoon salt
¼ teaspoon turmeric powder
3 tablespoons oil
2 green chilies, whole

DIRECTIONS:

- Heat oil in the Fagor Pressure Cooker, sauté onion for 1 minute on SAUTÉ mode.
- Stir in tomatoes, ginger paste, garlic paste, salt, chili powder, and turmeric powder and fry for 1 minute.
- Add the pork, and fry for about 10 minutes. Add carrots and fry until lightly tender.
- Add the chicken broth and green chili and cook for 30 minutes on MEAT mode.
- Add cinnamon and cumin powder and stir. Transfer to a serving dish and enjoy.

370. Spicy Pork Korma

(Time: 40 minutes \ Servings: 4)

INGREDIENTS:

½ lb. pork, boiled
½ teaspoon garlic paste
1 teaspoon salt
2 tomatoes, chopped
½ teaspoon chili powder

¼ teaspoon turmeric powder
1 cup vegetable broth
½ teaspoon cumin powder
½ teaspoon dry coriander powder
3 tablespoons oil

DIRECTIONS:

- Heat oil on SAUTÉ mode and fry garlic for 1 minute.
- Add the tomatoes with salt, chili powder, and turmeric powder and fry.
- Add in the pork pieces and stir fry with a few splashes of water until the oil disappears from the sides of pan. Simmer for 10 minutes. Pour in the vegetable broth and mix well.
- Cook on MANUAL mode for 30 minutes. Season with cumin powder and dry coriander powder.

371. Beef Orzo

(Time: 120 minutes \ Servings: 4)

INGREDIENTS:

1 cup orzo
¼ cup spinach, chopped
½ lb. beef, boiled
½ teaspoon garlic paste
1 teaspoon salt
2 tablespoons soya sauce

2 tomatoes, chopped
½ teaspoon chili powder
¼ teaspoon turmeric powder
2 cups vegetable broth
3 tablespoons oil

DIRECTIONS:

- In the Fagor Pressure Cooker, add all ingredients and cook on SLOW COOK mode for 120 minutes.

372. Hot Shredded Pork

(Time: 30 minutes \ Servings: 4)

INGREDIENTS:

2 pork fillets, boiled, shredded
½ teaspoon garlic paste
½ teaspoon salt
½ teaspoon soya sauce
2 tablespoons lemon juice

2 tablespoons barbecue sauce
½ cup chili garlic sauce
2 tablespoons vinegar
½ teaspoon chili powder
2 tablespoons oil

DIRECTIONS:

- Heat oil on SAUTÉ mode and fry garlic for 1 minute. Place the pork and fry well.
- Add soya sauce, chili garlic sauce, garlic paste, vinegar, barbecue sauce, salt, and chili powder and fry well. Transfer to a serving dish and drizzle lemon juice.

373. Mutton and Tomato Stew

(Time: 55 minutes \ Servings: 4)

INGREDIENTS:

1 cup tomato puree
1 cup mutton, pieces, boiled
2 tablespoons chili garlic sauce
2 cups chicken broth
1 garlic clove minced

1 red chili
¼ teaspoon salt
¼ teaspoon black pepper
2 tablespoons cooking oil

DIRECTIONS:

- In the Fagor Pressure Cooker, add the tomato puree, mutton, chicken broth, salt, pepper, garlic, chili, chili garlic sauce, oil and stir well.
- Cover with a lid and cook on CHILI mode for 40 minutes.Transfer the soup to a blender and blend to a puree. Transfer back to the cooker and let it simmer for 5 minutes. Pour to a serving dish and enjoy.

374. Mushroom and Mutton

(Time: 35 minutes \ Servings: 5)

INGREDIENTS:

½ lb. mutton, boiled
1 cup mushrooms, sliced
1 onion, chopped
2-3 garlic cloves, minced
2 tomatoes, chopped
1 carrot, chopped
¼ teaspoon cumin powder

¼ teaspoon cinnamon powder
1 teaspoon salt
½ teaspoon chili powder
4 tablespoons olive oil
½ cup chicken broth
1 green chili

DIRECTIONS:

- Heat oil in the Fagor Pressure Cooker and fry onion for 1 minute.
- Add in the tomatoes, chili powder, salt, and fry. Add the mutton and stir fry well.
- Then add the carrot and mushrooms and stir fry for about 5-6 minutes.
- Add the chicken broth in and cook on MANUAL mode for 15 minutes.
- Sprinkle cumin powder and cinnamon powder, toss well, and serve.

375. Fenugreek and Beef Curry

(Time: 35 minutes \ Servings: 5)

INGREDIENTS:

½ lb. beef, boiled
½ cup fenugreek, chopped
1 onion, chopped
2-3 garlic cloves, minced
2 tomatoes, chopped
¼ teaspoon turmeric powder
¼ teaspoon cumin powder

¼ teaspoon cinnamon powder
1 teaspoon salt
½ teaspoon chili powder
4 tablespoons olive oil
½ cup chicken broth
1 green chili

DIRECTIONS:

- Heat oil in the Fagor Pressure Cooker on SAUTÉ mode and fry onion for 1 minute.
- Add in tomatoes, chili powder, salt, and turmeric powder and fry.
- Then add the beef and stir fry for 5-10 minutes. Add the fenugreek and let it simmer for 5 minutes.
- Add the chicken broth in and cook on MANUAL mode for 10-15 minutes.
- Sprinkle cumin powder and cinnamon powder, toss well and serve.

376. Pork Chops with Gravy

(Time: 55 minutes \ Servings: 5)

INGREDIENTS:

½ lb. pork chops
1 onion, chopped
2-3 garlic cloves, minced
2 tomatoes, chopped
¼ teaspoon turmeric powder
¼ teaspoon cumin powder

¼ teaspoon cinnamon powder
1 teaspoon salt
½ teaspoon chili powder
4 tablespoons olive oil
½ cup chicken broth
1 green chili

DIRECTIONS:

- Heat oil on SAUTÉ mode and fry onion for 1 minute.
- Add in the tomatoes, chili powder, salt, turmeric powder and fry.
- Add the pork chops and stir fry for 5-10 minutes.
- Add the chicken broth on and cook on MANUAL mode for 10-15 minutes.
- Sprinkle cumin powder and cinnamon powder, toss well.

377. Mutton Masala

(Time: 60 minutes \ Servings: 5)

INGREDIENTS:

½ lb. mutton, boiled
1 onion, chopped
1 teaspoon ginger paste
½ teaspoon garlic paste

1 teaspoon salt
¼ teaspoon black pepper
3 tablespoons oil

DIRECTIONS:

- In the Fagor Pressure Cooker, add all ingredients and cook on SLOW COOK mode for 1 hour.
- Stir occasionally.
- Serve with boiled noodles and enjoy.

378. Mutton Broth

(Time: 60 minutes \ Servings: 4)

INGREDIENTS:

½ lb. mutton, pieces
3-4 garlic cloves
1 teaspoon salt
¼ teaspoon black pepper
½ teaspoon chili powder
1 onion, sliced

1-inch ginger slice
5 cups water
¼ teaspoon turmeric powder
¼ teaspoon dry coriander powder
1 cinnamon stick
3 tablespoons oil

DIRECTIONS:

- Add all ingredients and cook on SLOW COOK mode for 2 hours. Stir occasionally.

379. Pork Mutton with Potato

(Time: 35 minutes \ Servings: 5)

INGREDIENTS:

½ lb. mutton, pieces, boiled
1 onion, chopped

2-3 potatoes, peeled, diced
2-3 garlic cloves, minced

2 tomatoes, chopped
¼ teaspoon turmeric powder
¼ teaspoon cumin powder
¼ teaspoon cinnamon powder

1 teaspoon salt
½ teaspoon chili powder
4 tablespoons olive oil
½ cup chicken broth

DIRECTIONS:

- Heat oil on SAUTÉ mode and fry onion for 1 minute.
- Add in the tomatoes, chili powder, salt, turmeric powder and fry.
- Add the mutton and stir fry for 5-10 minutes. Then add the potatoes and fry well.
- After that, add the chicken broth on and cook on MANUAL mode for 10-15 minutes.
- Sprinkle cumin powder and cinnamon powder, toss well.

380. Mutton and Yogurt

(Time: 35 minutes \ Servings: 5)

INGREDIENTS:

½ lb. mutton, boiled
1 cup yogurt
1 onion, chopped
2-3 garlic cloves, minced
2 tomatoes, chopped
¼ teaspoon turmeric powder

¼ teaspoon cumin powder
¼ teaspoon cinnamon powder
1 teaspoon salt
½ teaspoon chili powder
4 tablespoons olive oil
½ cup chicken broth

DIRECTIONS:

- Heat oil in the Fagor Pressure Cooker on SAUTÉ mode and fry onion for 1 minute.
- Add in the tomatoes, chili powder, salt, turmeric powder and fry.
- Add the mutton pieces and stir fry for 5-10 minutes.
- Stir in yogurt and fry until the oil disappears from the sides of the pan.
- Then add the chicken broth on and cook on MANUAL mode for 10-15 minutes.
- Sprinkle cumin powder and cinnamon powder, toss well.

381. Mutton with Okra

(Time: 35 minutes \ Servings: 4)

INGREDIENTS:

½ lb. mutton, boiled
1 cup okra
1 onion, chopped
2-3 garlic cloves, minced
2 tomatoes, chopped

¼ teaspoon turmeric powder
1 teaspoon salt
½ teaspoon chili powder
4 tablespoons olive oil

DIRECTIONS:

- Heat oil in the Fagor Pressure Cooker and fry the okra until crispy. Set aside.
- In the same cooker, fry onion for 1 minute.
- Add in the tomatoes, chili powder, salt, turmeric powder and fry.
- Add the mutton and stir fry for 5-10 minutes. Then add the okra and mix well. Serve hot.

382. Fried Bitter Melon with Beef

(Time: 45 minutes \ Servings: 4)

INGREDIENTS:

½ lb. mutton, boiled, small pieces
1 cup bitter guard
1 onion, chopped
2-3 garlic cloves, minced
2 tomatoes, chopped

¼ teaspoon turmeric powder
1 teaspoon salt
½ teaspoon chili powder
4 tablespoons olive oil

DIRECTIONS:

- Heat oil in the Fagor Pressure Cooker and fry the bitter guard until golden brown; set aside.
- In the same cooker fry onion for 1 minute.
- Add in the tomatoes, chili powder, salt, and turmeric powder and fry.
- Add the mutton and stir fry for 5-10 minutes. Add the fried bitter guard and mix well.

383. Mutton and Turnip Stew

(Time: 60 minutes \ Servings: 4)

INGREDIENTS:

½ lb. mutton, boiled
3 turnips, peeled, diced
1 onion, chopped
2-3 garlic cloves, minced

2 tomatoes, chopped
¼ teaspoon turmeric powder
½ teaspoon chili powder
4 tablespoons olive oil

DIRECTIONS:

- In the Fagor Pressure Cooker, add all ingredients and toss around.
- Cook for 60 minutes on SLOW COOK mode. Serve hot and enjoy.

384. Beef and Turnips

(Time: 45 minutes \ Servings: 4)

INGREDIENTS:

½ lb. mutton, boiled
3 turnips, peeled, diced
1 onion, sliced
2-3 garlic cloves, minced

1 teaspoon salt
½ teaspoon chili powder
4 tablespoons olive oil

DIRECTIONS:

- Add all ingredients and mix well. Cook for 45 minutes on MEAT mode. Serve hot.

385. Slow Cooked Zucchini and Pork

(Time: 45 minutes \ Servings: 5)

INGREDIENTS:

½ lb. pork, pieces
2 zucchini, sliced
3 turnips, peeled, diced
1 onion, chopped
2-3 garlic cloves, minced

2 tomatoes, chopped
¼ teaspoon turmeric powder
½ teaspoon chili powder
4 tablespoons olive oil

DIRECTIONS:

- In the Fagor Pressure Cooker, add all ingredients and toss. Cook for 45 minutes on MEAT mode.

386. Beefalo Wings

(Time: 45 minutes \ Servings: 4)

INGREDIENTS:

2 lean meat fillets, cut into strips
1 teaspoon garlic powder
½ cup all-purpose flour
½ teaspoon salt

½ teaspoon chili powder
½ teaspoon cinnamon powder
1 cup oil, for frying
1 egg, whisked

DIRECTIONS:

- In a bowl, combine flour, salt, chili powder, garlic, cumin powder, pepper, and toss around.
- Dip each meat strip into the whisked egg and roll out into the flour mixture.
- Heat oil in the Fagor Pressure Cooker on SAUTÉ mode.
- Transfer the meat into the oil and fry until golden.
- Place on a paper towel to remove the excess oil.

387. Beef Fillets

(Time: 40 minutes \ Servings: 4)

INGREDIENTS:

4 beef fillets
1 teaspoon garlic paste
½ teaspoons ginger paste
½ teaspoon salt
½ teaspoon chili powder

½ teaspoon cinnamon powder
½ teaspoon cumin powder
2 tablespoons papaya paste
4 tablespoons oil

DIRECTIONS:

- In a bowl, add all ingredients and mix well.
- Place the fillets inside the Fagor Pressure Cooker and cook on MEAT mode for 35 minutes.

388. Cabbage and Carrots with Beef

(Time: 40 minutes \ Servings: 4)

INGREDIENTS:

2 cups cabbage shredded
¼ lb. beef, small pieces
1 potato, diced
1 teaspoon salt
1 teaspoon black pepper

1 cup tomato puree
½ cup spring onion, chopped
½ teaspoon garlic paste
3 tablespoons cooking oil
5 cups vegetable broth

DIRECTIONS:

- In the Fagor Pressure Cooker, add all ingredients and toss well.
- Cook on MEAT mode for 40 minutes.

389. Meatballs

(Time: 30 minutes \ Servings: 5)

INGREDIENTS:

2 cups ground beef
1 teaspoon garlic paste
2 tablespoons gram flour
½ teaspoon chili powder

½ teaspoon cinnamon powder
½ teaspoon cumin powder
1 onion, chopped
1 cup oil, for frying

DIRECTIONS:

- In a bowl combine beef, cinnamon powder, garlic, gram flour, salt, chili powder, cumin powder. Mix well.
- Make round balls and set aside. Heat oil in the Fagor Pressure Cooker on SAUTÉ mode.
- Put the meatballs in the oil and fry until golden. Place on a paper towel to drain out the excess oil.
- Transfer to a serving dish and serve with any sauce.

390. Hot Beef

(Time: 60 minutes \ Servings: 4)

INGREDIENTS:

½ lb. beef, boiled
1 cup tomato puree
1-inch ginger slice
½ teaspoon garlic paste
1 teaspoon salt

¼ teaspoon chili powder
1 cup water
½ teaspoon cumin powder
4 tablespoons oil

DIRECTIONS:

- Heat oil in the Fagor Pressure Cooker on SAUTÉ mode and fry tomatoes, chili powder, ginger, garlic and salt for 5-10 minutes.
- Add the beef and keep cooking. Add in water and cook on MEAT mode for 15-20 minutes.
- Sprinkle cumin powder and transfer to a serving dish.

391. Beef and Potato Stew

(Time: 45 minutes \ Servings: 7)

INGREDIENTS:

1 onion, chopped
2 tomatoes, chopped
½ lb. beef, pieces, boiled
2-3 potatoes, peeled, diced
2 cups chicken broth
½ teaspoon garlic paste
½ teaspoon ginger paste

½ teaspoon cumin powder
½ teaspoon cinnamon power
½ teaspoon chili powder
¼ teaspoon salt
¼ teaspoon turmeric powder
3 tablespoons oil
2 green chilies, whole

DIRECTIONS:

- Heat oil in the Fagor Pressure Cooker, sauté onion for 1 minute on SAUTÉ mode.
- Stir in tomatoes, ginger paste, garlic paste, salt, chili powder, turmeric powder and fry for 1 minute.
- Add the beef and fry for 10-11 minutes. Add potatoes and fry the beef until slightly tender.
- Add the chicken broth, green chili, and cook for 30 minutes on MEAT mode.
- Add cinnamon and cumin powder and stir.

392. Pressure cooker Beef Rice

(Time: 45 minutes \ Servings: 5)

INGREDIENTS:

2 cups rice, soaked
½ lb. beef, boiled, pieces
1 teaspoon cumin seeds
1 bay leaf
2 garlic cloves, minced
1 teaspoon black pepper

1 pinch turmeric powder
1 teaspoon cumin powder
2 tomatoes, chopped
2 medium onions, sliced
3 tablespoons olive oil
4 cups chicken broth

DIRECTIONS:

- Heat oil in the Fagor Pressure Cooker on SAUTÉ mode, fry onion until golden. Add the tomatoes, cumin seeds and bay leaf and fry well. Then add the beef and season with salt, turmeric powder, pepper, and garlic and fry well.
- Pour in the vegetable broth and add cumin powder, and cinnamon powder, boil.
- Add rice and let it simmer until bubbles appear on the surface, then cover the pressure cooker with a lid.
- Cook for 20 minutes on WHITE RICE mode.

393. Beef and Split Gram Curry

(Time: 55 minutes \ Servings: 6)

INGREDIENTS:

1 onion, sliced
2 tomatoes, chopped
1 cup split gram, boiled
½ lb. beef, boiled
2 cups chicken broth
½ teaspoon garlic paste
½ teaspoon ginger paste

½ teaspoon cumin powder
½ teaspoon cinnamon power
½ teaspoon chili powder
¼ teaspoon salt
¼ teaspoon turmeric powder
3 tablespoons oil

DIRECTIONS:

- Heat oil in the Fagor Pressure Cooker, sauté onion for 1 minute on SAUTÉ mode.
- Stir in tomatoes, ginger paste, garlic paste, salt, chili powder, turmeric powder and fry for 1 minute.
- Add the beef and fry for 5-10 minutes. Add the split gram and stir fry for 5 minutes.
- Add in chicken broth and cook for 20 minutes on MEAT mode.

394. Hot and Spicy Beef Gravy

(Time: 40 minutes \ Servings: 4)

INGREDIENTS:

½ lb. meat, cut into small pieces, boneless
1 cup tomato puree
1 onion, chopped
¼ garlic paste
1 teaspoon salt

½ teaspoon chili powder
½ teaspoon cumin powder
½ teaspoon cinnamon powder
2 tablespoons olive oil

DIRECTIONS:

- Heat oil in the Fagor Pressure Cooker on SAUTÉ mode and fry garlic and onion for a minute.
- Add the tomato puree, salt, chili powder and fry again for 4-5 minutes. Add in the boiled meat and stir fry for 10-15 minutes. Sprinkle cumin powder and cinnamon powder and mix well.

395. Red Beans and Beef

(Time: 120 minutes \ Servings: 4)

INGREDIENTS:

1 can red beans
½ lb. beef meat, pieces
2 tomatoes, slices
1 cup spring onion, chopped

1 teaspoon chili powder
1 teaspoon garlic powder
2 tablespoons olive oil
3 cups vegetables broth

DIRECTIONS:

- In the Fagor Pressure Cooker, add all ingredients and toss well. Cook for 2 hours on SLOW COOK mode.

396. Meat Pops

(Time: 25 minutes \ Servings: 6)

INGREDIENTS:

1 meat fillet, cut into small pieces
1 teaspoon garlic powder
1 teaspoon onion powder
½ cup flour
¼ cup water

1 teaspoon salt
½ teaspoon black pepper
½ teaspoon cinnamon powder
½ teaspoon cumin powder
1 cup oil, for frying

DIRECTIONS:

- In a bowl, mix flour, water, garlic powder, bread crumbs, onion powder, cinnamon powder, salt, pepper, and cumin powder. Set the Fagor Pressure Cooker on SAUTÉ mode.
- Dip the meat pieces into the flour mixture. Then transfer to the pressure cooker.
- Deep fry each meat pop until golden.

397. Spicy Beef Korma

(Time: 40 minutes \ Servings: 4)

INGREDIENTS:

½ lb. beef, boiled
½ teaspoon garlic paste
1 teaspoon salt
2 tomatoes, chopped
½ teaspoon chili powder

¼ teaspoon turmeric powder
1 cup vegetable broth
½ teaspoon cumin powder
½ teaspoon dry coriander powder
3 tablespoons oil

DIRECTIONS:

- Heat oil in the Fagor Pressure Cooker on SAUTÉ mode and fry garlic for 1 minute.
- Add the tomatoes, salt, chili powder, turmeric powder and fry.
- Add in the beef pieces and stir fry with a few splashes of water until the oil disappears from the sides of the pan. Let it simmer for 10 minutes.
- Pour in the vegetable broth and mix well. Cook on SLOW COOK mode for 30 minutes.
- Season with cumin powder and dry coriander powder.

398. Pulled Beef

(Time: 30 minutes \ Servings: 4)

INGREDIENTS:

2 beef fillets, boiled, shredded
½ teaspoon garlic paste
½ teaspoon salt
½ teaspoon soya sauce
2 tablespoons barbecue sauce

½ cup chili garlic sauce
2 tablespoons vinegar
½ teaspoon chili powder
2 tablespoons oil

DIRECTIONS:

- Heat oil on SAUTÉ mode and fry garlic for 1 minute. Transfer the beef and fry well.
- Add soya sauce, chili garlic sauce, vinegar, barbecue sauce, salt, chili powder and fry well.

399. Roasted Bell Pepper with Beef

(Time: 120 minutes \ Servings: 4)

INGREDIENTS:

4 yellow and red bell peppers, halved, seeds
½ lb. beef, boiled
½ teaspoon garlic powder

½ teaspoon salt
½ teaspoon black pepper
3 tablespoons olive oil

DIRECTIONS:

- In the Fagor Pressure Cooker, add all ingredients and toss well. Cook for 2 hours on SLOW COOK mode.

400. Beef and Peas with Gravy

(Time: 45 minutes \ Servings: 5)

INGREDIENTS:

½ lb. beef, boiled
1 cup peas
1 onion, chopped
2-3 garlic cloves, minced
2 tomatoes, chopped
¼ teaspoon cumin powder

¼ teaspoon cinnamon powder
1 teaspoon salt
½ teaspoon chili powder
2 tablespoons olive oil
½ cup chicken broth
1 green chili

DIRECTIONS:

- Heat oil in the Fagor Pressure Cooker on SAUTÉ mode and fry onion for 1 minute.
- Add in the tomatoes, chili powder, salt, and fry.
- Add the beef and stir fry well. Then add the peas and fry for 5-6 minutes.
- Add the chicken broth and green chili. Cook on MANUAL mode on high pressure for 10-15 minutes.
- Sprinkle cumin powder and cinnamon powder, toss well and serve.

401. Beef with Cauliflower

(Time: 45 minutes \ Servings: 5)

INGREDIENTS:

½ lb. meat, beef, boiled
1 cup cauliflower florets
1 onion, chopped
2-3 garlic cloves, minced
2 tomatoes, chopped
¼ teaspoon cumin powder

¼ teaspoon cinnamon powder
1 teaspoon salt
½ teaspoon chili powder
4 tablespoons olive oil
½ cup chicken broth
1 green chili

DIRECTIONS:

- Heat oil on SAUTÉ mode and fry the cauliflower for 3-4 minutes, set aside.
- In the same oil, fry onion for 1 minute. Add in tomatoes, chili powder, salt, and fry.
- Add the beef and the cauliflower and stir fry for 5-6 minutes.
- Add the chicken broth on and cook on MANUAL mode for 10-15 minutes.
- Sprinkle cumin powder and cinnamon powder, toss well and serve.

402. Beef and Spinach

(Time: 35 minutes \ Servings: 5)

INGREDIENTS:

½ lb. lean meat, boiled
1 cup spinach, chopped, boiled
1 onion, chopped
2-3 garlic cloves, minced
2 tomatoes, chopped
¼ teaspoon cumin powder

¼ teaspoon cinnamon powder
1 teaspoon salt
½ teaspoon chili powder
4 tablespoons olive oil
½ cup chicken broth
1 green chili

DIRECTIONS:

- In a blender, add the spinach and blend to a puree.
- Heat oil in Fagor Pressure Cooker on SAUTÉ mode and fry onion for 1 minute.
- Add in tomatoes, chili powder, salt, and fry.
- Add the beef and stir fry for 5-10 minutes.
- Add the chicken broth and the spinach and cook on MANUAL mode for 10-15 minutes.
- Sprinkle cumin powder and cinnamon powder, toss well.

403. Beef and Chickpea Stew

(Time: 35 minutes \ Servings: 4)

INGREDIENTS:

½ lb. beef, boneless, pieces
1 cup chickpea, boiled
1 tomato, chopped
1 onion, chopped
1 teaspoon garlic paste
¼ teaspoon ginger paste
¼ teaspoon salt

¼ teaspoon chili powder
¼ teaspoon cayenne pepper
1 carrot, sliced
¼ teaspoon cinnamon powder
½ teaspoon cumin powder
3 cups chicken broth
2 tablespoons olive oil

DIRECTIONS:

- Heat oil on SAUTÉ mode and add fry onion until transparent.
- Add in garlic, ginger, tomatoes, salt, cayenne pepper, chili powder, and fry for 4-5 minutes.
- Add the beef and stir fry for 10-15 minutes with a few splashes of water.
- Add the chickpea and carrots and stir fry for 5 minutes.
- Transfer the chicken broth, cover with a lid, and cook on MEAT mode for 30 minutes.
- Sprinkle cumin powder and cinnamon powder. Transfer to serving dish and enjoy.

404. Carrot and Beef Stew

(Time: 45 minutes \ Servings: 4)

INGREDIENTS:

½ lb. beef, pieces
3 carrots, peeled, sliced
1 tomato, chopped
1 onion, chopped
1 teaspoon garlic paste
¼ teaspoon ginger paste
¼ teaspoon turmeric powder

¼ teaspoon salt
¼ teaspoon chili powder
¼ teaspoon cinnamon powder
½ teaspoon cumin powder
3 cups chicken broth
2 tablespoons olive oil

DIRECTIONS:

- Heat oil on SAUTÉ mode and add fry onion until transparent.
- Stir in garlic, ginger, tomatoes, salt, chili powder, and turmeric powder and fry for 6 minutes.
- Stir fry the beef for 5-6 minutes.
- Transfer the chicken broth, cover with a lid and cook on MEAT mode for 40 minutes.
- Sprinkle cumin powder and cinnamon powder.

405. Tropical Beef Pineapple

(Time: 30 minutes \ Servings: 4)

INGREDIENTS:

½ lb. beef, boiled
1 cup pineapples, chunks
½ cup pineapple juice
1 teaspoon ginger paste

½ teaspoon garlic paste
1 teaspoon salt
¼ teaspoon black pepper
3 tablespoons oil

DIRECTIONS:

- Heat oil on SAUTÉ mode and fry the beef, ginger, garlic and salt for 5-10 minute.
- Stir in pineapple chunks and toss well. Season with pepper.
- Add in pineapple juice and simmer for 10-15 minutes on MEAT mode.

406. Beef with Pumpkin

(Time: 60 minutes \ Servings: 4)

INGREDIENTS:

½ lb. beef, boiled
1 cup pumpkin, peeled, chunks
½ teaspoons ginger paste
½ teaspoon garlic paste
1 teaspoon salt

1 onion, chopped
¼ teaspoon black pepper
2 cups chicken broth
3 tablespoons oil

DIRECTIONS:

- Heat oil in the Fagor Pressure Cooker on SAUTÉ mode and fry onion, ginger, and garlic for 5-10 minute.
- Add the beef, pumpkin, chicken broth, salt, pepper and cook on SLOW COOK mode for 50-60 minutes.
- Put in serving bowls and enjoy.

407. Slow Cooked Beef Turnips

(Time: 70 minutes \ Servings: 5)

INGREDIENTS:

½ lb. beef, boiled
3 large turnips, peeled, diced
1 tomato, sliced
1 onion, sliced
1 teaspoon ginger paste
½ teaspoon garlic paste

1 teaspoon salt
¼ teaspoon chili powder
3 cups chicken broth
1 cup baby carrots
3 tablespoons oil

DIRECTIONS:

- In the Fagor Pressure Cooker, add all ingredients and mix well.
- Set on SLOW COOK mode and cover with a lid. Cook for 60 minutes. Serve hot.

408. Mustard Leaves with Beef

(Time: 45 minutes \ Servings: 4)

INGREDIENTS:

3 cups mustard leaves, chopped
¼ lb. beef
2 onions, chopped
1 teaspoon salt
2 ripe tomatoes, chopped
1 teaspoon garlic paste

1 teaspoon red chili powder
2 green chilies whole
¼ cup tablespoons cooking oil
4 cups water
1 cup vegetable broth

DIRECTIONS:

- In the Fagor Pressure Cooker, add all ingredients and toss well.
- Cook on MEAT mode for 45 minutes.

409. Lentils with Beef

(Time: 60 minutes \ Servings: 4)

INGREDIENTS:

1 cup green lentils
¼ lb. beef, pieces
1 teaspoon salt
1 teaspoon chili flakes
½ teaspoon cumin powder

2 tomatoes, chopped
½ teaspoon cinnamon powder
2 tablespoons cooking oil
3 cups vegetable broth

DIRECTIONS:

- In the Fagor Pressure Cooker, add all ingredients and toss well.
- Cook on MANUAL mode for 1 hour.

410. Fried Okra with Beef

(Time: 45 minutes \ Servings: 4)

INGREDIENTS:

¼ lb. beef, boiled, boneless
1 cup okra, sliced
1 tomato, chopped
1 onion, sliced
1 teaspoon garlic paste
¼ teaspoon ginger paste

¼ teaspoon turmeric powder
¼ teaspoon salt
¼ teaspoon chili powder
3 cups chicken broth
¼ cup olive oil

DIRECTIONS:

- Heat oil on SAUTÉ mode and fry okra until golden. Transfer to a platter and set aside.
- In the same pressure cooker, add onion and fry until transparent.
- Stir in garlic, ginger, tomatoes, salt, chili powder, and turmeric powder and fry for 6 minutes.
- Stir fry the beef for 5-6 minutes. Add the fried okra and stir fry for 10-15 minutes.
- Sprinkle cumin powder and cinnamon powder.

411. Rice with Ground Beef

(Time: 25 minutes \ Servings: 5)

INGREDIENTS

1 finely chopped onion
5 tbsp. of coconut oil
2 chopped cloves of garlic
2 diced tomatoes
1 tsp. of sweet paprika
1 tsp. of saffron

2 cups of brown rice
3 cups of beef broth
1 cup of dry white wine
1 lb. of ground beef
1 tsp. of ground flax seeds
1 cup of soaked or dry beans

DIRECTIONS

- Melt the coconut oil into the Fagor Pressure Cooker and sauté the onion until soft.
- Add the garlic, tomatoes, salt, paprika, saffron, and beans; then stir well and keep cooking until the tomatoes soften. Add the ground beef and mix the ingredients. Add the rice, broth, wine, flax seed powder, and salt. Close the lid and press the MANUAL to high pressure for 25 minutes.
- Once the timer beeps, quickly release the pressure. Season with pepper and salt before serving.

412. Lamb with Pomegranate Seeds

(Time: 25 minutes \ Servings: 4)

INGREDIENTS

2 lb. of lamb chops
6 tbsp. of bacon fat
1 chopped onion

1 cup of pomegranate juice
½ tsp. of sea salt
seed of 2 pomegranates

DIRECTIONS

- Heat the Fagor Pressure Cooker and pour 2 cups of water. Add the lamb chops, juice and bacon fat.
- Press MANUAL on high pressure for 15 minutes. Close the lid and seal the valve.
- Once the timer beeps, release the pressure with the use of a towel. Pour 2 tbsp. of coconut oil on the lamb with a pinch of salt and a pinch of pepper. Add the onion and press SAUTÉ and cook the lamb for 5 more minutes.
- Keep stirring to avoid burning the lamb. Once the lamb is perfectly cooked, add the pomegranate seeds and cook for 5 minutes. Finally, press Keep warm button.

413. Ground Beef with Flax Seeds

(Time: 30 minutes \ Servings: 2)

INGREDIENTS

2 lb. of ground beef
1 package 4.6 oz. of sausage, cut in pieces
2 tsp. of dried, chopped onion
1 tsp. of garlic powder
1 tsp. of dried basil
1 tsp. of dried parsley

½ cup of flax seed meal
½ tsp. of salt
1 tsp. of ground fennel
1 cup of dried slices of tomatoes
2 beaten eggs
1 mango, cubed

DIRECTIONS

- In a deep bowl, mix the onion, garlic powder, dried basil, flax seed meal, salt, and ground fennel. Squeeze the sausage out of any casings and place in the bowl cut in very small pieces.
- Place the ground meat in the same bowl and mix the ingredients with hands. Shape the meat into the form of two loaves. Heat the Fagor Pressure Cooker and melt a tbsp. of coconut oil.
- Transfer the meat loafs and press MEAT mode. Close the lid and set the timer for 30 minutes. Serve the meat loaves with mango cubes.

Seafood and Fish

414. Lemon Fish Steaks

(Time: 25 minutes \ Servings: 3)

INGREDIENTS:

4 fish fillets
2 tablespoons extra virgin olive oil
1 teaspoon fine sea salt

1 teaspoon black pepper
Lemon wedges, for serving
2 tablespoons lemon juice

DIRECTIONS:

- Sprinkle salt and pepper on the fish. Drizzle lemon juice and oil, then rub all over.
- Place into a greased Fagor Pressure Cooker and cook for 15 minutes on STEAM mode.
- Serve with lemon wedges.

415. Fried Fish

(Time: 25 minutes \ Servings: 3)

INGREDIENTS:

4 fish fillets
½ tablespoon salt
½ tablespoon black pepper
2 tablespoons white vinegar
½ cup of tomato puree

½ tablespoon red paprika powder
1 clove of garlic, minced
1 onion, chopped
Bread crumbs as required
Oil for frying

DIRECTIONS:

- Place the fish fillets in a large bowl and sprinkle salt and black pepper.
- Roll in the bread crumbs and set aside.
- Heat oil in the Fagor Pressure Cooker and fry the fish until golden.
- Cut into chunks and set aside. In the Pressure cooker, heat 2 tablespoons of oil on SAUTÉ mode.
- Add another 1-2 tablespoons of oil, chopped onion, garlic and stir for 1-2 minutes.
- Add tomato puree, vinegar, salt, paprika, stir well and cook for 10 minutes.
- Add the fish chunks and add ½ cup of water.
- Cover with a lid and cook for 10 minutes on MANUAL mode.

416. Creamy Tilapia

(Time: 25 minutes \ Servings: 3)

INGREDIENTS:

½ lb. oz. tilapia fillets
2 tablespoons lemon juice
½ teaspoon of black pepper
2 tbsp of cream cheese

2 tablespoons chopped fresh dill weed
½ teaspoon salt
Cooking spray

DIRECTIONS:

- Grease the Fagor Pressure Cooker with a cooking spray and place the fish filets, sprinkle salt and dill.
- Drizzle lemon juice and toss around. Cook for 20 minutes on MANUAL mode.
- After that, add cream cheese and black pepper and combine. Simmer for 2 minutes.

417. Fried Fish

(Time: 25 minutes \ Servings: 4)

INGREDIENTS:

4 fish fillets, cut into pieces
½ tablespoon salt
½ tablespoon black pepper
2 tablespoons white vinegar

½ tablespoon red paprika powder
1 teaspoon garlic paste
3 tablespoons gram flour
Oil for frying

DIRECTIONS:

- In a bowl, add all the seasoning and mix well. Add in the fish fillets.
- Heat oil in the Fagor Pressure Cooker on SAUTÉ mode. Add in the fish and fry until golden.

418. Fish with Bell Peppers

(Time: 35 minutes \ Servings: 4)

INGREDIENTS:

2 fish fillets, fried, cut into pieces
½ tablespoon salt
½ tablespoon chili power
1 teaspoon ginger paste

2 tablespoons oil
1 cup tomato puree
2 green bell peppers, chopped
1 cup chicken broth

DIRECTIONS:

- Heat oil in the Fagor Pressure Cooker and fry the ginger garlic paste for 1 minutes.
- Add tomatoes and fry well. Season with salt and chili powder.
- Add the fried fish and bell pepper, toss well.
- Stir fry for 10 minutes. Pour in the chicken broth and cook on STEAM mode for 15 minutes.

419. Roasted Fish with Vegetables

(Time: 25 minutes \ Servings: 4)

INGREDIENTS:

2 tomatoes, sliced
1 avocado, chopped
1 onion, sliced
1 bunch green coriander, chopped
½ cup tomato puree

1 teaspoon garlic paste
Salt and black pepper to taste
2 fish fillets, cut into pieces
1 teaspoon lemon juice

DIRECTIONS:

- Heat oil in the Fagor Pressure Cooker and fry garlic and onion for 1 minutes.
- Add the fish and fry until golden. Add tomatoes and keep frying. Season with salt and chili powder.
- Add avocado, tomato puree, and lemon juice, simmer for 10 minutes. Sprinkle coriander and serve.

420. Creamy Tuna with Macaroni

(Time: 25 minutes \ Servings: 3)

INGREDIENTS:

¼ lb. tuna, cut into pieces
1 cup cream
1 teaspoon garlic paste

Salt and black pepper to taste
1 cup macaroni, boiled

DIRECTIONS:

- Heat oil in the Fagor Pressure Cooker and fry garlic for about 30 seconds on SAUTÉ mode.
- Add the fish and sauté it for 1-2 minutes. Season with salt and pepper.
- Stir in the macaroni and cream, mix well. Transfer to a serving platter and serve.

421. Maple Flavored Fish

(Time: 25 minutes \ Servings: 3)

INGREDIENTS:

2 fish fillets
4 tablespoons maple syrup
2 garlic cloves, minced

Salt and black pepper to taste
2 tablespoons soya sauce

DIRECTIONS:

- Heat oil in the Fagor Pressure Cooker and fry garlic for 30 seconds.
- Add the fish and sauté it for a 1-2 minutes. Season with salt and pepper.
- Drizzle maple syrup and soya sauce. Toss well, and let simmer for 5 minutes.

422. Halibut with Mustard

(Time: 25 minutes \ Servings: 3)

INGREDIENTS:

4 halibut fish fillets, skin on
2 tablespoons Dijon mustard

2 cups water

DIRECTIONS:

- Pour the water in the pressure cooker and bush the fish fillets with mustard.
- Place them in the steaming basket and close the lid.
- Set on MANUAL and cook for 3 minutes. Perform a quick pressure release and serve.

423. Fried Fish Fingers

(Time: 25 minutes \ Servings: 3)

INGREDIENTS:

2 fish fillets, cut into 1-inch stripes
½ tablespoon salt
½ tablespoon black pepper
1 teaspoon garlic powder

3 tablespoons gram flour
1 teaspoon rosemary
Oil for frying

DIRECTIONS:

- In a bowl, add all the seasoning and mix well. Add in the fish fingers and toss well.
- Heat oil in the Fagor Pressure Cooker on SAUTÉ mode.
- Fry the fish stripes until golden. Serve with green salad.

424. Tuna with Tamarind Sauce

(Time: 25 minutes \ Servings: 3)

INGREDIENTS:

3 tuna fish fillets
2 tablespoons extra-virgin olive oil
1 teaspoon fine sea salt

1 teaspoon black pepper
Lemon wedges, for serving
2 tablespoons lemon juice

DIRECTIONS:

- Sprinkle salt and pepper on the fish. Then drizzle lemon juice and oil, rub all over the fish.
- Place it into a greased Fagor Pressure Cooker and cook for 15 minutes on STEAM mode.
- Top with lemon wedges and serve.

425. Fish Fried with Green Beans

(Time: 25 minutes \ Servings: 3)

INGREDIENTS:

2 red bell peppers, chopped
1 teaspoon tarragon
1 cup green beans
1 teaspoon garlic paste

Salt and black pepper to taste
2 fish fillets, cut into pieces
1 teaspoon lemon juice

DIRECTIONS:

- Heat oil in the Fagor Pressure Cooker and fry garlic and onion for 1 minute on SAUTÉ mode.
- Add the fish and fry well until golden brown. Season with salt and chili powder.
- Add beans and bell pepper. Simmer for 10 minutes. Sprinkle tarragon and toss.

426. Crispy Crumb Fish

(Time: 25 minutes \ Servings: 3)

INGREDIENTS:

2 fish fillets
1 cup bread crumbs
1 egg, whisked
½ tablespoon salt

½ tablespoon black pepper
1 teaspoon garlic powder
Oil for frying

DIRECTIONS:

- In a bowl, add the bread crumbs, salt, pepper, garlic and toss well.
- Dip the fish fillet in the egg and then roll out in the bread crumbs.
- Heat oil in the Fagor Pressure Cooker and fry fish pieces until golden brown on SAUTÉ mode.

427. Soul Satisfying Fish Soup

(Time: 35 minutes \ Servings: 2)

INGREDIENTS:

1 teaspoon saffron
1 teaspoon garlic paste
Salt and black pepper to taste
2 fish fillets, cut into pieces

1 cup cream
1 pinch chili powder
1 cup milk

DIRECTIONS:

- Heat oil in the Fagor Pressure Cooker and fry garlic with onion for 1 minutes. Add the fish and fry well until golden brown.

- Season with salt and chili powder. Shred the fish with a fork and transfer back to the cooker.
- Add in the cream and milk, mix well. Simmer for 10 minutes. Top with chili powder and saffron.

428. Fish Patties
(Time: 35 minutes \ Servings: 3)

INGREDIENTS:

2 fish fillets, cut into pieces
½ tablespoon salt
½ tablespoon black pepper
1 tablespoon coriander, chopped

¼ teaspoon garlic paste
4 tablespoons of gram flour
1 potato, boiled
½ cup oil for frying

DIRECTIONS:

- Heat 2 tablespoons of oil on SAUTÉ mode. Fry the fish until lightly golden. Crumble with a fork and set aside. Combine the fish, potatoes, garlic, coriander, salt, pepper and mix well.
- Make small round patties with this mixture and place into a platter. Heat oil in the Fagor Pressure Cooker and shallow fry the patties on SAUTÉ mode until lightly golden.

429. Fish with Tomatoes
(Time: 25 minutes \ Servings: 2)

INGREDIENTS:

2 fish fillets, cut into pieces
½ tablespoon salt
½ tablespoon black pepper

¼ teaspoon garlic powder
2-3 tomatoes, sliced
2 tablespoons oil

DIRECTIONS:

- Heat oil on SAUTÉ mode. Fry the fish until lightly golden. Season with salt, pepper, garlic powder and tomatoes. Cover with a lid and cook on STEAM mode for 15 minutes.

430. Ground Fish with Macaroni
(Time: 25 minutes \ Servings: 4)

INGREDIENTS:

1 cup ground fish
½ tablespoon salt
½ tablespoon black pepper
¼ teaspoon garlic powder

1 cup peas, boiled
1 16 oz. package of macaroni, cooked
2 tablespoons oil

DIRECTIONS:

- Heat oil on SAUTÉ mode. Fry the ground fish until lightly golden adding the garlic powder, salt and pepper. Add the peas and macaroni and cook for 5 to 8 minutes on STEAM mode.

431. Salmon Bowl
(Time: 15 minutes \ Servings: 2)

INGREDIENTS:

2 salmon fillets, cut into pieces
½ tablespoon salt
½ tablespoon black pepper
¼ teaspoon garlic powder

1 cup lettuce leaves
1 tomato, chopped
2 tablespoons oil

DIRECTIONS:

- Heat oil on SAUTÉ mode. Stir fry the lettuce for 1 minute, then set aside.
- In the same pot, fry the fish until lightly golden. Season with salt, pepper and garlic powder.
- Transfer to a serving platter and serve with lettuce and tomatoes.

432. Fish Stew

(Time: 25 minutes \ Servings: 2)

INGREDIENTS:

1 fish fillet, cut into small pieces
½ tablespoon salt
½ tablespoon black pepper
¼ teaspoon garlic powder

2 cups chicken broth
1 tablespoon green onion
2 tablespoons oil

DIRECTIONS:

- Add all ingredients and stir well. Cook on BEANS mode for 25 minutes. Serve hot.

433. Tarragon Steamed Fish

(Time: 25 minutes \ Servings: 3)

INGREDIENTS:

2 fish fillets, cut into pieces
½ tablespoon salt
½ tablespoon black pepper

2 tablespoons tarragon
¼ teaspoon garlic paste
2 tablespoons oil

DIRECTIONS:

- In the Fagor Pressure Cooker, place a rack and fill the pressure cooker with 2 cups of water.
- Season the fish with salt, pepper, tarragon, and garlic. Rub well.
- Place the fish on the rack and cover with a lid. Cook for 25 minutes on STEAM mode or until soft.

434. Whitebait with Capers

(Time: 25 minutes \ Servings: 2)

INGREDIENTS:

3 whitebait fillets
½ tablespoon salt
½ tablespoon black pepper
¼ teaspoon garlic paste

1 tablespoon capers
1 tablespoon sun dried tomatoes
2 tablespoons oil
2 tablespoons lime juice

DIRECTIONS:

- Add all ingredients, except the lime juice. Cook for 5 minutes on MANUAL mode on high pressure.
- Sprinkle with lime juice and serve.

435. Fish with Tamarind Sauce

(Time: 45 minutes \ Servings: 3)

INGREDIENTS:

3-4 fish fillets, pieces
½ tablespoon salt
½ tablespoon chili powder
¼ cup tamarind pulp
½ cup of tomato puree

1 tsp. of paprika
1 clove of garlic, minced
1 onion, chopped
Oil for frying

DIRECTIONS:

- Take a large bowl and put the fish fillets inside. Sprinkle salt and black pepper and place into a platter.
- Heat oil in the Fagor Pressure Cooker and fry the fish until golden. Cut into chunks and set aside.
- Then heat 2 tablespoons of oil on SAUTÉ mode. Add 1-2 tablespoons of oil, chopped onion, and garlic and stir for 1-2 minutes.
- Add the tomato puree, tamarind pulp, salt, and paprika, stir well and cook for 10 minute.
- Add the fish chunks and add ½ cup of water. Cover with a lid and cook for 10 minutes on MANUAL mode.

436. Creamy Tuna
(Time: 35 minutes \ Servings: 3)

INGREDIENTS:

3-4 tuna fillets
½ tablespoon black pepper
1 clove of garlic, minced

2 tablespoons oil
1 teaspoon basil, chopped
1 cup cream

DIRECTIONS:

- Heat oil on SAUTÉ mode. Add the fish and fry. Put on a platter and scramble with a fork.
- Transfer back to the pressure cooker and add cream, salt, pepper, garlic and let it simmer for 2-3 minutes.

437. Coconut Fish
(Time: 45 minutes \ Servings: 3)

INGREDIENTS:

3-4 fish fillets, pieces
½ tablespoon salt
½ tablespoon chili powder
½ cup coconut, crushed

1 cup coconut milk
1 clove of garlic, minced
Oil for frying
3 oz. boiled rice

DIRECTIONS:

- Take a large bowl and put the fish fillets inside. Sprinkle salt and black pepper and place into a platter.
- Heat oil in Fagor Pressure Cooker and fry the fish until golden. Heat two tablespoons of oil on SAUTÉ mode. Add garlic and fry for another minute.
- Add fish, coconut, coconut milk and simmer on STEAM mode for 10 minutes. Serve it with boiled rice.

438. Glazed Salmon
(Time: 20 minutes \ Servings: 3)

INGREDIENTS

1 ½ cups of apricot nectar
2 tbsp. of honey
2 tbsp. of reduced sodium soy sauce
1 tbsp. of grated fresh ginger

2 minced cloves of garlic
¼ tsp. of cayenne pepper
¼ tsp. of ground cinnamon
¾ lb. of skinless salmon filet

DIRECTIONS

- Heat a 1 tbsp. of coconut oil in the Fagor Pressure Cooker. Mix the apricot nectar, honey, soy sauce, ginger, garlic, cinnamon, and cayenne.
- Press MANUAL and set the timer to 10 minutes on high pressure. Close the lid and let simmer.
- When the timer beeps, remove the ingredients, quick release the pressure, and remove around ¼ cup of the cooked glaze. Then remove the remaining glaze by putting it in a saucepan.
- Transfer the salmon into the Pressure cooker and brush it with some glaze; sauté it for 10 minutes. Serve with the remaining quantity of the glaze.

439. Teriyaki Salmon with Ginger

(Time: 10 minutes \ Servings: 3)

INGREDIENTS

¾ cup of Kikkoman Teriyaki Marinade
¾ cup of Teriyaki Marinade
2 tbsp. of brown sugar

1 tsp. of grated fresh ginger root
4 salmon steaks
1 tbsp. of coconut oil

DIRECTIONS

- In a large bowl, combine the Kikkoman Teriyaki, marinade, brown sugar, coconut oil, and grated ginger root.
- Heat 1 tbsp. of olive oil in the Fagor Pressure Cooker and place the salmon. Pour the mixture over the salmon and press SAUTÉ. Cook for 10 minutes.

440. Fish with Coconut and Rice

(Time: 25 minutes \ Servings: 3)

INGREDIENTS

2 tbsp. of coconut oil
3 thinly sliced onions
3 crushed garlic cloves
1 piece of fresh peeled and finely grated
    ginger
2 tbsp. of curry paste (Madras)
1 can diced tomatoes

½ cup of coconut milk
1 lb. white fish filets diced into2-inch pieces
½ cup of frozen peas
¼ cup of fresh coriander leaves
Steamed basmati rice for serving
1 lemon cut into wedges

DIRECTIONS

- Heat the oil in the Fagor Pressure Cooker. Press Sauté and add the onion, then cook for 10 minutes.
- Add the garlic and ginger and cook for several more minutes.
- Add the tomatoes and curry paste keep stirring until the ingredients are well combined.
- Add the coconut milk and a cup of cold water.
- Press MANUAL and close the lid. Then set on high pressure for 5 minutes.
- Once the timer beeps, add the fish and the peas and keep stirring.
- Cook the ingredients for 10 minutes, loose lid.
- Once the fish is perfectly cooked, add coriander leaves. Serve and enjoy with the cooked rice.

441. Tilapia with Chia Seeds

(Time: 15 minutes \ Servings: 4)

INGREDIENTS

½ lb. of tilapia filets
2 tsp. of coconut oil
3 tbsp. of chia seeds
¼ tsp. of Old Bay Seasoning
½ tsp. of garlic

½ tsp. of salt
1 sliced lemon
1 tsp. of grated ginger
1 package frozen cauliflower with red pepper
    and broccoli

DIRECTIONS

- Press SAUTÉ and melt the coconut oil. Put the tilapia filets on the bottom.
- Season with the Old Bay and garlic, ginger, and salt and sprinkle chia seeds.
- Top each of the salmon pieces with lemon slices.
- Arrange the frozen vegetables around the portions of fish; season with salt and pepper.

- Cover the lid of the Fagor Pressure Cooker and set to high pressure for 10 to 15 minutes.
- Once the timer goes off, quickly release the pressure and enjoy this delicious dish!

442. Scallops with Strawberries Salsa

(Time: 10 minutes \ Servings: 2-3)

INGREDIENTS

1 cup of strawberries, Ripe
½ minced shallot
2 tbsp. of minced arugula and basil
1 tbsp. of red wine vinegar
½ lb. of scallops, remove the tough membrane
1 pinch of salt

1 pinch of pepper
¼ cup of toasted, chopped almonds
1 tbsp. of chia butter
1 tbsp. of coconut oil
arugula and basil leaves.
1 pinch of salt, pepper
1 pinch of ginger

DIRECTIONS

- Start by combining the strawberries, shallot, vinegar, and minced arugula with the basil in a bowl. Salt and pepper to taste.
- Adjust the seasoning to a balanced, nice taste between sweet and sour.
- Place the Pressure cooker and melt the butter and the coconut oil and press SAUTÉ. Season the scallops with salt, pepper, and ginger.
- Then sauté the scallops for around 3 minutes.
- Flip and cook for 2 more minutes.
- Once cooked, remove the scallops from the heat and top with the strawberry salsa.
- Serve and garnish with the basil and the arugula; then sprinkle the almonds.

443. Salmon with Oat and Mustard

(Time: 10 minutes \ Servings: 3)

INGREDIENTS

2 tbsp. of mustard
1 tbsp. of maple syrup
2 tsp. of ground pepper
¼ cup of quick cooking oats
3 salmon filets

2 tbsp. of coconut oil
pickles of mustard
3 diced carrots
1 potato cut into cubes
1 ripe mango

DIRECTIONS

- Melt 2 tbsp. coconut oil and add the mustard, maple syrup, and pepper.
- Rub the salmon in the mixture of the mustard and syrup; sprinkle the oats on the salmon.
- Line the salmon in the Fagor Pressure Cooker and sauté it for about 10 minutes.
- Once cooked, remove the salmon and add the carrot cubes with the diced potatoes and a cup of water with a pinch of salt and a pinch of ginger.
- Set the Fagor Pressure Cooker to MANUAL on high pressure for 5 minutes.
- When the timer beeps, be sure the potatoes and carrots are cooked.
- Quickly release the pressure and add the mango cubes.

444. Sardine with Cauliflower Florets

(Time: 15 minutes \ Servings: 3-4)

INGREDIENTS

6 sardines
1 tbsp. of coconut oil
2 minced garlic cloves
1 thick slice of bread, crumbed

1 tsp. of paprika
1 handful of chopped parsley
1 medium cauliflower
lemon wedges

DIRECTIONS

- Heat the Fagor Pressure Cooker and melt 1 tbsp. of coconut oil.
- Season the sardines on both sides, then sauté them for about 5 minutes or until cooked.
- Remove the sardines and pour ½ cup of water.
- Press Soup and add the garlic, cauliflower florets, salt, and a pinch of ginger and ground pepper.
- Set the timer to 3 minutes on high pressure and lock the lid of the Fagor Pressure Cooker.
- Once the timer beeps, quickly release the pressure and add the crumbs and the paprika to the other ingredients, setting to Sauté for 3 minutes.
- Add the sardines and the parsley and cook for 2 minutes. Serve the sardines and garnish with spinach.

Desserts

445. Chocolate Pudding
(Time: 50 minutes \ Servings: 6)

INGREDIENTS:

1 cup milk
1 cup chocolate, melted
4 bananas, peeled, sliced
½ cup condensed milk

½ cup sugar
2 tablespoons butter
2 tablespoons cocoa powder
1 cup whipped cream

DIRECTIONS:

- Press SAUTÉ. Add the butter and the whipped cream and cook until it is reduced to half.
- Add the condensed milk, chocolate, sugar, cocoa powder and stir gradually.
- Pour half of the chocolate pudding into a large dish and place the banana slices evenly.
- Pour the remaining chocolate on top and freeze for 2 hours.

446. Strawberry Cake
(Time: 50 minutes \ Servings: 4)

INGREDIENTS:

2 cups all-purpose flour
1 cup fresh strawberries
2 cups of strawberry puree
1 teaspoon baking powder
1 cup butter
1 pinch salt

2 eggs
1 cup milk
1 cup sugar
1 cup whipped cream
2 tablespoons caster sugar
1 teaspoon vanilla extract

DIRECTIONS:

- In the Fagor Pressure Cooker place a trivet and add 2-3 cups of water in the pot.
- In a bowl, add flour, eggs, sugar, salt, baking powder, milk, butter, vanilla extract and beat well.
- Add the strawberry puree and stir. Pour into a greased cake pan and place on a trivet.
- Cook for 40 minutes on MANUAL mode. Toss the caster sugar with the whipped cream to mix well.
- When the cake is cooled, top it with the whipped cream and place the strawberries.

447. Carrot and Rice Pudding
(Time: 60 minutes \ Servings: 6)

INGREDIENTS:

6 carrots, shredded
1 cup pineapple, chunks
1 cup rice, boiled
½ cup sugar
1 cup raisins

2 green cardamoms
5-6 pistachios, chopped
2 cups milk
1 cup water
1 pinch of salt

DIRECTIONS:

- In the Fagor Pressure Cooker, transfer the boiled rice, shredded carrots, pineapple, sugar, milk, salt, and cardamom, and cover with a lid. Let it to cook on SLOW COOK mode for 45 minutes.
- Place pudding into the freezer for 15 minutes and top with pistachios.

448. Lemon Cake

(Time: 50 minutes \ Servings: 6)

INGREDIENTS:

2 cups all-purpose flour
2 tablespoons lemon zest
2 tablespoons lemon juice
1 teaspoon baking powder
¼ teaspoon baking soda
½ cup butter

1 pinch salt
4 eggs
1 cup coconut milk
1 cup sugar
½ cup honey
½ cup apple jam

DIRECTIONS:

- In the Fagor Pressure Cooker, place a stand or a trivet and add 2 cups of water.
- Combine the flour, sugar, salt, baking powder, baking soda, eggs, lemon juice butter, milk, and 1 tablespoon lemon zest and beat with electric beater.
- Transfer to a greased baking pan and place on a trivet, cover and cook on MANUAL mode for 40 minutes.
- Combine the apple jam with honey. Pour this mixture onto the cake and top with lemon zest.

449. Chocolate Crackers

(Time: 40 minutes \ Servings: 6)

INGREDIENTS:

1 cup all-purpose flour
1 cup cocoa powder
½ cup molten chocolate
½ teaspoon baking powder

½ cup butter
2 eggs
1 cup caster sugar

DIRECTIONS:

- Grease the Fagor Pressure Cooker with cooking spray. Combine all ingredients in a bowl and knead a soft dough. Roll out the dough on a clean surface. Cut with a cookie cutter.
- Place into the greased Fagor Pressure Cooker and cook for 30 minutes on MANUAL mode.

450. Pumpkin and Pineapple Cobbler

(Time: 50 minutes \ Servings: 4)

INGREDIENTS:

1 cup ripe pumpkin, peeled, chunks
1 cup pineapple, chunks
1 cup milk

½ cup sugar
1 teaspoon pumpkin pie spice
1 cup whipped cream for toping

DIRECTIONS:

- In the Fagor Pressure Cooker, add pumpkin, pineapples, milk, sugar, and pumpkin pie spice and cover.
- Cook on SLOW COOK mode for 50 minutes. Put on a serving dish and top with whipped cream.

451. Velvet Chocolate Pudding

(Time: 40 minutes \ Servings: 4)

INGREDIENTS:

1 cup raw chocolate, melted
1 teaspoon vanilla extract
1 cup cocoa powder
2 tablespoons butter
¼ cup caster sugar

½ cup chocolate syrup
2 cups milk
2 eggs
½ cup chocolate chips

DIRECTIONS:

- Beat eggs until fluffy. In the Fagor Pressure Cooker, add butter and milk and boil it on SAUTÉ mode.
- Add the cocoa powder and stir continuously. Add caster sugar and eggs by stirring gradually.
- Transfer the melted chocolate inside and mix thoroughly.
- Transfer into a serving dish and place inside the freezer for 20 minutes. Drizzle chocolate syrup on top.

452. Mango and Sweet Potato Smash

(Time: 50 minutes \ Servings: 4)

INGREDIENTS:

1 cup mango cubes
½ cup sugar
3 sweet potatoes, peeled, cubes

1 cup milk
1 cup cream
½ cup water

DIRECTIONS:

- In the Pressure Cooker add mangoes, sugar, milk, cream, sweet potatoes water, and cover with a lid.
- Cook for 50 minutes on SLOW COOK mode. Transfer to a bowl, mash it slightly with fork, and serve.

453. Chocolate Silk Bowls

(Time: 35 minutes \ Servings: 4)

INGREDIENTS:

2 cups raw chocolate
¼ cup cocoa powder
2 tablespoons brown sugar

1 cup milk
¼ cup heavy cream
3 tablespoons butter

DIRECTIONS:

- Melt the butter in on SAUTÉ mode.
- Add milk, brown sugar, chocolate, and cream, and cook well on SLOW COOK mode for 30 minutes.
- Stir occasionally. Place in small serving bowls and place inside the fridge for 10 minutes.

454. Pineapple and Mango Blossom

(Time: 50 minutes \ Servings: 3)

INGREDIENTS:

1 cup mango, chunks
1 cup pineapple slices
1 cup milk
½ cup sugar

½ teaspoons vanilla extract
1 cup whipped cream
½ cup pomegranates

DIRECTIONS:

- In the Fagor Pressure Cooker, add milk, pineapple, sugar and mangoes cover with a lid.
- Cook for about 50 minutes on SLOW COOK mode.Transfer to a serving dish when cooled.
- Add 2-3 spoons of whipped cream on top and sprinkle with pomegranates.

455. Cinnamon Spiced Apples

(Time: 30 minutes \ Servings: 3)

INGREDIENTS:

1 cup apple, peeled and diced
1 cup milk
½ cup sugar

½ teaspoon cinnamon powder
¼ teaspoon black pepper
4 tablespoons honey

DIRECTIONS:

- In a large bowl, toss apples, cinnamon powder, black pepper, salt and transfer into the Fagor Pressure Cooker. Stir in milk and sugar and cover with a lid. Cook for 35 minutes on SLOW COOK mode.
- Put on a serving dish and drizzle honey on top.

456. Sweet and Sour Pears

(Time: 25 minutes \ Servings: 3)

INGREDIENTS:

3 pears, sliced
¼ cup brown sugar
4 tablespoons maple syrup

1 tablespoon lemon juice
1 pinch salt
3 tablespoons butter

DIRECTIONS:

- Melt butter inside the Fagor Pressure Cooker and add the pears. Stir fry for 10 to 15 minutes on SAUTÉ mode. Add brown sugar and salt, dissolve it. Stir continuously.
- Transfer to a serving dish and top with maple syrup. Drizzle lemon juice.

457. Blackberry Smash

(Time: 40 minutes \ Servings: 4)

INGREDIENTS:

1 cup blackberries
2 tablespoons all-purpose flour
1 cup milk

1 cup cream
½ cup sugar
2 tablespoons butter

DIRECTIONS:

- In the Fagor Pressure Cooker, melt butter on SAUTÉ mode. Add flour and stir well.
- Pour in the milk and stir continuously. Add in the cream, blackberries, and sugar, and cook on SLOW COOK mode for 30 minutes.

458. Mouth-Watering Bread Pudding

(Time: 60 minutes \ Servings: 4)

INGREDIENTS:

6 slices of bread, roughly shredded
4 eggs
½ cup sugar
½ teaspoon cardamom powder
¼ teaspoon vanilla extract

1 cup milk
1 cup mozzarella cheese, shredded
1 pinch salt
1 tablespoon butter

DIRECTIONS:

- In a large bowl, beat eggs with a pinch of salt for 3-4 minutes. Transfer to the Fagor Pressure Cooker, add the bread slices, milk, cardamom powder, butter, cheese, sugar, and vanilla extract. Cook for 60 minutes on SLOW COOK mode. Serve hot.

459. Pistachio Cake

(Time: 50 minutes \ Servings: 4)

INGREDIENTS:

2 tbsp. pistachio powder
4-5 tablespoons mint leaves, finely chopped
½ cup sugar
1 cup all-purpose flour

1 teaspoon vanilla extract
1 tablespoon cocoa powder
2 eggs
½ cup butter

DIRECTIONS:

- In a large bowl, beat the eggs until fluffy.
- In another bowl, beat the butter with sugar, add vanilla extract and beat for 1-2 minutes.
- Add it to the eggs mixture and fold flour, vanilla extract, mint leaves, and pistachio powder.
- Pour the butter into the greased Fagor Pressure Cooker and cover with a lid.
- Cook on medium pressure cook mode for 45 minutes.

460. Banana and Strawberry Pudding

(Time: 40 minutes \ Servings: 3)

INGREDIENTS:

1 cup banana, slices
1 cub strawberries
2 cups milk

½ cup sugar
3 tablespoons honey
½ teaspoon cardamom powder

DIRECTIONS:

- In the Fagor Pressure Cooker, add milk, banana, strawberries, sugar, and cardamom powder.
- Cover with a lid, and cook for 40 minutes on SLOW COOK mode. Top with honey and serve.

461. Buttercream Dessert

(Time: 20 minutes \ Servings: 2)

INGREDIENTS:

1 cup sugar
3 tbsp. almond flour
3 egg whites

4 tbsp. granulated sugar
2 tbsp. food color
4 cups buttercream for filling

DIRECTIONS:

- Add flour and sugar into a bowl. Mix egg whites, sugar and food color. Pour the batter into a round baking tray. Cook for 15 minutes in the Fagor Pressure Cooker on MANUAL mode, high pressure.
- When ready, pour the buttercream over it to serve!

462. Butter and Cream Mix

(Time: 19 minutes \ Servings: 3)

INGREDIENTS:

2 tbsp. butter
2 tbsp. brown sugar
2 eggs
2 tbsp. vanilla extract
2 cups chocolate chips, chunks
2 cups flour

2 tbsp. baking powder
1 tbsp. baking soda
1 pinch salt
1 cup whipped cream
1 cup strawberries, sliced

DIRECTIONS:

- Blend butter and brown sugar in a bowl.
- Add in the eggs, vanilla extract, chocolate chips, flour, baking powder, baking soda and salt.
- Pour the batter into a round baking tray. Cook on MANUAL mode for 15 minutes in the Fagor Pressure Cooker. When ready, cover the cake with whipped cream. Top with strawberries and serve!

463. Apples Dessert

(Time: 19 minutes \ Servings: 2)

INGREDIENTS:

2 cups apples, sliced
2 tbsp. lemon juice
2 tbsp. sugar
2 cups flour
2 tbsp. rolled oats

2 tbsp. brown sugar
2 tbsp. cinnamon powder
3 tbsp. butter
1 cup nuts, chopped

DIRECTIONS:

- Mix flour and sugar in a bowl. Add lemon juice, rolled oats, brown sugar, cinnamon powder, butter and nuts. Mix well.
- Pour the batter into a round baking tray. Cook for 15 minutes on MANUAL mode.
- When ready, top with apples and serve.

464. Puff Pastry Dessert

(Time: 17 minutes \ Servings: 3)

INGREDIENTS:

2 cups Milk
1 tbsp. Vanilla bean extract
3 Egg yolks
2 tbsp. Sugar

2 tbsp. Cornstarch
3 tbsp. Butter
2 sheets Puff pastry
½ cup Confectioners' sugar

DIRECTIONS:

- Place puff pastry into a round baking tray. Add milk and vanilla bean extract into a bowl.
- Mix in the egg yolks, sugar, cornstarch and butter. Pour the mixture into the baking tray.
- Cook for 15 minutes on MANUAL mode. When ready, powder with confectioners' sugar.

465. Chocolate Cake

(Time: 14 minutes \ Servings: 3)

INGREDIENTS:

½ cup heavy cream
2 tbsp. vanilla extract
2 cups flour
½ tbsp. salt

3 egg whites
1 cup sugar
2 cups chocolate chips
chocolate shavings to garnish

DIRECTIONS:

- Add flour and vanilla extract in a bowl. Mix in the salt, egg whites, chocolate and salt.
- Pour the mixture into a round baking tray. Cook for 10 minutes on MANUAL mode.
- When ready, cover the cake with heavy cream and chocolate shavings.

466. Honey Pistachio Cake

(Time: 12 minutes \ Servings: 2)

INGREDIENTS:

2 cups butter
2 cups flour
2 tbsp. sugar
1 tbsp. brown sugar

¼ cup honey
3 egg whites
1 tbsp. baking powder
1 cup chopped pistachios

DIRECTIONS:

- Add butter and flour in a bowl. Mix in the brown sugar, egg whites and baking powder.
- Pour the mixture into a round baking tray. Cook for 10 minutes on MANUAL mode.
- When ready, cover the cake with honey and garnish with pistachios.

467. Lemon Flavored Cake

(Time: 23 minutes \ Servings: 3)

INGREDIENTS:

2 eggs
2 tsp. sugar
¼ tbsp. salt
2 tbsp. lemon zest

2 cups heavy cream
1 tbsp. vanilla extract
2 cups flour

DIRECTIONS:

- Add eggs and sugar in a bowl. Mix in the salt, lemon zest, heavy cream, vanilla extract and flour.
- Pour the batter into a round baking tray. Cook for 20 minutes on MANUAL mode.

468. Vanilla Cherries Dessert

(Time: 17 minutes \ Servings: 2)

INGREDIENTS:

2 tbsp. butter, melted
1 cup milk
2 tbsp. sugar
2 tbsp. vanilla extract
3 eggs

¼ tbsp. salt
2 cups flour
2 cups black cherries
powdered sugar for dusting

DIRECTIONS:

- Add butter and milk in a bowl. Mix in the sugar, vanilla extract, eggs, salt and flour.
- Pour the batter into a round baking tray. Cook for 15 minutes on MANUAL mode.
- When ready, cover the cake with black cherries and powdered sugar.

469. Vermicelli Dessert

(Time: 23 minutes \ Servings: 2)

INGREDIENTS:

3 cups vermicelli
2 cups milk

1 cup sugar
1 tbsp. cardamom powder

DIRECTIONS:

- Add milk and vermicelli into the pressure cooker. Mix in the sugar and cardamom powder.
- Cook for 20 minutes on high pressure. When ready, serve and enjoy!

470. Cocoa Dessert

(Time: 23 minutes \ Servings: 2)

INGREDIENTS:

1 tbsp. butter, melted
1 cup flour
3 eggs
2 tbsp. sugar

2 tbsp. brown sugar
3 tbsp. cocoa powder
2 tbsp. vanilla extract
1 pinch salt

DIRECTIONS:

- Add butter and flour in a bowl.
- Mix in the eggs, sugar, brown sugar, cocoa powder, vanilla extract and sugar.
- Pour the batter into a round baking tray. Cook for 20 minutes on MANUAL mode.

471. Cherry Cake with Peaches

(Time: 18 minutes \ Servings: 3)

INGREDIENTS:

1 can (21 oz.) cherry pie filling
2 cups white cake mix

2 cups butter, melted

TOPPING:

2 cups peaches, sliced
2 tbsp. butter

1 cup whipped cream

DIRECTIONS:

- Mix cherry pie filling and white cake mix in a bowl. Add butter.
- Pour the batter into a round baking tray. Cook for 15 minutes on MANUAL mode.
- Prepare the topping by mixing together peaches, butter and whipped cream in a bowl.
- When the cake is ready, spread the topping and serve.

472. Kiwi and Strawberry Dessert

(Time: 17 minutes \ Servings: 2)

INGREDIENTS:

2 cups flour
2 tbsp. baking powder
1 pinch salt
2 cups sugar
2 tbsp. butter

2 tbsp. vanilla extract
2 eggs
2 kiwi, sliced
2 cups strawberries, sliced
2 cups whipped cream

DIRECTIONS:

- Add flour and baking powder into a bowl. Mix in the salt, sugar, butter, vanilla extract and eggs.
- Pour the batter into a round baking tray. Cook for 15 minutes on MANUAL mode.
- When ready, spread whipped cream on the cake. Place kiwi and strawberries on top and serve.

473. Almond Chocolate Cake

(Time: 15 minutes \ Servings: 3)

INGREDIENTS:

5 tbsp. almond flour
3 tbsp. cocoa powder

3 tbsp. sugar
1 tbsp. baking powder

3 tbsp. water
2 tbsp. avocado oil

¼ tsp. banilla extract
1 pack chocolate chips

DIRECTIONS:

- Add flour and cocoa powder in a bowl. Mix in the sugar, baking powder, water, avocado oil and vanilla extract. Add chocolate chips.
- Pour the batter into a round baking tray. Cook on MANUAL on high pressire for 15 minutes.

474. Pecan Bread Pudding

(Time: 20 minutes \ Servings: 2)

INGREDIENTS:

2 tbsp. butter
1 lb. brioche bread – 1 loaf
1 cup pecans , chopped
1 cup half and half
½ cup whole milk
2 eggs

2 cups brown sugar
2 tbsp. vanilla extract
2 tbsp. cinnamon powder
a pinch of salt
1 tbsp. nutmeg powder

DIRECTIONS:

- Place the bread on a round baking tray. Add butter and whole milk in a bowl.
- Mix in the half and half, eggs, brown sugar, vanilla extract, cinnamon powder, salt, and nutmeg powder.
- Cook for 20 minutes on MANUAL on high pressure. When ready, garnish pecans and serve.

475. Chocolate Sour Cream Cake

(Time: 20 minutes \ Servings: 3)

INGREDIENTS:

2 cups butter
2 cups flour
2 tbsp. sugar
2 eggs

3 tbsp. sour cream
2 tbsp. almond extract
1 cup chocolate chips

DIRECTIONS:

- Add butter and flour in a bowl. Mix in the sugar, eggs, sour cream, almond extract and chocolate chips.
- Pour the batter into a round baking tray. Cook for 20 minutes on high pressure.

476. Light Chocolate Cake

(Time: 15 minutes \ Servings: 3)

INGREDIENTS:

2 tbsp. milk
2 tbsp. sugar
2 cups chocolate, chopped

2 egg yolks
2 egg whites
2 cups flour

DIRECTIONS:

- Add milk and sugar in a bowl. Mix in the chocolate, egg yolk, egg whites and flour.
- Pour the batter into a round baking tray. Cook for 15 minutes in the pressure cooker.

477. Pretzel Pecan Dessert

(Time: 15 minutes \ Servings: 3)

INGREDIENTS:

1 cup pecan, halves
1 cup pretzel twists
1 cup caramel
2 cups milk chocolate, melted

2 cups flour
2 tbsp. sugar
2 tbsp. vanilla extract

DIRECTIONS:

- Add flour and sugar in a bowl. Mix in the pecans, pretzels, caramel, milk chocolate and vanilla extract.
- Pour the batter into a round baking tray. Cook on MANUAL mode for 15 minutes.

478. Apple Sauce

(Time: 30 minutes \ Servings: 4)

INGREDIENTS:

1 cup water
1 tsp. cinnamon powder
juice of half lemon
10 apples, quartered

1 tbsp. honey
1 tbsp. ghee
1 pinch of salt

DIRECTIONS:

- Add all ingredients in the Fagor Pressure cooker. Set to MANUAL and cook for 30 minutes on high pressure. Discard half of the cooking liquid. Blend the rest until smooth in a blender.

479. Apple Brandy Pastry

(Time: 15 minutes \ Servings: 2)

INGREDIENTS:

2 cups butter
1 cup sugar
½ tsp. salt

3 apples, chopped
½ cup brandy
3 phyllo dough sheets

DIRECTIONS:

- Add butter and sugar in a bowl. Mix in the salt, apples and brandy.
- Place the phyllo dough sheets on a round baking tray.
- Pour the batter into a tray. Cook for 15 minutes on MANUAL on high pressure.

480. Cardamom Banana Pudding

(Time: 20 minutes \ Servings: 3)

INGREDIENTS:

4 ripe bananas, mashed
2 cups milk

½ cup sugar
2 green cardamoms

DIRECTIONS:

- In the Pressure cooker, add milk and boil on pressure cooking mode. Add sugar and stir well.
- Add the mashed bananas, and cardamom and stir for 5-10 minutes.

481. Carrot and Honey Pie

(Time: 40 minutes \ Servings: 4)

INGREDIENTS:

1 cup shredded carrot
1 cup of milk
1 cup shredded mozzarella cheese
½ cup condense milk

1 teaspoon cardamom powder
4-5 almonds, chopped
4-5 pistachios, chopped
¼ cup sugar

DIRECTIONS:

- In the Fagor Pressure Cooker, place carrots, milk, condense milk, mozzarella cheese, cardamom powder, and sugar and cover. Cook for 40 minutes on SLOW COOK mode.
- Transfer into a serving dish and top with chopped pistachios and almonds.

482. Rice Pudding with Chocolate Chips

(Time: 120 minutes \ Servings: 4)

INGREDIENTS:

1 cup rice, boiled
1 cup mango, chopped
2 cups of milk
½ cup sugar

½ cup chocolate chips
2 tablespoons honey
1 pinch salt

DIRECTIONS:

- In the Fagor Pressure Cooker, add mangoes, rice, milk, sugar, chocolate chips and pinch of salt.
- Cook for 2 hours. Stir occasionally. Serve with honey on top.

483. Cherry Delight

(Time: 40 minutes \ Servings: 3)

INGREDIENTS:

1 cup fresh cherries, chopped
½ cup pomegranates
2 cups milk
1 cup whipped cream

½ cup sugar
1 tsp. vanilla extract
1 pinch of salt
½ cup pineapple slices

DIRECTIONS:

- In the Fagor Pressure Cooker, add cherries, milk, sugar, vanilla extract and salt, cover with a lid.
- Cook for 40 minutes on low pressure. Top with pomegranate, whipped cream and pineapples slices.

484. Coconut Peach Crumble

(Time: 30 minutes \ Servings: 3)

INGREDIENTS:

1 cup peach chunks
1 cup milk
½ cup sugar
1 pinch of salt

½ cup coconut powder
1 tbsp. almond powder
½ tsp. cardamom powder
½ cup pineapple slices

DIRECTIONS:

- In the Fagor Pressure Cooker, add peaches, milk, sugar, coconut powder, almond powder, cardamom powder, and salt. Cook on STEAM mode for 30 minutes. Stir occasionally.
- Serve with pineapple slices on top.

485. Cheese Fruit Smash

(Time: 40 minutes \ Servings: 4)

INGREDIENTS:

1 cup mango chunks
1 cup banana chunks
1 cup peach chunks
1 cup strawberries, chunks
1 cup blueberries, chopped
½ cup pomegranate

1 cup whipped cream
1 cup cherries, chopped
¼ cup sugar
1 cup coconut milk
1 cup mozzarella cheese, shredded

DIRECTIONS:

- In the Fagor Pressure Cooker, add pineapples, mangoes, bananas, cheese, sugar, coconut milk, strawberries and blueberries, cover with a lid.
- Cook for 40 minutes on SLOW COOK mode. Serve with pomegranates and whipped cream on top.

486. Coconut Milk Apple Crumble

(Time: 40 minutes \ Servings: 4)

INGREDIENTS:

1 cup apple, diced
1 cup coconut milk
½ cup sugar

1 banana, chopped
1 tsp. cardamom powder
3-4 almonds, crushed

DIRECTIONS:

- In the Fagor Pressure Cooker add apples, coconut milk, cardamom powder, banana and sugar.
- Cook on SLOW COOK mode for 40 minutes.
- When the apples are tender, smash with fork and transfer to a serving dish. Top with almonds.

487. Bloody Plum Pudding

(Time: 40 minutes \ Servings: 5)

INGREDIENTS:

1 cup ripe plums
½ cup sugar
2 cups of water

1 tbsp. sesame seeds
1 pinch of salt

DIRECTIONS:

- In the Fagor Pressure Cooker, add whole plums, sugar, water, sesame seeds and pinch of salt.
- Cook for 40 minutes on SLOW COOK mode. Discard the seeds of the plum and serve.

488. Strawberry Sauce

(Time: 40 minutes \ Servings: 3)

INGREDIENTS:

2 cups strawberries
1 cup pineapple juice

½ cup sugar
1 pinch of salt

DIRECTIONS:

- In the Fagor Pressure Cooker, add all ingredients and cover with a lid.
- Set the pressure cooker on SLOW COOK mode and cook for 40 minutes.

489. Quinoa Chocolate Balls

(Time: 20 minutes \ Servings: 5-6)

INGREDIENTS

¼ cup of pre-rinsed quinoa
1 cup of coconut milk
16 whole, pitted dates
½ cup of raw almonds with skin

¼ cup of natural, crunchy peanut butter
¼ cup of dark chocolate chips
¼ cup of shredded coconuts

DIRECTIONS

- Place a trivet or a steaming basket into the Fagor Pressure Cooker.
- Add the quinoa and coconut milk to the saucepan; cover and bring to boil for 10 minutes.
- In a food processor, add the dates and pulse until they become smooth and can be shaped into balls.
- Add the almonds to the food processor and pulse until they are finely minced.
- Add the date balls to the minced almonds, peanut butter, and warm quinoa and place all the ingredients into a food processor; then pulse.
- Add the chocolate chips to the mixture, return to the bowl, and shape small balls.
- Roll the balls into the crushed almonds and shredded coconuts.
- Line the balls in a baking form in the steaming basket of the Fagor Pressure Cooker and cover it tightly with the use of tin foil. Close and lock the lid. Set to high pressure for 5 minutes.
- Once the timer beeps, quickly release the pressure or let it release naturally.

490. Chia Seeds Balls

(Time: 5 minutes \ Servings: 4-6)

INGREDIENTS

1 cup of raw almonds
8 Medjool dates
2 tbsp. of unsweetened, shaved coconut
1 tbsp. of chia seeds

2 tbsp. of melted coconut oil
1 tbsp. of coconut nectar
1 tbsp. Tahini
Shredded coconuts

DIRECTIONS

- Add a trivet or a steaming basket and make sure to keep it from touching the bottom of the Fagor Pressure Cooker.
- Combine all the ingredients into a food processor and pulse until it becomes a smooth ball.
- Form the mixture of dates into the form of balls with hands or use an ice-cream scoop.
- Line the rolls on a dish and dip, then coat. Roll the balls in the shredded coconuts, almonds, and chia seeds or the cacao nibs.
- Line the balls in a baking form in the steaming basket in the Fagor Pressure Cooker and cover it tightly with the use of tin foil. Close the lid, lock it, and press MANUAL on high pressure for around 5 minutes.
- Once the timer beeps, quickly release the pressure or let it release naturally.

491. Whole Wheat Brownies

(Time: 7 minutes \ Servings: 6-8)

INGREDIENTS

¼ cup of coconut milk yogurt
¼ cup of vegan butter
1 tsp. of vanilla extract
1 cup of maple syrup
2 tbsp. of chia seeds

6 tbsp. of water
¼ cup of cocoa powder
¾ cup of wheat flour
¼ tsp. of salt
¼ tsp. of baking powder

DIRECTIONS

- Mix the water and chia seeds and place them in the fridge for 15 minutes.
- Meanwhile, prepare the Fagor Pressure Cooker by adding the trivet or the steaming basket and make sure to keep it from touching the bottom.
- Place the melted butter, yogurt, and maple syrup in a mixing bowl. Once the chia seeds mixture becomes a syrup, add it to a bowl and mix. Beat the cocoa, flour, salt, and baking powder.
- Spread the ingredients in a greased, floured baking dish that fits in the Fagor Pressure Cooker, or you can pour the mixture into ramekins. Slide the baking tray or the ramekins in the steamer of the Fagor Pressure Cooker and close the lid.
- Press Manual and use the buttons [+] or [-] and set the timer to 7 minutes of high pressure cooking. When the timer beeps, release the pressure naturally and serve the brownies.

492. Oatmeal Bread with Strawberries

(Time: 30 minutes \ Servings: 12)

INGREDIENTS

3 and ½ cups of whole wheat flour
1 ½ cups of rolled oats
2 cups of white sugar
1 tbsp. of ground cinnamon
2 tsp. of baking powder

1 tsp. of salt
1 ½ cups of vegetable oil
4 large eggs
1 lb. of fresh and sliced strawberries
¼ cup of rolled oats

DIRECTIONS

- Start by pulsing the oats in a food processor to obtain fine oat flour.
- Prepare the Fagor Pressure Cooker by placing the rack or steamer basket in it.
- Grease a tall, long, skinny, heat-proof container of 4 cup capacity with 1 tsp. of vegetable oil.
- Combine the flour with 1 ½ cups of the rolled oats, sugar, cinnamon, baking powder, and salt in a mixing bowl.
- In a separate bowl, whisk the oil and eggs; then add the flour mixture until the ingredients becomes moistened.
- Add the strawberries and pour the mixture into the container and sprinkle the top with ¼ cup of the rolled oats.
- Place the container in the steaming basket; close and lock the lid and set on high pressure for 30 minutes.
- Once the timer beeps, let the strawberry bread cool down for around 5 minutes before serving it. Serve and enjoy this healthy and yummy bread.

493. Raspberry Crumbles

(Time: 10 minutes \ Servings: 5)

INGREDIENTS

4 cups of fresh frozen raspberries
1 tbsp. of lemon juice
¾ cup of packed brown sugar
½ cup of flour

1 tbsp. of cinnamon
½ cup of mango sauce
¼ cup of organic butter
1 cup of flake whole oats

DIRECTIONS

- Prepare the Fagor Pressure Cooker by pouring 2 cups of water and a trivet or a steaming basket.
- Grease the ramekins or the steel muffin cups with organic butter.
- Spread the raspberries on the bottom of each steel ramekin and sprinkle the lemon juice on the top of the ramekins. Combine all the ingredients into a bowl. If the dough is not moist enough, add more mango sauce. Spread the mixed ingredients over the raspberries in the ramekins.

- Press Steam at high pressure for around 10 to 15 minutes. When the timer beeps, naturally release the pressure. Enjoy these healthy raspberry crumbles.

494. Blueberry and Blackberry Cookies

(Time: 10 minutes \ Servings: 7)

INGREDIENTS

4 cups of frozen blackberries
2 cups of frozen blueberries
¼ cup of honey

2 tbsp. of freshly squeezed lemon juice
2 tbsp. of cornstarch
1 cup of almond flour

DIRECTIONS

- Pour 2 cups of water and place the trivet/steaming basket inside. Grease the ramekins or the steel muffin cups with organic butter. Add the blackberries, blueberries, and honey to a deep saucepan and cook the ingredients on SAUTÉ mode. Mix the lemon juice, cornstarch, and almond flour; then add to the berries and stir gently.
- Spoon the batter into the oiled ramekins and top with almonds and crumbs.
- Press the setting button to high pressure for 10 minutes. When the timer beeps, naturally release the pressure and serve the cobblers.

495. Quinoa Chocolate Cake

(Time: 35 minutes \ Servings: 5)

INGREDIENTS

2 cups of cold, cooked quinoa
¾ cup of melted butter
4 beaten eggs
¼ cup of milk
1 ½ tsp. of vanilla extract
1 ¼ cups of white sugar

1 cup of cocoa powder
1 ½ tsp. of baking powder
1 tsp. of baking soda
½ tsp. of salt
½ cup of chocolate chips
½ cup of chopped pecans

DIRECTIONS

- Grease a square baking pan that fits inside the Fagor Pressure Cooker and set it aside. Blend the quinoa, butter, eggs, milk, and vanilla extract in a blender until the mixture becomes smooth. Combine the sugar, cocoa powder, baking powder, baking soda, and salt in a deep bowl.
- Add the quinoa mixture into the mixture of sugar until the batter is well combined. Fold the chocolate chips and pecans into the batter; then pour into the already prepared baking pan.
- Cook the cake in the preheated Fagor Pressure Cooker and press the high pressure for 35 minutes. Naturally release the pressure and remove the cake from the cooker. Serve cold.

496. Chocolate Squares with Chia Seeds

(Time: 10 minutes \ Servings: 4)

INGREDIENTS

4 oz. of unsweetened chopped chocolate
1 ½ tsp. of organic stevia
½ tsp. of vanilla crème stevia
2 tbsp. of dried, diced apricots

2 tbsp. of dried, diced mango
2 tbsp. of chopped almonds
¼ tsp. of chia seeds
¼ tsp. of coarse sea salt

DIRECTIONS

- Prepare the Fagor Pressure Cooker by pouring 2 cups of water and putting the trivet or the steaming basket inside. Grease the ramekins or the steel muffin cups with organic butter. Add the chocolate, stevia, and e vanilla crème stevia to heat proof ramekins; then stir to mix the ingredients. Immediately, pour the

167

mixture to the ramekins and sprinkle the rest of the ingredients.
- Line the ramekins in the steaming basket. Set to high pressure for 10 minutes and close the lid.
- When the timer beeps, naturally release the pressure and serve!

497. Cinnamon Raisin Cookies

(Time: 10 minutes \ Servings: 4)

INGREDIENTS

½ cup of palm sugar
2 egg whites
¾ cup of unsweetened organic applesauce
1 tsp. of raw ground vanilla
1 ½ cups of whole wheat flour
1 tsp. of baking soda

½ tsp. of himalayan salt
1 ½ tsp. of cinnamon
¼ tsp. of organic nutmeg
1 ½ cups of oatmeal
¾ cup of raisins
½ cup of walnuts

DIRECTIONS

- Prepare the Fagor Pressure Cooker by pouring 2 cups of water and putting the trivet or the steaming basket inside.
- Grease 4 heat proof ramekins with organic butter. Mix the vanilla with the sugar. Add the flour, soda, and cinnamon with the nutmeg. Combine the raisins with the walnuts and the oatmeal.
- Pour the cookies mixture into the greased heat proof ramekins covered with coconut oil. Flatten the mixture with a fork and place it in the Fagor Pressure Cooker.
- Set on high pressure for 10 minutes.
- Close the lid, and when the timer beeps, naturally release the pressure. Serve and enjoy these delicious and energy boosting cookies!

498. Coconut Carrot Cake

(Time: 25 minutes \ Servings: 7-8)

INGREDIENTS

3 beaten eggs
¾ cup of coconut milk
½ cup of shredded coconut
¾ cup of vegetable oil
1 ½ cups of white sugar
2 tsp. of vanilla extract
2 tsp. of ground cinnamon
¼ tsp. of salt

2 cups of all-purpose flour
2 tsp. of baking soda
2 cups of shredded carrots
1 cup of flaked coconut
1 cup of chopped walnuts
1 can crushed pineapple
1 cup of raisins

DIRECTIONS

- Prepare the Fagor Pressure Cooker by pouring 2 cups of water and putting the trivet or the steaming basket inside.
- Grease a baking dish that fits the Fagor Pressure Cooker with organic butter.
- In a deep bowl, sift the flour, baking soda, salt, and cinnamon together.
- Set it aside. In another bowl, combine the eggs, buttermilk, oil, sugar, and vanilla.
- Then mix the ingredients very well.
- Add the flour mixture and combine it. In a bowl, combine the shredded carrots, coconut, walnuts, pineapple, and raisins. Using a spatula, spread the carrot mixture and fold in very well.
- Sprinkle with shredded carrots.
- Pour the mixture into the heat-proof baking dish and set on high pressure for 20 minutes.
- Once the timer beeps, naturally release the pressure and serve it.

499. Pear and Ginger Muffins

(Time: 20 minutes \ Servings: 4)

INGREDIENTS

1 tbsp. of ground flax seeds
3 tbsp. of water
1 ¾ cup of self-rising oat flour
1 tsp. of baking powder
2 tsp. of turmeric
1 tsp. of pumpkin pie spice
1 pinch of salt

½ cup of grapes seed oil
¼ cup of sugar
½ cup of maple syrup
¾ cup of coconut milk
1 tsp. of grated fresh ginger
2 Small peeled, cored, and diced pears

DIRECTIONS

- Prepare the Fagor Pressure Cooker by pouring 2 cups of water and putting the trivet or the steaming basket inside.
- Grease 4 heat proof ramekins with organic butter. In a deep bowl, combine the ground flax seeds and the water; set the mixture aside.
- In another bowl, combine the flour, baking powder, turmeric, pumpkin pie, spice, and salt. In a deep bowl, whisk together the grape seed oil, sugar, and maple syrup until they are very well combined.
- Pour the flax mixture with the milk and whisk very well. Add the grated ginger
- Add the flour gradually to the mixture and keep mixing until the ingredients combine well, but do not over mix. After that, stir in the chopped pears
- Fill the ramekins with the mixture and place it in the steaming basket.
- Set the timer for 20 minutes on high pressure.
- When the timer beeps, naturally release the pressure and muffins are ready!

500. Pumpkin Cake

(Time: 10 minutes \ Servings: 10)

INGREDIENTS

3 cups of wheat flour
1 tbsp. of baking powder
2 tsp. of baking soda
2 tsp. of ground cinnamon
1 tsp. of ground nutmeg
½ tsp. of ground cloves
1 tsp. of ground ginger

1 tsp. of salt
4 beaten eggs
1 cup of granulated sugar
1 cup of light brown sugar
1 can 15 oz. of pumpkin
1 cup of coconut oil

DIRECTIONS

- Prepare the Fagor Pressure Cooker by pouring 2 cups of water and putting the trivet or the steaming basket inside.
- Grease a heat proof baking tray with organic butter.
- Then, sift the flour, baking powder, soda, salt, and spices all together in a bowl and set the ingredients aside. In a deep bowl, beat the eggs until you obtain a foamy mixture.
- Add the sugars and beat it until thick.
- Add the pumpkin and oil and beat again until the mixture becomes smooth. Blend the dry ingredients into the mixture of the pumpkin.
- Pour the batter into the already greased baking pan and set to high pressure for 10 minutes and close the lid. When the timer beeps, naturally release the pressure and serve the ramekins warm.

Made in the USA
Middletown, DE
15 April 2018